ENTER THE BODY

When the body comes on stage, how does it 'play'? And how do spectators read it? *Enter the Body* offers a series of provocative case studies of
the work women's bodies do on Shakespeare's intensely body-conscious
stage. Carol Chillington Rutter looks at:

- Ophelia in the grave
- Cordelia in Lear's arms
- Cleopatra's blackness
- Helen of Troy's beauty

Rutter's topics are sex, death, race, gender, culture, politics, and the
'excessive' performative body that exceeds the playtext it inhabits. She
focuses on performances domestic and iconic – Emilia gossiping,
Cressida handing over her glove.

As well as drawing upon vital primary documents from Shakespeare's
day, Rutter offers close readings of women's performances on stage
and film in Britain today, from Peggy Ashcroft's (white) Cleopatra
and Whoopi Goldberg's (whiteface) African Queen to Sally Dexter's
languorous Helen and Alan Howard's raver 'Queen' of Troy. Zoe
Wanamaker, Imogen Stubbs, Jean Simmons, Helena Bonham-Carter,
Janet Suzman, Kate Winslet and Claire Benedict put in stunning
appearances in this timely and theatrically sophisticated study.

Carol Chillington Rutter is Senior Lecturer in English at the University
of Warwick. She is the author of *Clamorous Voices: Shakespeare's Women
Today* – a classic account of a decade of women's performance – and *The
Documents of the Rose Playhouse*.

ENTER THE BODY

Women and representation on Shakespeare's stage

Carol Chillington Rutter

London and New York

First published 2001
by Routledge
11 New Fetter Lane, London EC4P 4EE

Simultaneously published in the USA and Canada
by Routledge
29 West 35th Street, New York, NY 10001

Routledge is an imprint of the Taylor & Francis Group.

© 2001 Carol Chillington Rutter

Typeset in Galliard by
M Rules
Printed and bound in Great Britain by
Biddles Ltd, Guildford and King's Lynn

British Library Cataloguing in Publication Data
A catalogue record for this book is available from the British Library.

Library of Congress Cataloging in Publication Data
Rutter, Carol Chillington
Enter the body/Carol Chillington Rutter.
p. cm.
Includes bibliographical references and index.
1. Shakespeare, William, 1564–1616 – Characters – Women.
2. Shakespeare, William, 1564–1616 – Stage history.
3. Body, Human, in literature. 4. Women in literature. I. Title
PR2991.R87 2000
822.3'3–dc21 00–044637

ISBN 0 415 14164 8 (pbk)
ISBN 0 415 14163 X (hbk)

IN MEMORY OF MY FATHER
Rev. J. H. Chillington

12 December 1906–13 January 2000

who said of dying,
'You're going to find this fascinating. It's like
being in a Shakespeare play.'

CONTENTS

PLATES

PREFACE

When the ghost of Hamlet's father urgently needs to incite his son from paralysed sympathy to sweeping revenge, he remembers his living body and the murder performed upon it. Indeed, he re-performs the ghastly business, transferring it to Hamlet's memory by re-citing the narrative in graphic detail. This 'telling' is not unlike the First Player's 'telling' of another murder of another 'unnerved father', limb-lopped Priam. In that later performance, the Player subjects his actorly body to his narrative, and forces 'his whole function' to 'his own conceit' so entirely that the blood drains from his face while tears spring to his eyes. He remembers the body of Trojan Priam, the 'reverend' king whose age-enfeebled arms can no longer heave a sword, whose 'milky head' incites no pity in killer Pyrrhus. In turn, Grecian Pyrrhus is remembered as another body graphically re-cited and transformed by slaughter, 'total gules', as revenge literally incorporates itself into his deadly physical frame, 'bak'd and impasted' with 'blood of fathers, mothers, daughters, sons', monstrously 'o'ersized with coagulate gore.' Prompting his son to revenge as ruthless as Pyrrhus's, the Ghost remembers how his own body was monstered, how the effects of the poison corrupted, boiled and burst through his mortal flesh, the 'leprous distilment' coursing like 'quicksilver' through 'the natural gates and alleys of the body' to 'posset' and 'curd' his blood then to erupt in an 'instant tetter', 'most lazar-like'. 'All my smooth body,' cries the Ghost, remembering feelingly the sensuous pleasure of his living flesh, was 'bark'd', scabbed with a 'vile and loathsome crust'. Audience to this appalling re-embodiment, Hamlet reacts by trying to hold off sensation – whose effect is working upon his sensible body already. 'Hold, hold, my heart,' cries the prince, feeling it crack. 'And you my sinews, grow not instant old, / But bear me stiffly up.' Spectator, that is, to the spectre whose re-citation makes his body 'instant old', Hamlet turns into an obscene spectacle – theatrical 'telling' works as violently on his body as his uncle's bizarrely theatrical poison worked on his father's.

Citing *Hamlet* citing bodies that remember in and on the flesh the sto-ries they're compelled to enact, helps me stake out the territory I want to explore in this book. In the theatre, the body bears the brunt of perfor-mance; it is the material Shakespeare's text works on, works through. No body in the theatre is exempt – least of all, the spectator's. So how does the body play on Shakespeare's stage? What work does it do, and how can I account for it, bring it on stage within this text? Famously, when Hamlet wants to think about the imperative relationship between remembered action, enactment and acting (both 'playing' and 'doing'), he theorizes the body, framing it abstractly – 'the body of the time' – as he moves from material bodies to the figurative body politic. He lectures the Players (who are, just then, readying themselves to play *The Murder of Gonzago* before the king) on the social work performance does in culture-at-large. 'The purpose of playing,' he tells them, 'was and is' to hold 'the mirror up to nature', to show 'the very age and body of the time his form and pressure'. Thus speaks the academic on study leave from Wittenberg, and his conceit is persuasive enough until Ophelia's entrance some scenes later arrests its intellectual force. Mind-shattered Ophelia devastates theory. She shows instead that 'the purpose of playing' in a theatre of cruelty like the Ghost's or a theatre of bared nerve endings like the Player's is to remember in the body. So, pressing into numbed hands a flower 'that's for remembrance' to urge 'love, remember', mad Ophelia plays out on her wrecked body yet another synoptic reprise of *Hamlet*: *Hamlet* 'with a difference', not a repeat of the prince's political farce, *Gonzago* re-scripted as *The Mousetrap*, but a lunatic improvisation stand-ing surrogate for the wooing play *Hamlet* has kept well offstage. This impromptu wants to end as a comedy – perhaps called *A Lover and His Lass* – but won't. In any case, it requires Ophelia to play all the parts, parts her body re-cites even as she transfers them affectively on to the bodies of her spectators. 'O heat, dry up my brains,' says Laertes, facing a sister 'anticked' 'in deed' by madness that Hamlet only 'played'.

Ophelia's intensely body-conscious theatre – and the traffic it conducts between memory and re-citation, actor and spectator, telling, re-telling with a difference, and enacting – is the subject of this book. Indeed, this book began its life in the theatre. It began with performances like Ophelia's that interrupted intellect to fix my interest on bodies. They momentarily suspended whatever work Shakespeare's words were doing to gather up meanings that exceeded language, locating expressiveness in the articulate materiality of the actor's body instead. Sometimes what arrested my viewing was fleeting: a casual turn of head or hand, an elbow propped at an angle on a table. Sometimes it was a sight that staggered spectatorship, that left it reeling or raw: a corpse, slumped in the cradle of her father's arms; a lunatic, matted hair falling over her face, bent to her fixed project of sorting a posy of bones; a fist beating time on a heart, and then later, that same hand clawing the air for life; black shoulders swaying in slow pleasure, recalling a memory bigger than a dream; fingers snapping and pointing; a head, thrown back, opening its mouth in a soundless wail of animal grief. From its beginning in today's theatre, however, this book likewise travels back to Shakespeare's 'original' theatre, to try to recover something of early modern performance practice by calling as witness a variety of contemporary texts that help me understand his culture's body consciousness: documents, letters, playhouse accounts, portraits, tomb effigies, official and unofficial notices. The 'stage' I refer to in my title, then, occupies a site on at least two maps, one of urban London around the turn of the seventeenth century, another of contemporary cultural Britain.

Offering readings of performance, this book gives a series of specific case studies of the work bodies do on Shakespeare's stage, both with and beyond his words. As I argue, the body in play bears continuous meaning onstage, and always exceeds the playtext it inhabits. My business is to pay attention to that 'excessive' performance text, to register and analyse it. My practice is borrowed from Hamlet's Ghost (who, bringing a body into play and on to the stage when people least expect it, coercively reanimates their attention to body work). Like him, I re-perform performance, retelling telling to new listeners and generating what Clifford Geertz calls 'thick descriptions' to produce the kind of archival record of my own viewing that remembers it accurately for subsequent readers – even as I acknowledge its inaccuracy.[1] For like the Ghost, I am partial, selective in remembering. Like him, I have certain axes to grind. First as a reader of performance texts, then a writer of performances remembered, I know that I am engaged in a circular practice or translation exercise that, converting what Barbara Hodgdon calls the 'thisness' of performance into the 'thatness' of analysis, retells 'with a difference'.[2] In its limitations, my writing imitates theatre production: it intends to be rigorous, committed, grounded, but knows it is provisional, contingent, never definitive. In its aspirations, it engages, in Joseph Roach's terms, the two 'necessarily problematic' procedures any reconstruction of performance depends upon – 'spectating and tattling'.[3] These chapters circulate memory as serious gossip.

Some bodies concern me only tangentially in this book; others, not at all. I'm not interested, for instance, in the body that's been so excitingly, if alarmingly, man-handled by certain new historicist and feminist materialist critics over the past decade, prompted, perhaps, by Stephen Orgel's mischievously punning subtitle to 'Nobody's Perfect, Or, Why

Did the English Stage Take Boys for Women?' (1989) – the body, that is, of the cross-dressed professional player on the all-male Elizabethan stage.[4] After Orgel, the practice of theatrical cross-dressing was increasingly politicized, sensationalized (even hystericized) in historicist criticism that figured the London playhouse as a veritable sweat tub of sodomitical desire, a place where men in women's clothes were sexually ambivalent, even androgynous, erotically provocative, certainly seductive, even more certainly threatening to a stable sex-gender system – a place where boys were 'taken' for women and where English culture's 'intense anxieties', fixed on the 'problematics of the flesh', could be staged and their 'transgressive erotic impulses' released.[5] It's certainly a lively place, this eroticized, historicized playhouse, but it's not a place I recognize as a theatre historian and close reader of Elizabethan playhouse documents, no doubt because, as David Cressy mildly observes in surveying this criticism, historicists exploit 'history' very differently than historians do and make very different arguments out of the texts they read as evidence. For him, as for me, this sensationalized theatre turns out to be more a rhetorical than a historical construct, and one that serves post-, not early-modern discursive ends. By contrast, the 'history' I read (including eyewitness accounts) brings me to conclude with Anthony Dawson that cross-dressing was an unremarkable stage convention, no more sensational, anxious or transgressive when practised by the Chamberlain's Men in 1601 than by Cheek by Jowl in 1991 – or indeed, by Shakespeare's 'replica' players playing *Antony and Cleopatra* in his 'replica' Globe theatre in 1999.[6] The English stage didn't 'take' boys for women any more than it 'took' commoners for aristocrats or Richard Burbage for Henry V. It did 'take' players for the parts they played: that is, Elizabethan spectators, understanding actors as professionals whose business was role play, read the role played, not the player beneath the role. When I'm thinking about 'original' performances on Shakespeare's stage, the bodies I focus on belong to the play, not to the players who played them. I read Cordelia as 'she', not 'he'.

I emphasize the point because the bodies in play I observe in this book, the roles and performances I document, are, almost exclusively, women's. This concentration of focus I intend as a corrective to feminist criticism's preoccupation with discursive bodies, and materialist and performance criticism's exaggerated attention on men. The former derives from a fascination with power, the latter, from a logocentric fascination with Shakespeare's words as the bearers of authorial meanings; as everyone knows, men have more to say in Shakespeare than women do. To concentrate criticism on words, on Shakespeare's playtext, then, is to concentrate on men – a habit that doesn't end with academic readings of these plays but spills over into theatre practice, to affect how plays are cast, rehearsed, directed, designed, publicized, reviewed. To affect, that is, the entire politics of contemporary theatre production. Without diminishing the work Shakespeare's words do in the theatre, I want to argue that his playtext tells only part of the story: that, until the text he didn't write down – the performance text – is recuperated, re-imagined, put back into play and accounted for by spectators, we're reading only half Shakespeare's play. Reading performance texts means reimagining the canon, opening up its supplementary physical, visual, gestural, iconic texts, making more space for the kind of work women do in play (particularly as Shakespeare situates their roles to play off men). It also means writing about it in a body-conscious language attentive to feeling, to the itch and pleasures of desire, and to pain. It means attending to theatre's 'feminine' unruliness and the unpredictable, not to say promiscuous, theory-resisting effects performance generates. And it means registering and fixing scrutiny on the woman's body as bearer of gendered meanings – meanings that do not disappear when words run out or characters fall silent. Discursive criticism finds such textual absence a form of erasure or mysterious opacity: a symptomatic instance of this is Elaine Showalter's interesting failure, in a seminal essay on the 'Responsibilities of Feminist Criticism' some years back, to register Ophelia's appearance in her final scene – where she's a corpse.[7] For Showalter, it seems, the silent body of dead Ophelia simply vanished. More recently, Philippa Berry ends her elegantly word-attentive study of *Shakespeare's Feminine Endings* with 'uncertainty' surrounding the dead body of Cordelia, who remains, says Berry, 'the play's central riddle', 'a mystery even in her death'.[8] Perhaps rhetorically that is true, but as a body in play, Cordelia's corpse is clearly, concretely and extensively legible and generates many more certain, if provisional, readings than Berry allows for. Discursive bodies in criticism may disappear, get erased. Material bodies in the theatre remain in view. Where Berry's work on Cordelia's ending ends, mine on that same ending begins.

In my opening chapter I propose the corpse as a limit case for the work a body in play can perform. Moving between the narrative and performative endings of *King Lear* and seeing the appalling illegibility of his daughters's bodies (which drove Lear's abdication crisis) remembered at the end, I speculate on Cordelia, seeing her dead body as an 'instructive object' and asking 'What does it instruct?'. What do they see when Lear demands of spectators, 'Look on her, look there'? Historicizing those questions, I survey the apparatus Shakespeare's first *King Lear* spectators may have had culturally to hand to make sense – or not – of Cordelia's corpse and the spectacle of theatrical death. Finally, I return to the present to review three re-presentations of *Lear*'s ending, on film and stage, to see how subsequent performances exploit the 'naught-y' body to frame Lear's death as tragedy.

Chapter 2 takes these ideas further, applying notions of 'vexed looking' and 'unruly bodies' – the actorly corpse who, playing dead, plays up – to a feminist critique of four film *Hamlet*s that, I argue, achieve their heroic ending by erasing the body that contests it, the body of Ophelia in the grave. I move between the structuring absence of the Shakespearean playtext (which these films – quite legitimately – mostly cut) and the images film produces in its place to analyse the performance work Ophelia's funeral does in Shakespeare's script. I produce a reading of her funeral that is attentive to the early modern practices Shakespeare is both invoking and inverting, and then I count the cost of what is lost when films commit a body snatch of dead Ophelia.

The politics of performance, representation and celebrity that I see circulating around the hijacked body of Ophelia becomes a central issue in Chapter 3 where the erasure I observe is not of the woman's gendered body but the woman's raced body. Shakespeare's Cleopatra tells us she is black, as his Othello tells us he is black. The Egyptian queen, however, captured early on by white western culture (a capture which, in the play, she commits suicide in order to avoid) and installed as one of its chief feminine icons, is everywhere whited out in her subsequent high-cultural representation. I examine this phenomenon in productions of *Antony and Cleopatra* by the Royal Shakespeare Company since 1953 – coronation year – and I link Egypt's queen 'of infinite variety' both to post-war Britain's young Elizabeth and to England's first Elizabeth. But I also read the black narrative that hovers around the margin of the dominant white history, aligning Shakespeare's Cleopatra with another contemporary 'black' queen, Anna of Denmark. Ironically on the modern stage, the same productions which continue – even in multi-cultural Britain – to white out Cleopatra habitually insert black bodies at her side. So what work – political, cultural, theatrical – does the black body of the woman do in Shakespeare today?

The politics of representation I see operating so prejudicially in Chapter 3 are taken up, reframed, in Chapter 4. My topic is the designed body. Seeing Shakespeare himself as the first designer of Shakespeare and surveying some of his original design instructions, I argue that costume in the theatre is the most conspicuously charged material for writing a politics of the body, and assess the power the designer has in our contemporary 'designer's theatre' to determine both the discursive space a role occupies and how the audience reads it. Seeing women's roles as particularly vulnerable to design decisions – such that costume changes habitually mark changes in character – I use *Troilus and Cressida* to study the problematics of design. As its core conceit this Shakespeare playtext foregrounds 'change' (from changed minds and changed husbands to hostages exchanged) and locates in an exchange of tokens a costume change that plays against the text to register visually the crisis that annuls the lovers' vows. Reading Helen as Shakespeare's design coup for his play, I read productions at the RSC since John Barton's (in)famous 1968 *Troilus and Cressida* as setting a very different agenda for the work design performs in a theatre of theatricalized sexuality.

My last chapter offers a close reading of one body in play: here, I remember Zoe Wanamaker playing Emilia in *Othello*. As an act of memory that re-performs performance, this chapter serves as a practical demonstration of the kind of performance studies theorized throughout the rest of the book. Emilia's need to remember, to gossip, to re-cite Desdemona's ending and retell it 'with a [crucial] difference' brings *Othello*'s narrative to a conclusion unanticipated by Iago's ugly manipulation of the cultural tropes that successfully stifle her voice – until she's confronted with the body of Desdemona stifled. But Emilia's remembering and her 'tattling' likewise collect up ideas about performance and bodies in play that have been circulating from my opening chapter, and reconfigure them. Thus, Emilia's need to tell, to 'bode', and to 'bode' in the body, offers me a final paradigm for what I want this book to offer.

Just as I understand that in writing performance I'm writing myself and staking a claim in theatre that is as much heuristic as historic – I want to 'see better' – so I understand that all the bodies in play on Shakespeare's stage are anamorphs. They're bogus proxies whose fake effects produce, in spectators, real affect, 'real tears' that we shed, as Tony Dawson says, 'on account of what we recognize as unreal feelings'.[9] Theatrical bodies work like those optical instruments, those 'perspectives' Bushy describes in *Richard II*, 'which rightly gazed upon / Show nothing but confusion; eyed awry, / Distinguish form' (2.2.16–24). 'Eyeing awry', like 'vexed looking', is a standard viewing procedure in the theatre, where we know, as the Chorus in *Henry V* tells us, we're looking at 'mockeries'. Paradoxically, however, theatre's equivocating bodies 'lie like truth'. Seeing those bogus, feigning, anamorphic bodies in play, we spectators learn to 'distinguish form', to re-cite and remember our own histories, by 'minding true things by what their mockeries be.'

ACKNOWLEDGEMENTS

This book begins and ends with scenes of women silenced. In between, however, its engagement with theatre, history and performance depends upon conversation. It is a pleasure, now, to remember and credit the conversations that went into its writing, most particularly with Barbara Hodgdon, Bill Worthen, Tony Howard and Skip Shand, my closest collaborators as readers and writers, spectators and cultural historians, friends who constantly challenge me to 'see better', and, by commenting on successive drafts of this book, to write better, too. Hodgdon's *The Shakespeare Trade*, Worthen's *Shakespeare and the Authority of Performance*, Shand's work on actorly reading and Howard's forthcoming *The Woman in Black* are the inter-texts that inform my work; my debt to them is everywhere and obvious. I'm grateful also to a wider group of friends and colleagues who share their research with me: Tony Dawson, Miriam Gilbert, Ric Knowles, John Stokes, Marion O'Connor, Bill Ingram, Peter Mack, Jim Bulman, Peter Holland, Russell Jackson, Peter Donaldson, Leeds Barroll, Joyce MacDonald and Mick Jennings (whose crash course in the cultural history of post-war Britain was as invaluable as it was entertaining). Colleagues in the Film, History, and English Departments at Warwick gave me invaluable help in things big and small: Richard Dyer, Victor Perkins, Bernard Capp, Mike Bell, Liz Cameron and Stephen Shapiro. Ed Gallafent and Kate Chedgzoy read various chapters at various times and offered criticism that was as smart as it was supportive. Peter Davidson chased rumours of black bodies in Scotland down to their sources and helped me decipher some devilishly difficult secretary hand.

Invitations in recent years to lecture at York University, the Shakespeare Institute, and on the Shakespeare in Performance circus at Cambridge University have given me opportunities to present preliminary versions of this work. I'm grateful to my hosts on those occasions both for attentive audiences and warm hospitality: Michael Cordner,

ACKNOWLEDGEMENTS

Stanley Wells, Peter Holland, Jean Chothia, Adrian Poole and Wil
Sanders (who also acted as go-between in a series of communiqués on
Cleopatra's family history from John Ray, Reader in Egyptology at
Selwyn College). I particularly appreciate the intelligent conversation of
students at Warwick and the Shakespeare Institute; the up-and-coming
generation of Shakespeare scholars is indeed impressive. Much of the
impetus to write the book came from meetings of the Shakespeare
Association of America (and their after-shocks), particularly Ric
Knowles's 'After the Shakespeare Revolution' seminar in 1994. My
thanks, too, to all who contributed such thoughtful work to my
'Performing Race' seminar in 2000, especially Bill Worthen, Denis Salter
and John Drakakis, Sujata Iyengar, Ian Smith and David Schalkwyk.
Initial versions of Chapters 1 and 2 appeared as 'Eel Pie and Ugly Sisters
in *King Lear*' in *Essays in Theatre/Études Théâtrales* 14:1 (November
1995) and 'Snatched Bodies: Ophelia in the Grave' in *Shakespeare
Quarterly* 49:3 (Fall 1998). My thanks to both journals for permission to
republish.

Librarians at the Shakespeare Centre – Sylvia Morris, Karin Brown, Jo
Lockhart – and the Shakespeare Institute – Jim Shaw – provided a level
of expertise and personal attention that was simply astonishing and were
responsible not just for much material but for much good humour, good
sense and sanity. I appreciate the time Peter Higgs at the British Museum
took to answer queries on a certain Syrian lady, and the whole day
Christopher Lloyd, Surveyor of the Queen's Pictures, devoted to me.
'The Family' being out of town, he showed me, at St James's, the
Jacobean collection and taught me to read the van Somer portrait of
Queen Anna. Garry Nickols of Warwick University's Audio-Visual
Department made production pictures happen. Janet Costa and Sophie
Holroyd supported me both personally and professionally beyond the
call of duty or even love, doubling as chief wizard and good angel,
knowing how to work computers and when to turn them off, to pull on
Wellies (or unwrap chocolate).

Anyone who writes about theatre in Britain relies on a corps of critics
whose business is today's news; their reviews comprise a rich archive of
observation, anecdote and analysis. I'm fortunate to know some of the
best eyes and ears in the business: Michael Billington, Michael Coveney,
John Peter, Robert Butler and Paul Taylor. I'm deeply grateful to them
for writing that keeps theatre alive after the event and for serious gossip
in theatre foyers and on the telephone. I continue to appreciate the
friendship and sceptical conversation of theatre practitioners – actors,
directors, designers, photographers – who first taught me to think theatre through the body and who remain bemused by my interest in

performance past, since theirs is in performance present and future. My thinking on black Cleopatra began with Claire Benedict's Charmian: I thank her for that performance, for the later interview, and for making white Cleopatra forever strange. Chapter 3 is hers.

This project was supported by awards from the Arts and Humanities Research Board of the British Academy, the Jubilee Education Fund of the Shakespeare Birthplace Trust (Stratford-upon-Avon), and by generous study leave provision and a publication grant from the University of Warwick.

My dearest debt is to the women I live with, my daughters, Bryony and Rowan, who, when they were younger, used to shove notes under the door of the former pig sty where I work to see if I were still in there – and alive. In their father, the actor, they see the struggle to make theatre happen; in their mother, the academic, the struggle to write about it well. Despite this double inoculation from the 'old stock', it looks like neither of them will go in for banking or brain surgery. I thank my daughters for their conversation; without it, this book wouldn't have happened.

1

BODY PARTS OR PARTS FOR BODIES

Speculating on Cordelia

Gonerill and Regans bodies brought out.
Enter Lear with Cordelia in his armes
Folio Stage Direction

A dead body is an instructive object.
Michael Bristol, *Carnival and Theatre*, 1985

Death may usurp on nature many hours,
And yet the fire of life kindle again
The o'erpressed spirits. I have heard
Of an Egyptian nine hours dead,
Who was by good appliances recovered.
Pericles, Scene 12, 80–85

Dead Reckoning

When Cordelia makes her final entrance in Lear's arms, Kent will not believe what he is seeing. 'Is this the promised end?' he asks. Cordelia plays her last scene dead. Or maybe she's playing dead. For she isn't meant to die. It wasn't what audiences were expecting. The old *King Leir*, the *True Chronicle* which they had seen at Henslowe's Rose playhouse in 1594 and (perhaps) again, revived, in 1605 before it went into print, had a happy ending. That 'true' story (which, clearly, had saturated Shakespeare's mind, for memory traces of *Leir* turn up in *Lear*) ended in return, recognition, reconciliation.[1] So maybe Cordelia in Lear's arms is only pretending, like Hero, Helena, Juliet, Thisbe in Peter Quince's *Pyramus and Thisbe*, the Player Queen in Hamlet's *Mousetrap*. Or, like Desdemona (momentarily) or Cleopatra (chronically) – and with Hermione, Thaisa, Imogen to come in plays not yet written – perhaps

1

Cordelia will revive. As Cerimon testifies over Thaisa's body, 'I have heard of an Egyptian . . .'

'Playing dead', of course, is precisely what the actor does in the scene. But it is also what the scene mocks the audience and Lear with imagining that Cordelia is doing. 'She's dead as earth,' says Lear. But then: 'This feather stirs; she lives!'. So is she 'gone for ever!', or will she 'stay a little'? Does she breathe? Will 'her breath . . . mist' 'a looking-glass'? Lear's invitation (rough? urgent? gentle? querulous?) to Cordelia to speak ('What is't thou say'st'?') and his command to his spectators to 'Look on her, look, her lips' opens up the miraculous possibility of resurrection. Are we, along with Kent, Albany, Edgar and the huddle of soldiers who circle King Lear, looking at a miracle or an hallucination, at a corpse stiffening in rigor mortis or at 'a chance that does redeem all sorrows'?

Like Kent, whose gaze towards Cordelia's entrance forces him to speculate, I want to question this ending, to think not just about narrative closure and the meaning of Cordelia's death, but about the theatrical significance of Cordelia-as-corpse. Indeed, I want to use Cordelia as a case study for the kinds of work a body in play performs on stage as it focuses a whole series of paradoxical speculations. Only the most conspicuous of these is the way, in performance, a real body fakes the role of bogus corpse for the purposes of the narrative, a discrepancy Shakespeare manipulates most disturbingly in *King Lear* to set the finality of the narrative ending – 'she's dead' – at odds with the ambiguity of the performative ending. We know the actor who plays Cordelia 'lives'. Cordelia could come back to life. Any body on stage, potentially, might. The actorly body who plays dead, works, in performance, at the margin. Speechless, motionless, reduced by death from somebody to *the* body, the corpse, the actor's body occupies a theatrical space of pure performance where it has most to play when it has least to act. It is a subject-made-object whose presence registers absence and loss. Narratively, too, though, the body that plays dead works at the margin: it comes in at the end; it collects up final meanings. The scrutiny of the body, the interpretations attached to it through last rites and contemplations, the final stories told about it in consolation or in rage work to fix the narrative's final form. Looking at the body as a sign loaded with 'story', we discover whether what we have been watching is desolate tragedy or grotesque comedy; whether what we feel is pity or other, wilder emotions.

The questions that inform these speculations are very simple. How does Shakespeare 'play' the body? How do audiences – his, ours – read it? I want, first, to think about the status of the theatrical corpse to try to theorize the areas of cultural work it performs; then to view its performance historically, to attempt to recuperate some of the interpretational apparatus that might originally have been in place for making sense – or not – of death. Next, I return to *King Lear*'s playtext to argue that the ending replays the beginning: once again, the crisis turns on interpretation and is located in the staggering illegibility of bodies. Finally, having proposed some modes of reading the ending, I come clean on 'speculation', admitting that a textual body 'means' nothing until it's performed. Cordelia's body becomes legible only in performance. And not finally or definitively legible, but provisionally, plurally, and variously readable, for every subsequent performance of *King Lear* elaborates additional meanings, written through the body. That being the case, I mobilize another mode of 'speculation', looking closely at three versions of Cordelia's final scene in performance.

Parts for Bodies

Theorizing the relationship between art and anatomy, Ludmilla Jordanova understands the body as a 'cultural resource' where any number of 'social constituencies' converge to 'find meanings that are immediately relevant to them'. Because the body 'is simultaneously abstract and concrete, symbolic and intimate, familiar and dangerous, ordinary and mysterious, material and sacred', it is 'used in all societies for doing . . . much business'.[2] One of those 'societies', Keir Elam would argue, is the 'Shakespearean critical industry' where, over the past ten years, a 'boom of "corporeal" criticism' has transformed it, via what Elam imagines as a kind of academic takeover bid, into 'Shakespeare Corp'.[3] Elsewhere, Anthony Dawson reminds readers of Shakespeare how much we (already) knew about the body before Elam's crit/corps got hold of it: from Mary Douglas, we knew how the body figured as 'natural symbol, a site of circulating, intersecting, clashing meanings'; from Foucault, 'how power and discourse make themselves felt in relation to the body of the criminal, the madman, the lover.'[4] Bakhtin taught us about the carnivalised body; Laqueur, the sexualised body. Bodies sodomised (Goldberg); patriarchally enclosed (Stallybrass); effeminised (Levine); embarrassed (Paster); anatomised (Sawday) have all been mustered in what Elam calls 'a veritable ghost army of early modern organisms.'[5]

In Dawson's terms, the body constructed by new historicist and cultural materialist critics works discursively: it's a textual body that figures as a site of 'struggle', 'differentiation', 'appropriation'. As a politicized 'discursive nexus', it functions as a kind of inscriptive surface: 'differences of power are *written* on the body.'[6] But against this 'discursive' body Dawson posits another body, what he calls the 'theatrical' (or 'performative') body of the actor. This body is 'of' the text, but always exceeds the text. Reading Shakespeare requires us to read double, both discursively and theatrically, as 'the text puts the ideological reading into play and at the same time engages it with a theatrical one.'[7] So as we read 'words, words, words', we also read bodies. For Dawson, the space between the two kinds of reading is 'both contested and negotiated': neither displaces the other. Instead, 'What is staged is a contest between alternative ways of making meaning, of turning theatrical experience into meaning', a contest between body and meaning which Shakespeare stages in such a way as to locate 'fundamental' though 'not exclusive, signifying power in the theatrical body'.[8]

Both bodies, the discursive and the theatrical, are at work in the final scene of *King Lear*. Death is a gendered topic in Shakespeare. Mostly, men die onstage, their violent deaths fulfilling the terms and conditions of male adventure, struggle, antagonism and contest, in a pattern that costs life but legitimates male heroism and male law. The *Lear* stage has just been occupied with this business, brother killing brother in a combat that restores legitimacy to the kingdom. Usually, male death ends the story as the dead exit heroizes (sometimes problematically) the corpse. Hamlet, borne 'like a soldier, to the stage', is the archetype; Antony, heaved ingloriously up the side of Cleopatra's monument and comically denied his final speech, the parodic anti-type. Women, however, mostly die offstage, accessories, both 'adjunct' and 'means to' heroic male dying. But before those deaths occur, women's corpses are returned onstage, re-presented for speculation. The physical material of their death works like the Queen's tears in *Richard II,* analogized to 'perspectives' – optical instruments – 'which, rightly gazed upon, / Show nothing but confusion; eyed awry, / Distinguish form' (2.2.18–20). That is, the dead body of the woman has a part to play in which the paradoxical looking economy it sets up with the spectator is skewed, 'awry'. And that requires us to bend our sight in order to see better.

At the end of *King Lear*, Shakespeare requires Cordelia's dead presence on stage, and he requires three audiences to study her body. Is the body there to provide material on which to write male performances and male reactions? Perhaps, for Cordelia's body is Lear's sole speculation. He constructs his own final performance upon it: he plays across it, plays over it, plays with it. Or is it there to signify, mutely, a recuperation of patriarchal power? Perhaps, for, dead silent, Cordelia finally achieves female excellence and redeems the fault she committed by faulty speaking in the opening scene where Lear's 'Mend your speech' rebuked the 'Nothing' she wanted to say. Now, saying nothing, Lear approves her: 'Her voice was ever soft, / Gentle and low, an excellent thing in woman'. Of course, speechless, Cordelia is deprived of obvious power to construct her own meanings. Dead, she is a *tabula rasa* or collection of signs, like Desdemona, the 'fair paper', the 'goodly book' Othello writes 'whore upon', or like Lavinia, whose 'martyr'd signs' Titus will 'wrest' into 'an alphabet' to read her as a 'map of woe'. On this surface Lear will inscribe his particular desires and fantasies, for Cordelia is Lear's object – her evacuated subjectivity a cause for lament and her body, as Janet Adelman puts it, 'a prop for Lear's anguish'.[9] As object, her corpse is situated to occupy what Elisabeth Bronfen explores as the prime iconic space reserved for the female body in western culture.[10] 'Look on her,' says Lear. Cordelia-as-corpse is the spectacle that holds and directs the all-male gaze, passive, unresisting, whatever Lear makes her.

Or not. For the body I have just been describing, positioned inside a gendered discursive nexus, is attached to that other, performative body. Dead, her text exhausted, Cordelia has nothing to act yet everything to play for. She is indeed a prop, but not in Adelman's sense; rather, she's a theatre prop, 'property' – belonging to – Lear's performance.[11] And, like all Shakespeare's properties from Desdemona's handkerchief and Cressida's glove to Yorick's skull and Antony's sword, she is both a troubled and troubling signifier. Performing death, her corpse alienates – in the Brechtian sense – Lear's performance by challenging the anguish Lear attempts to fix upon it. The discursive effect of this is to frame the theatrical site of female death not as a conformable but as a subversive site. Cordelia's body does not behave in death. Her corpse plays up. Even as the audience is required to 'Look on her', the demand that we look is most intense at the very moment when what we are looking at is most vexed.[12]

How are we invited to look at this body? To address that, I want to begin by considering how Shakespeare's audience might have looked.

Instructive Objects

Michael Bristol's dry comment, 'A dead body is an instructive object', prompts a come-back. What (and whom) does it instruct? Death, certainly, is universal, but its practices are historically constituted.[13] How we imagine it, react to it, dress up for it (as mourners and as corpses), repress, discuss, remember, mystify and profane it, are all elaborated in customary rituals that formulate death as a social text, a cultural performance, whose conventions are open to revision and subversion. To be legible, whatever instruction death offers requires historicized reading.

Consider the Londoner, a householder in the Liberty of the Clink on the South Bank, who lived through the first week of August 1593. In that single week, 1,305 Londoners out of a population of some hundred thousand died of plague. This imaginary Londoner's real neighbour, Philip Henslowe, whose Rose playhouse down Southwark High Street, on Maiden Lane, had been enlarged and refurbished eighteen months earlier to accommodate the Admiral's Men, their stellar lead player, Edward Alleyn, and the bustling increased business the move anticipated, was an eyewitness who wrote to Alleyn telling him the appalling news.[14] The players were on tour and the Rose shut by order of the Privy Council to prevent the spread of infection, attributed by some to the 'profanity' of playhouses by a logic that construed epidemic death as God's punitive, if dreadfully promiscuous, judgement upon players. A week later, Henslowe wrote further. 'As for newes of the sycknes,' he told Alleyn, 'I cane not seand you no Juste note of yt be cause there is command ment to the contrary but as I thincke doth die with in the sitteye and with owt [i.e. in the suburbs] of all syckneses to the nomber of seventen or eyghten hundreth in one weacke.' Henslowe's own household was 'flytted with ffeare': 'Rownd a bowte vs' the 'sycknes . . . hathe bene all most in every howsse . . . & wholle howsholdes deyed . . . . Robart browne's wife in shordech & all her chelldren & howshowld be dead & heare dores sheat vpe.'[15]

Ten years later, in the summer of 1603, London went through it all again. Entire households died. Doors, again, were shut up. This time it was Joan Alleyn who wrote to the absent players. Her stepfather, Henslowe, was 'at the Corte but wheare the Court ys I know not.' (As a Groom of His Majesty's Chamber, Henslowe was required to attend upon the new king, whose coronation on 25 July would be curtailed to the bare ceremony for fear of the infection.) In the final week of June, 158 Londoners were listed dead of plague; by mid-July, 917; in August, Bartholomew Fair was cancelled as the week by week total rose from 1,922 to 2,713 to 3,035. John Chamberlain wrote to Dudley Carleton that he had returned to London from the country 'and meant to have tarried here till the coronation, but seing yt wilbe so private, and the sicknes increseth so fast upon us, I wish myself there again, and will make all the haste I can out of towne, for yt growes hot here.' London was deserted – at least of its gentry. 'Powles grows very thin,' Chamberlain wrote, 'for every man shrinckes away' – most conspicuously, the king, removed from London to his hunting lodge in the country.[16] His meaner subjects were not so fortunate. While Joan Alleyn rejoiced that her own household were 'in good healthe & about vs the sycknes dothe Cease' and reported that 'All the [playing] Companyes be Come hoame & well for ought we knowe', she sent desolate news of another player: 'Browne of the Boares head is dead & dyed very pore, he went not into the Countrye at all.'[17]

How did people who lived through these deadly years, who avoided death in their houses and gardens to perform it on stage or observe it, as spectators, from the theatre's yard or galleries, look upon the spectacle of theatrical death? What apparatus did their culture propose for addressing the representation of death?

Grief Work: Consolation

One available apparatus was the elegy, the poetic genre that did for them the work of mourning. Elegy expressed the inexpressible. Remembering lost objects, it shaped unutterable loss into utterance under pressure of tropes conventionalized long before Sidney, Spenser and Shakespeare found them, already old, in Theocritus and Ovid. This poetry set mourning in a conventional pastoral landscape animated by vegetation deities and informed by myths of return and rebirth, a landscape that felt desolation but held it in tension with potential restoration, not as fantasy but as miracle, as resurrection. Like the pastoral eclogue, elegy was characterized, formally, by repetition and refrain, reiterated questions, interruptive outbreaks (in elegy, of rage and cursing), a sense of internal contestation and debate that, finally, resolved into consolation, 'all passion spent'. As the conventional procession of mourners moved across this poetry from grief to consolation, their voices, speaking in counterpoint, even in competition, raised questions that mourning wanted answered – about blame, reward, inheritance, but also, crucially, about affect. Elegy, that is, interrogated the very work of consolation it purported to be doing. As Peter Sacks points out in his fine study of the genre, while, by convention, the elegist needed 'to draw attention, consolingly, to his own surviving powers', he was forced, at the same time, to concede 'reluctant submission to language itself'.[18] He was forced to admit, as the work of poetry proceeded, that words failed, that mourning could reach only an accommodated settlement with loss through elegy's fictions of consolation.

Elegy, in short, offered Shakespeare's culture a formal poetic model for managing bereavement. By association, it might have offered Shakespeare's spectators more, a paradigm for managing *Lear*'s ending, for that ending works like elegy, calling up one elegiac convention after the other – then disrupting them, refusing to play them straight. It produces the expected repetitions ('Howl, howl, howl'; 'Never, never, never, never, never'; 'Look there, look there!'). And questions ('Is this the promis'd end?'; 'Or image of that horror?'; 'Why should a dog, a horse, a rat, have life . . . ?'). The anticipated movement towards consolation is, predictably enough, interrupted by vengeful cursing ('A plague upon you, murderers, traitors all!') and repaired by promised rewards ('All friends shall taste / The wages of their virtue . . .') and the distribution of inheritance ('you twain / Rule in this realm . . .'). But – unpredictably – that movement is blocked, consolation refused, as the scene works utterly to derange elegy's most precious conventions. It re-imagines the scene of nostalgic mourning and travesties it, the landscape of Lear's loss not Arcadian but apocalyptic, bounded on one side by the barren heath, on the other, the limitless, empty, sterile sands – a bizarre, pastoral dystopia. It plays cruelly with elegy's optimism about poetry's power. 'Pray you, undo this button' perhaps sounds like Lear's hopeful attempt to release whatever 'surviving powers' remain to him, a trope for his need to keep on talking. But his quizzing of the corpse – 'What is't thou say'st?' – insanely registers what he still doesn't recognize, that language, spectacularly, has failed. If Lear's journey through madness (3.2, 3.4, 3.6, 4.6) and catatonic sleep (4.7) into waking to new life in new clothes is seen to mimic resurrection (4.7), his cradling of Cordelia's body at the end perhaps puts spectators in mind of another cradled corpse, another longed-for resurrection. Or maybe what's striking is not how Shakespeare's ending reproduces elegiac convention, but nihilistically confounds it. Elegy, crucially, desires metamorphosis. As in Ovid, it wants translation of lost objects into substitutes, 'found' signs, like Daphne, fleeing Apollo's pursuit, metamorphosed into the laurel that Apollo, mourning her loss, fashions into something new, a wreath, a 'consolation prize'. This remembers Daphne even as it self-promotes the god. The laurel is Apollo's crown which he awards to prize-winning poets, his own celebrants. What elegy desires, though, *Lear* denies. There is no transformation, resurrection. In *Lear* the Ovidian metamorphosis that translates mourning into consolation fails.

Reading *Lear*'s ending as elegy – or failed elegy – suggests one strategy available to Shakespeare's spectators for viewing that ending. But there were also others.

'Memento Mori': Contemplation

While the elegy worked to translate lost objects into signs and mourning into consolation, the *memento mori* stubbornly stuck on the thing itself, charging man to know his end by gazing on his future, the skull beneath the skin. The *memento mori* found house room everywhere in early modern English culture, for as Roy Strong observes, it was one of the few subjects collected as avidly by the plebs as the aristos. The Earl of Leicester collected *memento mori*. So did Edward Alleyn – one of Leicester's Men.[19] Schooled, as Roland Mushat Frye says, in the contemplation of death, Renaissance man conned core texts from Seneca and scripture. The philosopher taught him that man's mind was 'never more divine than when it reflects upon its mortality, and understands . . . that the body is not a permanent dwelling but a sort of inn' where 'sojourn' is 'brief'. The gospeller instructed him that 'ripeness' was 'all', for since 'That day and hour' of death 'no man knoweth', man's 'lively' discipline was to be prepared. 'Therefore,' said Matthew, rounding off the parable of the wise and foolish virgins, 'be ye also ready'.[20] The *memento mori* objectified that preparation.

Thus, Mary Queen of Scots wore on a chain around her neck a silver-gilt skull-shaped timepiece, designed ingeniously to tell her the hour but also the truth, that her every minute took her closer to death.[21] Thus, too, a vogue arose among the gentry in the mid-1500s for collecting the small ivory skull or *vanitas*, a conceit that found its way into English portraiture via, it appears, Holbein (in *The Ambassadors, c.* 1533). Both the skull and the skeleton are used in an unknown artist's *memento mori* portrait of the ageing Queen Elizabeth, her head resting on her hand, her cheekbones standing out from her shrunken flesh. Flanking her, Time waits at her elbow like an obsequious, geriatric courtier; opposite, a skeleton leans towards her attentively, proffering an hourglass and coffin. The queen is not so much weary as thoughtful, her pose registering that her contemplation of death is not just the subject but the object of this portrait as artefact. These same elements and sense of purpose found their way into domestic portraiture intended as *memento mori*, in, for example, the unsigned *Judd Memorial* (*c.* 1560), a painting Edward Alleyn may once have owned.[22] Husband and wife, standing in three-quarter profile at opposite sides of the panel, reach towards each other, hands touching as they rest on the head of a skull. At the foot of the painting, a naked cadaver draped in his shroud lies prone, the horizontal composition mirroring the line across the painting above, formed by the Judds' clasped hands – husband and wife connected in death as in life.

Where portraiture worked *memento mori* into curious compositional discourse with the subject, monumental masonry laid out its contemplation starkly in stone. From the mid-fifteenth century the fashionable dead were represented in tomb effigy as twin bodies, stacked one upon the other. Above lay the gorgeously memorialized *gisant*, representing the body of the prince (temporal or spiritual) in all the splendour of his worldly substance; below lay the parallel text, the ghastly *transi*, the same body exposed post mortem as a naked corpse, a rotting cadaver feasting worms, a mummy so desiccated that the skeleton threatened to pierce the skin stretched over it.[23] A hundred years later tombs like the

Cornwall Triptych (1588) and the Foljambe monument (*c.* 1592) approximated what the Judd memorial achieved in painting by representing life and death as somehow coterminous, occupying the same visual space. Richard Cornwall and his parents, in gown and armour, gaze out of the triptych; below them a predella opens to reveal Richard's corpse bizarrely enclosed in a transparent shroud – designed to let the spectator gaze upon the body's decay. The Foljambe tomb reads horizontally, frame upon frame, like the great stained glass windows of York Minster and Bath Abbey. At the top of the tomb, centre, skeletal Death presides, his deadly dart in one hand, a sexton's shovel in the other, his foot resting on a skull. Age, bent over a walking stick, and Youth, a plump naked boy, flank him. Below them, the corpse awaits the grave laid out on a bier, its shroud knotted head and foot.

Memento mori prepared the spectator for death by stimulating the imagination into active contemplation. It 'remembered' the future – in some cases, literally. Archbishop Chichele's *transi* tomb was carved twenty years before he died.[24] John Donne sat for his death portrait in advance, as Issac Walton relates:

> Several charcoal fires being first madde in his large study, he brought with him into that place a winding sheet in his hand, and having put off all his clothes, had this sheet put on him, and so tied with knots at his head and feet, and his hands so placed as dead bodies are usually fitted, to be shrouded and put into their coffin, or grave . . . with his eyes shut and with so much of the sheet turned aside as might show his lean, pale and death-like face.[25]

Close to death in August 1598, Philip II of Spain 'made himself most familiar, not only with the thought of death but with the details . . . thereof,' ordering his servants 'to bring into his room and to his bedside a shirt of lead into which he is to be wrapped after he has breathed his last.'[26]

Ghosting all these *memento mori* is a conceit that found full embodiment in one final representation, the *portrait macabre*. What the *transi*, the *vanitas*, the tomb effigy only intimated, the *portrait macabre* materially constituted by representing its subject as an anamorph to show life and death as merely different spectator positions on the same object. Thus, Mary Queen of Scots, in her *portrait macabre*, showed from one perspective the gorgeous queen; from another, a death's head.

I want to propose that, for spectators in Shakespeare's theatre, the actorly corpse reworked the *vanitas* tradition, that the body on stage worked like Mary Stuart in the portrait. Cordelia at *Lear*'s end is there to be read as an anamorph, a *memento mori*.

10

Unruly Bodies: Controversy

The culture that used the elegy and the *vanitas* to organize its thoughts on death was perhaps signalling a desire to settle men's minds, to compose them against the indignities of such hysterical terrors as shake, for one, Shakespeare's Claudio, anticipating death – 'To lie in cold obstruction, and to rot' (*Measure for Measure*, 3.1.120). The *memento mori*, elegy, even *portrait macabre* steadied man for death by displaying dead bodies that observed decorum, that behaved themselves. But not all corpses were so tractable – or comfortingly instructive. Elsewhere, this culture speculated on corpses that misbehaved, that struggled against mortal limitation as they aggressively, uncannily reinserted themselves back into life, unsettling both closure and composure to puzzle understanding of mortality with controversy.

In two early Shakespeare plays of the 1590s unruly corpses make unexpected returns (one staged, one reported) to confront, even confound the living. In *1 Henry VI* Warwick produces the ghastly body of Humfrey, Duke of Gloucester, not 'Dead in his bed' as Suffolk reported, but 'traitorously . . . murdered' (3.2.29, 123). 'Come hither gracious sovereign,' Warwick directs the king, 'view this body' while he himself conducts a 'survey' of the 'dead and earthly image', reading it for signs of violence:

> See how the blood is settled in his face . . .
> But see, his face is black and full of blood;
> His eyeballs further out than when he lived,
> Staring full ghastly like a strangled man;
> His hair upreared; his nostrils stretched with struggling;
> His hands abroad displayed, as one that grasped
> And tugged for life and was by strength subdued.
> Look on the sheets . . .
> It cannot be but he was murdered here.
> The least of all these signs were probable.
>
> (3.2.160, 168–178)

In *Titus Andronicus* the psychopathic comic genius Aaron self-delightedly catalogues his atrocities: murder, rape, false witness, arson. And necrotomy. Aaron robs graves, exhumes bodies, translates them into life-sized *memento mori*:

> Oft have I digged up dead men from their graves
> And set them upright at their dead friends' door,

11

Even when their sorrow almost was forgot,
And on their skins, as on the bark of trees,
Have with my knife carvèd in Roman letters,
'Let not your sorrow die though I am dead.'

(5.1.135–140)

Such bodies, returning, their 'signs' or 'Roman letters' demanding to be read, wreck consolation as they wildly deflect the gaze from composed contemplation to horrified fascination, repulsion. As objects, they appal, but as props (in Warwick's theatre of arraignment, or Aaron's theatre of cruelty) they turn the gaze back on to their spectators, to interrogate the subjects whose objectives they serve. They won't let matters lie.

Even more controversial were performances put in by two real bodies. On 8 February 1586, Mary Queen of Scots was beheaded at Fotheringay Castle. Fifteen signatories put their names to a brief account, only some 400 words, that ended unremarkably. According to the official report, the Queen kissed her women servants,

> willed them to depart the scaffold, and again with a cross, with her hands toward her said servants, she bade them farewell, and so resolutely kneeled down, and having a kerchief bound over her eyes, laid down her neck, whereupon the executioners proceeded, and she repeating these words, 'In manus tuas domine commendo spiritum meum,' and certain other verses of the Psalms.[27]

Seventeen years later, in 1603, her cousin, Elizabeth, Queen of England, who had ordered Mary's execution, lay in state in Whitehall. She had died on March 24 and would remain in the palace that was also her seat of government until her funeral on April 28. The Venetian ambassador wrote to his Doge:

> Meantime the body of the late Queen by her own orders has neither been opened [embalmed], nor, indeed, seen by any living soul save by three of her ladies. It has been taken to Westminster near London, and lies there in the Palace, all hung with mournings. There the Council waits on her continually with the same ceremony, the same expenditure, down to her very household and table service, as though she were not wrapped in many a fold of cerecloth, and hid in such a heap of lead, of coffin, of pall, but was walking as she used to do at this season, about the alleys of her gardens.[28]

In these official accounts, the scaffold and the household figure as sites of political theatre where both royal bodies played out their final acts of state with flawless decorum, in spectacles that affirmed the absolute authority of the state in the unbroken continuity of state power. Mary, on the raised platform that made her visible to the 300 spectators who witnessed her death, laid her own neck on the block, enacting submission to the monarch she was supposed to have plotted to usurp. Elizabeth, her corpse elsewhere, figured in a domestic performance (its props, 'her very household and table service') whose conceit was to represent her absence as presence: meals continued to be served to her vacant chair, meals that figured the vigour of the appetite that troped her power. Both performances (on the scaffold, in the household) were uncontroversial, 'continent': Mary's, contained by literal inscription within the commissioners' report; Elizabeth's, by symbolic inscription within the court protocol.

But there was more to both stories, reported by observers who kept on watching beyond the formal close, and what they saw registers those spectacles not as settled solemnity but as sensational return and grinning slapstick. Mary's head mocked the executioner. When he raised it to the customary 'view of all the assembly' and validating cry, 'God save the Queen,' he was left foolishly clutching a 'dressing of lawn' attached to an empty scalp of 'borrowed hair', the auburn wig Mary wore for the occasion. Meanwhile, the decapitated head (which, though Mary was only forty-four, was 'as grey as one of three score and ten years old and polled very short') rolled across the scaffold. Even then, it wouldn't play dead. 'Her lips stirred up and down almost a quarter of an hour after her head was cut off.'[29] Elizabeth's corpse was even more grossly incontinent. One of her ladies witnessed her spectacular comeback:

> now her bodie being seared up [Robert Cecil having overruled her command and ordered embalming, which involved 'scouring' and 'searing' the trunk cavity] was brought to whit hall. where being watched everie night by 6 severall Ladies. my selfe that night there watching as one of them being all about the bodie which was fast nayled up in abord cofin with leaves of lead covered with velvet, her bodie and head break with such a crack that spleated the wood lead and cer cloth. whereupon the next daie she was fain to be new trimmed up.[30]

In these unofficial accounts, the mumbling lips and exploding corpse display the excessive, grotesque vitality of Mikhail Bakhtin's carnivalized body, where a theatre of ritual gives way to a theatre of the absurd.

The unruly queens play up with travesties of themselves that interrogate the temporal authority once vested in them when alive. Their antics rupture what was meant to be closed by ceremonies organized to produce consensus. Officially, looking positions in those scenes were meant to be fixed. The plan that assigned everyone his seat in the Great Hall of Fotheringay was 'plotted' in detail; the procession of servitors and observers who laid her table, presented the queen's dishes, tasted them, removed them, was meticulously choreographed. As looking positions were fixed, so, too, reactions, it seems, were meant to be composed around an edifying spectacle of death. But then the head leaped from the executioner's hand, the corpse exploded. Like Duke Humfrey's eyes straining from their sockets or Aaron's carved-up gossips lounging at the door, the unruly bodies of Elizabeth and Mary unsettle death with controversial speculation that wrecks consensus. Now, everyone must speculate: 'Is this the promis'd end?' 'Or image of that horror?'

What was the currency of such stories? Did they circulate as common knowledge, as gossip? In the week of Elizabeth's death the story John Chamberlain reports (having heard the news on his own Rialto, the walkways of St Paul's) tells nothing of unseemly eruptions, but then refers to rumours he thinks better dismissed undisclosed than repeated.[31] For Shakespeare himself, the cultural trope of the *revenant* corpse – a female corpse, as it happens – may have been lodged deep in local folk memory. At Holy Trinity, Shakespeare's parish church in Stratford, there was a story, already old when he might have heard it, that a daughter of the prominent Clopton family, dead of the plague and placed in the family's tomb under the chancel, was buried prematurely.[32] When the vault was next opened, she was found leaning against the wall at the bottom of the stairs, still in her shroud.

Illegible Bodies

Arguing that Shakespeare's culture equipped itself by representational practice to look at death both iconically and iconoclastically, sometimes in the same object, and further, that Cordelia's body was just such an object, I understand that the performative body works much more promiscuously than those prototype mementos. Her corpse may compose, or console, or comfort, or, grotesquely, confound contemplation in wild resistance, for Cordelia, unlike the *memento*, remains stubbornly illegible of any single reading. But then, reading bodies has troubled *Lear* – and Lear – from the beginning.

With the map of the kingdom spread out before them, its gross materialism troping 'bounty' with inventoried property ('shadowy forests . . . champains rich'd . . . plenteous rivers . . . wide-skirted meads') Lear's daughters are required to 'Tell . . . love' – that is, both to 'say' and 'quantify' that love. For Cordelia, this requires a kind of vivisection or grotesque anatomy, for her love is written on her heart. Wanting love told, Lear wants the heart made visible, wants to read 'bounty' on the body as clearly as on the map. But Cordelia 'cannot heave / My heart into my mouth', a metaphor that becomes increasingly intensified and deranged as the play progresses. Early on, Lear performs a bizarre organ transplant where he is both patient and surgeon. 'Disclaim[ing] . . . blood', he 'give[s] / Her father's heart from her', only later to feel that missing organ rising in his own throat – 'O! how this mother swells up toward my heart; / *Hysterica passio!* . . . / . . . my heart, my rising heart!'. This imagery culminates, appallingly, in the mad assizes of 3.6 where Lear wants to peel back flesh and prise ribs apart to 'anatomize Regan' to 'see what breeds about her heart'.

As Lear's anatomical images probe deeper and deeper into the body's interior, his failure to recognize his daughter's meaning tropes her increasing bodily estrangement. In 1.1 Lear alienates Cordelia, makes her 'a stranger to my heart and me', makes her 'the barbarous Scythian / Or he that makes his generation messes / To gorge his appetite' – the monster, that is, who cannibalizes his own children. Again the play pursues images in both directions. It searches Goneril's womb – 'Into her womb convey sterility! / Dry up in her the organs of increase.' It penetrates Gloucester's eyes and Edgar's vision – 'Oh thou side-piercing sight!'. It plumbs the 'sulphurous pit' of female sexuality. Simultaneously, it writes women's exterior forms as increasingly monstrous, illegible of human meaning, incomprehensible. Lear, 'child-changed', is daughtered by hags, Centaurs, sharp-toothed serpents, bloody pelicans. When he mocks Cordelia with deprivation – 'thy truth then be thy dower' – and strips her to her smock, 'dismantl[ing]' so many 'folds of favour' that she becomes unrecognizable in her 'little seeming substance', Lear anticipates the inability to recognize Goneril that he feigns later – 'Your name, fair gentlewoman?' – and so opens the rhetorical abyss into which his self-recognition disappears. 'Does any here know me? . . . / . . . who am I?'. The body is illegible.

But staggeringly, the play proposes precisely the opposite. 'Time shall unfold what plighted cunning hides,' Cordelia comments simply, invoking, as if it were an anatomical datum, the *Nuda veritas* of the emblem books who, standing naked, is legible to all.[33] Which of these bodies does Lear see at the end? And what about us, Shakespeare's modern spectators?

Playing Dead

When 'Howl, howl, howl!' turns all eyes to Lear's entrance, what we see perhaps suggests to us the *pietà*, Lear as Mary cradling the broken child. Or maybe *The Bacchae*, Lear as Agave, coming out of her rhapsodic but murderous ecstasy – bacchic madness – dawningly recognizing the head on her lap as her child's.[34] The spectacle presents itself as tragedy: Cordelia is brought to the spoil heap of death by Mater Dolorosa. But perhaps equally as black comedy, for the scene produces a grotesque visual joke. Lear, having finally learned the Fool's language, and learned, too, the mangled sense in which 'nothing can be made out of nothing', is made, clownishly, to carry in his arms the terrible burden of his learning, the Cordelia-as-corpse who is 'nothing'. Rivetted to this terrible spectacle, Albany and the rest are petrified – 'men of stones'. But are they 'stones' because, like Lear in the first scene of the play, they have hardened their hearts to Cordelia? That is what Lear seems to mean. Or is it rather that they have been turned to stone by gazing upon a new Gorgon? In the opening scene, Lear cursed Cordelia, making her a monster, like 'the barbarous Scythian'. Has Cordelia, dead, finally come to occupy, like her sisters, the monstrous space of Lear's imagination?

Playing dead, Cordelia-as-corpse offers no 'kind nursery' to the father who will shortly die of a broken heart. Wanting death to release the king's old body, Kent urges heartbreak upon him – 'Break, heart; I prithee break!', and given Lear's original hard-heartedness brought on by Cordelia's inability to speak love, it is apt enough, this final heart failure. Instead of comfort, Cordelia, as in the opening scene, turns aside to replay that original scenario of refusal. Lear bends over the body to ask, 'What is't thou say'st?' But naught-y Cordelia again says nothing. 'Stay a little,' he commands, or perhaps implores. Again, she defies him, for this 'sometime daughter' will 'never, never, never, never, never' come again.

Of course, Cordelia does 'stay'. Dead, she can hardly do otherwise. And yet, this kind of staying is only more playing up, more naughtiness, for she is there, but significantly *not* there. So this staying is merely perverse, like speaking but not speaking, like answering 'Nothing' when Lear says 'Tell me.'

In his futile, fumbling way, Lear continues to fantasize compliance from this utterly resistant material. As he slides from Cordelia to 'my poor fool . . . hang'd', bizarrely collapsing identities (as when, earlier, he made his daughters his mother), spectators see the body accumulating meanings, becoming a saturated sign that defamiliarizes to refamiliarize – that is, it re-presents in disturbed replica what has been troubling this

16

play from the beginning. Lear looks up from his hallucination at Kent and suddenly asks, 'Who are you?' That, of course, is the core question the play poses, and it returns us to Lear, originally needing to know his daughters; to Cordelia 'stranger'd'; to Goneril, mocked with non-recognition; to Lear, self-strangered – 'who am I?'. His new question now – 'Who are you?' – is followed by devastating understatement: 'Mine eyes are not o'th'best.' And haven't been, since the opening scene when Kent urged him to 'See better, Lear.'

It is entirely apt that this scene mobilizes tropes of the 'familiar' and locates them in bodies, for what it is doing theatrically is to reassemble all of Lear's family for the first time since the family met to divide the kingdom. Shakespeare's text directs that all of Lear's daughters, not just Cordelia, are on stage. The bodies of Goneril and Regan are produced at Albany's command (while Edmund's body, not insignificantly, is removed: no distraction is going to disturb the stage picture of family reunion). The audience looks at a stage crowded with female – *only* female – death and remembers the opening scene, only now all the 'sometime daughters' are estranged by death, as though Holbein's *Family of Sir Thomas More* has been reassembled as Picasso's *Guernica*.

This idea of dead Cordelia's performative body as a 'saturated sign' that pulls into representation a re-presentation of the play's troubled interests is relevant to the spectacle of female death everywhere on Shakespeare's stage. Desdemona dies, as she was accused, in a love triangle, only it is Emilia, not Cassio, who lies between husband and wife. Lady Macbeth's ending, like the witches', is a weird vanishing, prepared for by that strange spectacle that embodies her absence, the sleepwalking. Cleopatra's ending is a spectacle that, spectacularly, re-genders the Roman triumvirate, making her, in death, queen, wife, and mother suckling the serpent. Gertrude drinks the poison intended for Hamlet and so unwittingly re-enacts a version of the older Hamlet's murder. Ophelia's funeral – the subject of my next chapter – mocks the 'maimed rites' that have blighted her play from the beginning; finally, she occupies the grave that the Ghost and Yorick have both vacated. All of these scenes play out near-parodic re-enactments of original theatrical moments – and render them as devastating critiques. At the end of *King Lear* Cordelia and her sisters, dead silent, replay, with a difference, the problematics of female speech that wrecked the opening and that matter again here. They are, finally, monsters, though not quite as Lear made them: not Scythian cannibal nor lustful Centaur nor monster Ingratitude, but *monstrances*, shows of violence, one poisoned, one stabbed, one strangled. The spectacle of their death constructs them as the play's Gorgon. Medusa, too, had two sisters. As Lear demands that we 'Look . . . look!' the answer

17

comes back, 'See better, Lear.' It may be that such looking, such intense, pitiless looking, is what finally kills Lear.

Bodies in Play

Having offered, speculatively, a number of potential readings of Cordelia's body, among them, readings that resist reading, I want to shift positions, to argue that meaning resides in performance and that what we understand about Cordelia is written and rewritten in the theatre and on film. How does Shakespeare 'play' the body? Three performances address that question differently.

When Peter Brook directed this final sequence on grainy black and white film in 1971 with Paul Scofield as Lear and Anne-Lise Gabold as Cordelia, he constructed a visual replica of the playtext's metaphoric 'vexed looking'.[35] He edited the film to cut disconcertingly between realism and wish-fulfilment, constructing the final sequence as an hallucination fantasy that plays out Lear's desires as a surreal return to Cordelia, *revenant*, alive.

Seconds earlier spectators saw Cordelia's neck broken as she dropped from a gibbet. Now, in long shot, as Lear weaves across a smouldering wasteland, the only sound the wind whipping the dust, the corpse he carries has the noose still tightened around her throat. Lear's 'Howl, howl, howl!' is an animal wail that staggers vocally as his feet do under him. We watch him coming at us from a long way off, the body awkward in his arms, but then the film cuts – disconcertingly, Lear is striding past us – and cuts again. He's turned his back on us. No one occupies this vast space but Lear and Cordelia, and we are forced to look on from afar. By such editing, Brook signals in the looking relations which this editing constructs that the manipulation of those relations is going to be central to the meanings this sequence makes.

Kneeling, Lear puts Cordelia down. The low-angle shot fills the background with sky, drawing a bleak line across the horizon that makes Cordelia, laid out on that plane, an offering to the void on some pagan altar. The film cuts awkwardly from long- to mid-shot as though it is having difficulty fixing its distance from the scene. 'Oh! you are men of stone,' is barely audible – Lear, shot from behind, is a huddle kneeling on the horizon above Cordelia. His line seems to have no audience, for there is no one to hear it, no spectators in the frame, no on-screen monitors of affect that intensify or dilute the focus on Lear, or that interpret it. We are still looking at his crouched back – excluded from his point of view.

'Had I your tongues' is spoken in close-up. We see Lear looking down on Cordelia, only from now on, the dead daughter will be absent. We shall never 'see / That face of hers again'. (This visual lacuna perhaps represents Lear's latest wish-fulfilment. The corpse that isn't there: absent Cordelia may be alive.) As Lear talks to her, the camera puts Cordelia always just out of shot, just beyond reach, then takes her point of view, becomes Cordelia gazing at her father, the camera lens the very surface on to which Lear projects his desire. So, as he calls, 'Cordelia, Cordelia! stay a little', he leans further and further into the camera. Accommodatingly, the camera-as-Cordelia co-operates with Lear's fantasy to project his desire on to the screen: the next shot shows Lear stepping into the frame asking 'What is't thou say'st?' to a Cordelia who stands in the centre of the shot, impassive, looking straight to camera, very much alive. Her face might be a Greek mask. She turns her head towards her father. The next shot, though, exposes mirage as delusion. Following the cut, Lear steps backwards out of the frame as though into the previous shot, and Cordelia is gone.

This same sur-realizing of desire recurs on 'my poor fool is hang'd!'. Lear in mid close-up speaks to camera; Cordelia stands just behind him, at his shoulder, looking too. This is the same Cordelia of the film's opening scene, the Cordelia who returned to Lear as hallucination in the mad scene in the storm-battered hovel, a slender, almost childish figure in a simple white tunic, her dark hair pulled back into a bun, unsmiling, her dark eyes intent, but her face an expressionless mask. In the next shot, she's gone. Now the camera takes her point of view as Lear tells her, 'Thou'lt come no more.' Behind him, the space of hallucination is vacant, Cordelia 'no more' there. From a head-shot on Lear droning 'Never, never' the film cuts to a mid-shot. We're behind King Lear as he kneels, watching his huddled back – an echo of that earlier shot, only now there is no body, just Lear, a dark hump framed by the grey, universal void.

Speech brings the camera into tight close-up on Lear's chest, the rough tunic laced up over his heart. 'Do you see this?' his voice asks as his hand, pointing a finger, comes into shot and drags itself up through the frame. (It's as though the screen isn't big enough to comprehend the whole Lear experience and can only deal with it in fragments. Or maybe Lear is directing our view of the experience, and directing from the heart.) The finger moves, and the camera travels up to Lear's face – 'Look on her, look, her lips.' He is pointing to what he sees, and the camera once again takes Cordelia's point of view. But this time it refuses to give back anything more than is written on the surface of Lear's face. It will not give us a final image of Cordelia alive – or dead. It remains watching as Lear's eyes, like his hand, travel upwards, looking at a Cordelia somewhere above him – elevated, an apotheosis. Or perhaps there is no 'vision'; perhaps his dying head is simply falling backwards as his eyes lose sight and close and his head slides slowly, slowly down the frame and out of shot. That is the last we see in the film, the grey expanse of sky – that resolves to blank white.

This sequence is not, however, as I've described it, continuous; rather, it's intercut, even interchopped, with Kent's violent reaction to Edgar's moves to save the king. 'Vex not his ghost,' Kent roars, shoving away both the younger man and the gestures that 'ought to' be performed. Again, the editing works disjunctively. What the eye sees next is a *non sequitur*, like an hallucination, which produces the uncanny sensation of two spatial or existential frames spliced into one. Camera tricks duplicate the tricks of Lear's mind. Indeed, they duplicate the faulty looking, the tampering with images – verbal, visual – that have plagued Lear's view of Cordelia from the beginning.

Brook's filmed scene denies the audience the morbid pleasure of looking at Cordelia's body. Once Lear puts her down, the corpse is not on camera again. Denying us the body, it denies our cultural fascination with the death of the beautiful woman, a trope of classic Hollywood cinema. But in refusing us the voyeuristic panning across the body, the close-up

Plate 1 'Cordelia! stay a little.' Paul Scofield and Diana Rigg in Peter Brook's 1962 staged *King Lear.*
Source: Jar Svoboda photograph. Courtesy of The Shakespeare Centre Library, The Shakespeare Birthplace Trust, Stratford-upon-Avon.

that eroticizes death but at the same time frames sexuality inside the ultimate taboo of unattainability, morbidity, Brook refuses sentimentality.
His film denies the emotion that attaches to the spectator roles that
Shakespeare writes inside the scene – by cutting them – for in Brook, Kent
and Edgar do no looking at Cordelia, or feeling for her, and there are no
reaction shots placed to mediate, to normalize what is happening. What
Brook denies them, he denies us too. And by refusing us the conventional
filmic gaze, he refuses us the conventional repertoire of emotions that go
with it. What he gives us in their place, though, is staggering, for Brook's
camera, instead of looking at Cordelia, looks *as* Cordelia – that is, it sees
the scene, *post mortem*, momentarily through her eyes, and so turns Lear's
looking back on him. Here, the performative body, proxied by the film
camera, works discursively to make the spectator look hard at Lear, a
strategy that makes for a final scene that is cerebral, not sentimental,
about the shattering of Lear's mind, not the breaking of his heart. As it
happens, Brook's film is interested in only one death. It disposed of
Goneril's and Regan's corpses a long while back in quick shots before
Cordelia dropped from the gibbet, and it doesn't remember them now.
Reanimating Cordelia through tricks of photography, it tropes a deep
emotional desire to edit life as we edit film. In this way, the scene is about

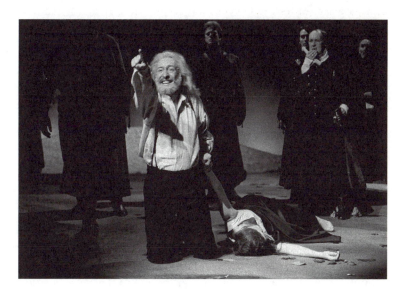

Plate 2 'Look there, look there!' Robert Stephens and Abigail McKern in Adrian
        Noble's 1993 *King Lear*.
Source: Mark Douet photograph. Courtesy of Mark Douet.

tragic absurdity, about the insane desire, holding death on one's lap, somehow to rewind the tape, to recover the moment before the horror, and to return to the Cordelia who does not have to play dead.

At the Royal Shakespeare Theatre (1993), Adrian Noble reversed the deep resonances of Brook's conceit to make Cordelia (Abigail McKern) not an 'absent presence' but a trivialized 'present absence'.[36] She and her sisters could hardly manoeuvre inside the overdetermining clichés that straitjacketed them – at the beginning, dressed in colour-coded costumes (the Albanys in green, the Cornwalls, mauve) as though they were Margaret Atwood's tractable *Handmaid*s (Ofalbany, Ofcornwall), and at the end, caricatured by pop-art imagery that borrowed its stereotypes from Gothic melodrama. Brook used Cordelia's body to reveal, to interrogate the desiring male imaginary; Noble, to indulge and flatter it.

Robert Stephens (Lear) was too frail to carry his dead Cordelia. He backed on to the stage wailing 'Howl, howl, howl!', eyes fixed upon the body brought on by three soldiers who laid her out on the stage, on her back. She was partly undressed: below the waist, still in her skirt, above it, stripped to her corset. Who had undressed her? Cordelia, accommodatingly, preparing for hanging? The 'slave' who did the hanging? Lear, after he cut her down? Of course, to 'consider so' was 'to consider too curiously', for spectators were not meant to pursue the logic of the costume very far nor to read Cordelia too deeply. Another sign system was operating here, one raided from popular television and print culture, a historically decontextualized aesthetic dependent on strobe imaging, instant gratification, short-term memory. The immediate effect of the corset was to eroticize Cordelia, to invite spectators to look at her as they hadn't looked before – voyeuristically. It might have worked to disrupt Lear's patriarchal claims upon his daughter's body, for in 1993 the corset had achieved pop-icon status as an instrument of cultural subversion and feminist critique – at least, as designed by Jean Paul Gaultier and worn, in-your-face, by Madonna. Madonna's corsets satirized male fantasy – they sprouted spiked nipples. But there was nothing satirical about the corset on McKern. Rather, its deeply conservative, even reactionary 'authenticity' (the corset is, after all, an apparatus for controlling women's bodies, and it remembers a culture that was very sure it knew how to control them) located Cordelia in a nostalgic Victorian costume drama, a Mills & Boon bodice ripper, where its titillation – which both restricts and reveals – troped women's 'faulty' sexuality and the punishment it deserved. The corset, in short, recruited to this representation the standard clichés of misogynist fantasy – dead, dumb, Cordelia was still sexy, and obviously 'asking for it'.

Meanwhile, Goneril and Regan played out a different cliché. They had

22

exited to their deaths at stage level, but now, as corpses, were flown in, like the architraves of a Gothic reredos designed by Edgar Allan Poe for the tomb of Ligeia. They hung suspended over the scene, their supine bodies arranged symmetrically and draped in hanging folds of red that looked like blood dripping from the ceiling – Bram Stoker's Dracula brides, a trope that aestheticized and tamed their murderous, anarchic sexuality by coercing it into the restrictive frame of the literary Gothic. For however sensationally the Gothic imagines female eroticism, the genre ultimately works to inscribe sexual repression by its codes of containment. As Noble directed Lear's daughters, two were vampires, the third, a vamp. All three, then, evacuated subjectivities.

The queasily incestuous love story Stephens's Lear played out on Cordelia's sexualized body read like necrophilia – he pawed the corpse, then straddled it as he loosened the noose. Women, it seemed, were easier to love dead than alive. And this Cordelia was very definitely 'dead as earth', as the old man demonstrated by kicking the corpse. It flopped over. Lear's need to punish Cordelia fitted the production's reactionary gender politics. This was a *Lear* that got applause every night on Albany's line, 'Shut your mouth dame', a *Lear* that nostalgically flattered male supremacist fantasies by writing an ending where uppity women got what they deserved. The traffic in images went one way. The body earned its abjection – 'naturally'. Lear's need to humiliate was not questioned. Indeed, any interrogation of Lear was simply denied in the sentimental apotheosis of the ending. Bent over the corpse, Lear looked up, his attention caught by something. He pointed towards it, a light, shining from the dark auditorium 'Look there. Look!' he urged, holding Cordelia's corpse by the arm, moving towards the light, pointing so that all eyes looked there too. He dragged behind him the body he'd forgotten but not released. Even in death, she went where he wanted. Still, it wasn't dead Cordelia spectators saw. Following Lear's instruction, they searched for what he was squintingly discovering in the intensifying light, the Cordelia 'off' who transfigured his face, 'redeem[ed] all sorrows', transformed the ending into sentimental triumph – not the dead-as-earth Cordelia who, tugged behind, might, in another production, have been trying to catch at Lear's heels.

When Albany heard 'Howl, howl, howl!' in Nick Hytner's 1990 RSC production, he was standing over the body of his wife,[37] brought on like a butchered carcass slung between two soldiers. Before they covered her face Albany stood looking, head bowed. This woman had been 'worth the whistle', and his stance over her corpse was a reference point for the deeply complicated narratives this production made legible on women's bodies. Then Lear's 'Howl' turned Albany upstage, and his body

Plate 3 'What is't thou say'st?' John Wood, Alex Kingston and David Troughton
in Nick Hytner's 1990 *King Lear*.
Source: Joe Cocks photograph. Courtesy of The Shakespeare Centre Library, The
Shakespeare Birthplace Trust, Stratford-upon-Avon.

crumpled as he saw the king (John Wood), half stumbling, half capering,
his St Vitus's dance of flailing hands and jerking head signalling something worse behind – the soldier carrying Cordelia in his arms like a
child.

The dead, wrecked daughter sat propped up; the prim, mad father
knelt beside her. They were replaying the play's opening, but they'd
swapped roles, Lear in the place of the postulant child, the corpse in the
place of the king. She looked like a broken doll, her head flopped on the
twisted neck, her arms akimbo, legs and feet at bizarre angles, her history
written on to her body. She also looked androgynous in the military
doublet and breeches she'd put on to lead the invasion, but she'd lost her
helmet so her long hair hung loose. This sexual ambiguity played teas-
ingly upon the retina, like *déjà vu*, for the audience knew it had seen this
body, or a version of it, before. Who was it? The Fool. (Played, cross-cast,
by Linda Kerr Scott, who made the Fool an under-fed Munchkin of inde-
terminate age and gender, put together like a marionette and acting like
one, jerking into life without warning.) Somehow, Lear's dead, broken-
jointed daughter collected up memories of his vanished 'boy' – more of
what would never be fixed, uncannily *revenant*.

24

Placed centre stage Cordelia was the apex of a heap of death. Her sisters' bodies lay further downstage, and Kent and the rest stood well clear so the family structure claimed attention. Lear spoke only to Cordelia, tender, wheedling, then devastatingly matter of fact – 'I kill'd the slave that was a-hanging thee.' The movement of voice registered Lear's moves into and out of lucidity, a mercurial sequence where individual images – like strobe flashes – were clipped, so that when Lear picked the feather ('This feather stirs!') out of the air (or out of his mind?), his squawk, 'She lives!', made everyone jump. Their gaze rivetted on Cordelia, they bent towards the miracle that did not happen, but for one split second, might have.

In this version, Kent's distracting intervention – 'O my good master' – was the 'murderer', the 'traitor' who killed Cordelia; thereafter, as Albany spoke the lines that condemned the kingdom to a future, Lear heard nothing. His eyes never left Cordelia. He stroked her face and hair. But then in a violent gesture of possession marked by Albany's shocked 'O, see, see!', Lear pulled Cordelia's body on top of him, covering him with her death. It was a grotesque parody of an erotic embrace that remembered something from the opening scene, the father's evidently incestuous desire as he leaned forward to suck Cordelia's 'mended speech' off her lips. Then, she pushed the kiss roughly away. The mystery of her heart was not to be plucked out of her. Now, the father 'mended' his action. He began simply to rock his child back and forth across his lap, his voice the sing-song of a nursery rhyme, high-pitched and keening – 'and my poor fool is hang'd!' Even his ultimate interrogation of existential absurdity contained no rage, just a reedy-voiced geriatric bewilderment – 'Why should a dog, a horse, a rat, have life, / And thou no breath at all?' As 'Never, never, never, never, never' faded into silence, the rocking stopped.

Just as violently, Lear rolled her away from him. His voice – virile, peremptory – commanded Kent to 'undo this button', Cordelia's button. It sounded like the preliminary to another autopsy – 'anatomize Regan' – to discover what might be breeding about this heart. 'Do you see this?' was suddenly urgent: Cordelia was arousing in him the same passionate reaction as in the opening scene. But with 'Look on her, look, her lips!', Lear collapsed into the silence of those lips. 'Break, heart; I prithee, break!' Kent howled, but was he addressing Lear's heart or his own? The final stage picture of Lear sprawled in the dead embrace of Cordelia, set against her sisters, remembered the opening scene and gave back an ironic echo of 'I lov'd her most, and thought to set my rest / On her kind nursery.' Here, then, was a final scene that literalized Lear's desiring imaginary, simultaneously to critique it, to expose male fantasy as episodes in madness. Such indulgence would not evade consequence. The stage laid out the cost clearly – the waste of Britain's daughters. History, this final stage picture suggested, could ill afford the fantasies men fed their hearts.

* * *

King Lear isn't finished. The play's ending is still being compiled out of the subsequent endings performed upon it: Kathryn Hunter's Lear (Leicester Haymarket, 1997) pushing Cordelia in a wheelchair, once the geriatric king's 'throne', now wobbling across the final scene with its cargo of dead daughter like a baby in a pram; Ian Holm's Lear (National Theatre, 1998) dwarfed by the corpse he carries, dumping her on a heap he only later discovers are his other daughters, cupping his hand round his ear to listen to Cordelia, and waving her silence away with anxious flapping; Barrie Rutter's Lear (Northern Broadsides, 1999) picked out in a single searchlight at the far end of the derelict mill-room theatre, demented now with grief, toiling doggedly the distance into the company of his wrecked court, with each step, the little body he holds in his arms juddering. This play has continuous work to do in contemporary culture as a core text for organizing our own thoughts on death.

The apparatus that served Shakespeare's culture – effigy, *memento mori*, *vanitas* – survives in the modern world, but not as viable forms, only as relics of an age that did death differently. Poetry persists: it is the poet who initiates most of us, born post-war, into death and keeps us up to date in our conversations with it. So, Ted Hughes, near death, gave us *The Birthday Letters*, written to, and about, Sylvia Plath, but by extension, to, and about, ourselves and our own anniversaries – birth days – that take us towards death.[38]

For the experience of death, though, contemporary culture looks not to the poet (and certainly not to the pathologist, mortician or funeral arranger, since 'real' death no longer belongs colloquially to our daily lives) but to the playwright. It is the playwright who makes death 'real', who arranges for us to experience 'conclusions infinite', which invite us, through them, to rehearse our own ending. In the theatre, we look on death hundreds, thousands of times, and learn to 'do' death by imitation. The dead body in performance serves as an instructive object because it tells us about original cultural moments, but more pertinently, perhaps, our own cultural moment. For us, as for Shakespeare, the experience of death is gendered, and death is a site where the work of gender gets (finally) done. If you want to know what any culture thinks of women, read its representations. Read the theatre. Read Cordelia. Read the body.

2

SNATCHED BODIES
Ophelia in the grave

The story is seen through his eyes and, when he is not present, through his imagination . . . I saw the camera seeing most things through Hamlet's eyes.

> Laurence Olivier, *On Acting,* 1986

Ophelia appears in only five of the play's twenty scenes.

> Elaine Showalter, 'Representing Ophelia', 1990

Because they are so familiar, so evident, we are culturally blind to the ubiquity of representations of feminine death. Though in a plethora of representations feminine death is perfectly visible we only see it with some difficulty.

> Elisabeth Bronfen, *Over Her Dead Body,* 1992

the desire to explore the female body, to cut beneath the skin and open it to the admiring gaze of fellow observers (whether poets, painters, or anatomists) was impossible to resist . . . Hesitation before the female form . . . is a nineteenth-century invention, one entirely foreign to the ruthless dynamism of Renaissance explorations of the human figure – particularly the female human figure.

> Jonathan Sawday, *The Body Emblazoned,* 1995

Absent Bodies

These voices supply a background conversation for my own reading of Ophelia in four filmtexts that invite thinking about how they use her scripted role – and body – to serve what they each construct as a resolutely masculinist *Hamlet.* Laurence Olivier (1947), Grigori Kozintsev (1964), Franco Zeffirelli (1990) and Kenneth Branagh (1997) place their cameras to see 'things through Hamlet's eyes'. Locating the essential 'story' of Shakespeare's tragedy in the prince's narrative, each directs that narrative towards a celebration of heroic masculinity by privileging moments that spectacularly define it.[1] But they have to achieve their heroic Hamlet

27

under erasure. They suppress the countertext voiced by Ophelia who rises from the dead to interrogate the prince who quizzed the skull.

Ultimately I want to look at Ophelia in the grave. Shakespeare's play-text positions the grotesquely conflicted scene of Ophelia's burial (5.1), with its 'maimed rites', its staggering disruptions, its vexed looking, to radically subvert Hamlet's (and *Hamlet*'s) heroic project.[2] The body is the scene's 'matter', and it forces speculation under the scrutiny of that 'ruthless dynamism' which does not hesitate to 'open it to the . . . gaze' (Sawday). But when I look for what ought to be perfectly legible in these films – the representation of female death – I discover, like Bronfen, that 'we only see it with some difficulty'. The body isn't there. It's been snatched. Like Showalter failing to register Ophelia's appearance in her final scene – her sixth scene – these films erase the body in the grave, thereby foreclosing the insistent questions Shakespeare's playtext requires me to consider. *Hamlet* is crowded with male bodies presented in all stages of post-mortem recuperation, from ghost-walking Hamlet to fresh-bleeding Polonius to mouldering Yorick to Priam of deathless memory; it's a playtext whose core issue exhaustively and excessively examines the imperatives of male reaction to the death of men ('remember'; 'revenge'); a playtext that valorizes killing and heroic death (but nicely condemns murder). When it finally arrives at the grave, however, *Hamlet* lays out a woman's body for speculation. What performance work does this body do? How do we look at it? What do we see?

Is the body actually there to begin with? What if Ophelia's corpse is shrouded, or 'played' by a dummy or brought to the grave in a closed coffin?[3] Although *Hamlet*'s three texts give contradictory instructions, each ultimately argues for the body in play – Q2 calls for a 'corse', Q1 and F, for a 'coffin'. Q2, the 1604 so-called 'good' quarto, which apparently derives from manuscript, contains the stage direction '*Enter K.Q. Leartes and the corse*', literalizing what is implicit in Hamlet's line (spoken in all texts) as he gazes on the funeral's 'maimed rites' and sees 'the corse they follow' as a suicide. It signals, too, the presence of a body for Laertes to embrace when, crying 'Hold off the earth awhile / Till I have caught her once more in mine arms' (variants occur in all versions), he leaps into the grave, desiring to be buried with her: 'Now pile your dust upon the quick and dead.' Ophelia's body arrived on Shakespeare's stage on a bier, like Juliet borne 'uncovered on the bier' in *Romeo and Juliet* (4.1.110), or in an open coffin, the customary practice, or perhaps in a stage version of a parish coffin. This last was a certain way of signalling her 'maimed rites'.[4] The coffin Q1 and F call for, in any case, is the means by which the 'corse' is carried onstage, not a substitute for it.

But Ophelia's body brings me to another problem. For I have already admitted that she has been snatched from the filmtexts I want to read. So is my project merely perverse? Does it locate me among those (shrewdly observed by Barbara Hodgdon) who look at any film of a Shakespeare play as a 'text of loss' and watch it most attentively to see what's missing?[5] Hodgdon is right to argue for a plurality of Shakespeare texts that includes the playtext, the theatrical performance text and the filmtext. She is right too, that 'filming Shakespeare involves shifting textual authority from the playscript to the filmtext', with the film emerging as a completely 'new text', possessing its own integrity and authority and inviting analysis on its own terms.[6] But what, then, of films that absent Ophelia from the funeral? How can we think about performances that weren't filmed, performances that Shakespeare's playtext writes but the shooting script cuts? Hodgdon believes we must attend to these 'texts of loss', for 'if the performance is not there, the film spectator is not aware of the gap and is all too willing to accept the erasure'.[7] Ophelia's role simply vanishes when her body is snatched, and that's bad news, I want to argue, not just for her but *Hamlet* too.

Reading Hodgdon's 'text of loss' means returning frequently to the structuring absence of Shakespeare's playtext, but I begin by mapping Ophelia's role across each of the films – leaving Branagh's for separate consideration – to observe what they make of her and therefore what is at stake when they cut her. I want to discover what narrative is silenced in these filmtexts, and to what cultural end.

Reel Bodies

Zeffirelli and Kozintsev open their *Hamlet*s with title credits that frankly declare the shift of authority from playtext to filmtext. Zeffirelli's *Hamlet* is 'Based on the play by William Shakespeare'; Kozintsev's is 'After the tragedy by . . .'; Olivier is more hesitant. In a later essay he proposes that his film 'should be regarded as an "An Essay in *Hamlet*," and not as a film version of a necessarily abridged classic'.[8] But Olivier is as much the *auteur* of his *Hamlet* as Zeffirelli and Kozintsev are of theirs. All three cut speeches, scenes and roles and alter continuity by repositioning not just speeches but entire scenes. All three invent new scenes and sometimes new lines. And Ophelia – played by Jean Simmons in 1947, Anastasia Vertinskaya in 1964, and Helena Bonham-Carter in 1990 – is prime material for visual invention.[9] All three directors expand the role by adding two scenes the playtext merely reports: Hamlet's intrusion, 'doublet . . . unbrac'd', into Ophelia's closet (2.1) and the drowning (4.7). But they also diminish the role. None of these Ophelias speaks her single soliloquy,

29

'O what a noble mind is here o'erthrown' (3.1.152ff). These directors cut her only unmediated articulation of subjectivity, thereby denying her access, performatively, to the speech act that constructs her as most like Hamlet even as the speech itself marks her utter alienation from him. One effect of such cuts and interpolations is to objectify Ophelia. In all three films, the camera finds Ophelia and settles on her, observing what she is doing – usually from the middle distance – and monitoring behaviour that it sometimes represents as charming, sometimes as ambiguously disturbing. Always, Ophelia's is a body to be watched. Until we get to the grave. Then things change. Then, like Showalter, they shrink from looking at Ophelia-as-corpse.

In Olivier's *Hamlet* the body we watch in Jean Simmons's performance is oddly dislocated from the mock-Tudor Elsinore invented for the film. Olivier dresses Claudius and Gertrude 'as the king and queen of universal playing cards, Hamlet in the timeless doublet and hose of a young romantic prince.' Ophelia, though, he puts in 'an innocent Victorian dress'.[10] This sounds as if Olivier is mixing his cultural metaphors. In 1947, 'Victorian' was the standard reactionary metonym in British culture for strait-laced values and sexual repression. 'Innocent' troped the infantile, and, in dress, 'Victorian' coded stricture – women's fleshly desires were tightly corseted in whalebone. (Before 1914, the average English waistline measured 21 inches.) But 'Victorian' for Olivier in 1947 also coded a profound and sentimental nostalgia for an invincible empire, a self-confident patriarchy. So which of these conflicted cultural references was Olivier alluding to in an Ophelia he cast as a Victorian innocent? Sexuality? The absence of sexuality? The repression of sexuality? A nostalgic paternalism operating upon female sexuality? All of these are possible and, as it turns out, all collapse into Olivier's direction of the role.

Simmons plays an Ophelia at home in this semiotic shambles. Her dress could never have been worn in any Victorian public place. It belongs to the Victorian boudoir, chaise longue – or nursery. It makes her a sensuous child who projects disturbingly contradictory signals, her silhouette offering her, quite literally, as the film's 'loose' woman, in some lights, sweet and artless, oblivious to her erotic appeal; in others, almost lascivious, a probationary 'novice' on her way to the 'nunnery'. Fooling with her brother while her father drones on with his tedious sententiae, she grapples Laertes from behind, half-unsheathing his dagger, then illustrates Polonius's advice on borrowing and lending by groping his purse which hangs over his groin.

If the dress fractures any coherent interpretation of Ophelia's body it likewise splits body from head. Ophelia's hair is neither Tudor nor

30

Victorian but pure Hollywood, for she is represented as the platinum blonde of cult and cliché – a cliché Olivier intensifies by making Gertrude brunette – the film's 'dark' lady. (Later, Kozintsev will parody the same cliché and Zeffirelli, reverse it: in the one, Ophelia and Gertrude are both blonde, but Gertrude's platinum is vulgarly fake, poured out of a bottle; in the other, Gertrude is 'fair', Ophelia, 'dark'.) Such hair codes Simmons as the 'good girl' as unerringly as the white horse codes the 'good guy' in the western, but it also codes her as the pin-up girl, the dumb blonde. This makes for strange traffic between images in an Elsinore where the only other blond Dane is Hamlet. Later, there is yet stranger traffic on offer when, in the preparations for the play scene, the company's boy player momentarily 'becomes' Ophelia in a lookalike wig as he dresses to play the queen in *The Mousetrap*. Since Olivier's is a film that clearly announces its Oedipal interests from the outset,[11] this moment makes it clear that Ophelia is a stand-in for certain uncanny doubles: for Gertrude, Denmark's 'player queen'; for the alluring boy, another 'player queen', towards whom Hamlet is here momentarily drawn; and also for Hamlet himself, for Ophelia is Hamlet's feminine double, the girl in himself from whom he recoils. Simmons' Ophelia is herself inscribed with ambiguity. She looks like a schoolgirl, not a grown woman, with her hair loose down her back and looped in childish plaits that frame her face. But there is something out of place here – the impossibly symmetrical eyebrows scored in black. They make her look like Rebecca of Sunnybrook Farm trying to vamp herself up as Jean Harlow.

In Olivier's black and white Elsinore – an Elsinore eerily empty of people – the vacant, brooding corridors and stairways belong to Hamlet.[12] The camera finds him in the dark, slumped in a chair, collapsed on the battlements, distant at the end of a dark tunnel of receding arches. Reversing this perspective, however, the camera finds Ophelia framed in light at the tunnel's opposite end. This is a shot the film will quote time and time again, Ophelia standing in a frame that makes her picturesque while the camera seems to stand back, detached, never doing for Simmons' Ophelia what it does for Olivier's Hamlet, circling round behind the head then dissolving through the cranium into his thoughts. Ophelia in this film 'think[s] nothing' that the camera records. Instead, she is visually constructed as a child of nature. Only Ophelia has access to a world outside prison-Elsinore. Her room, painted with flowers, looks on to a pastoral landscape through a window that frames a willow tree.[13] By these visual allusions Ophelia's sexuality is suggestively inscribed within the natural, and it will be to wild 'natural' instincts that she reverts in madness. The un-making of the artificially constructed female courtier falling into the wild disarray of madness will be imagined as a return to wild flowers, and the move from the empty bedroom to the teeming brook naturalized.

In Kozintsev's *Hamlet* nature is no prettily wild 'mother' but a blighted hag. Elsinore looks like the Hermitage, only located at Chernobyl, and Vertinskaya's Ophelia is a young Catherine the Great being made over as a functionary of the Soviet collective. Her hair is scraped back into a tight bun that pulls her face taut, like an oriental mask. When Laertes first finds her, she is learning the steps of a dance, jerking mechanically from one struck pose to the next, accompanied on a lute by the female minder who, a hunchbacked crow, flaps at her side. This Ophelia is under constant surveillance. But there is a bizarre discontinuity here. The music we hear isn't from the lute; it's from something mechanical, and its effect is to render the girl a mechanical puppet.

Kozintsev's Elsinore is both cosmopolitan and depressingly primitive. German, French and Italian are spoken in the corridors, but chickens scratch in the dirt courtyard, and the bleak interiors are functional boxes ill-relieved by Stalin-sized murals. Outside, on the wasteland plain that spreads out behind the castle, slack-jawed serfs lift their heads from their own scratching in the dirt to watch Hamlet gallop home across an epic horizon and clatter into Elsinore over a drawbridge that is raised by hand labour. More serfs, backs bent, turn a massive winch. This workplace Elsinore reifies politics (quite unlike Olivier's filmset Elsinore that privileges performances). Outside, the serfs' faces are furrowed with hardship; inside, the politburo are as sleek and jewel encrusted as the fat rats metamorphosed into royal footmen in *Cinderella*. Kozintsev frames shots to emphasize their social content; rarely does his camera move into close-up. He keeps it far enough back to pick up the business at the margins that complicates or contradicts what's happening at the centre. So, as Gertrude consoles her son with platitudes – 'all that lives must die' – at the bottom of the frame an attendant hands her a mirror, and she glances at her image, mending her coiffure, and registering consolation as mindless vanity. Such images, juxtaposed, show how the machinery of state grinds in this Elsinore, and how Ophelia is material for grinding. The point is made at the end of her first scene as the film cuts to a clock in a tower where the hour is striking. A door opens mechanically. Mechanical figures, as on a temporal assembly line, pursue each other; the king, the queen, the merchant, the reaper who is also Death. Life in Elsinore is a clockwork *danse macabre*, and Ophelia is learning its steps.

Zeffirelli's Elsinore comes straight out of Saxo Grammaticus via

Rossetti and the Pre-Raphaelites, its 'authentic' medievalism idealized, romanticized, glamorized in vibrant colours shimmering off sun-bleached walls. Rationality is given space to spread in this Elsinore where Claudius administers Denmark from a scriptorium, his bureaucracy bookishly monastic, and where Hamlet's apartment is cluttered with the apparatus both of chivalry and learning. An upright stone effigy of an armed knight sits among books, writing implements, manuscripts, a classical sculpture in white marble, an astrolabe. Women's work is 'authentically' situated in a sewing room among tapestry frames and cutting tables, a convivial space where women sing and joke and men enter freely.

Still, contradiction is built into it all: Elsinore's colour frequently seems overwrought, flushed, and its light, an intrusion, as when Gertrude swings open the tapestry shutter in Hamlet's darkened room and blinds him with the glare from the stone window. In this Elsinore, speculation is not just intellectual pursuit but surveillance, for the castle is fretted with high-level catwalks that let everybody play 'I Spy'. Even the singing women prove ambiguous, for their signature tune is the lewd ballad Shakespeare introduces in Act 4, the one about St Valentine's Day. Early on, Ophelia hums it under her breath as she concentrates on threading her needle; later, it returns, belted out in a bizarre reprise when, mad, only the song can articulate the 'sense' of her experience.

Bonham-Carter's Ophelia personalizes Elsinore's contradictions, has them written on her gawky body. The child in her that she has not yet outgrown is hiding out in her motor co-ordination: she sizes up the eye of her needle as if aiming to thread a camel through it. But her face is older than her movements, and too old for her dress. Her rough wool smock, topped by a linen tabard like a school pinafore, her white embroidered bonnet tied under her chin over thick, dark plaits that hang down to her waist all infantilize an Ophelia whose face registers the thoughts and emotions of a woman. All of this signifies what needs no other elaboration: Ophelia, with her crumpled little brooding face that makes her old, is in competition with Gertrude, the grown woman who ought by now to be a grandmother. But the queen is behaving like an adolescent only just discovering the 'hey day in the blood', skittishly careering down the castle steps to leap on to her hunter, her Pre-Raphaelite hair loose in the wind, her shy glances and smiles and lingering kisses failing to discriminate between Hamlet and Claudius. The camera cannot keep up with Gertrude. It's constantly left standing, watching her disappear into long shot.

By contrast, the camera frequently finds Ophelia in head-shot or close-up, a move that makes legible Ophelia's internalization of Elsinore's contradictions. Most of Bonham-Carter's performance happens in her head, and close-ups pick up what is written on her face in the muscle spasms that map her reactions as resistance, offering a gestural counter-text to the words she hears and does not believe. When Laertes launches into his earnest homily in 1.3 her eyebrows knot and her mouth twitches until her snort of scepticism – 'No more but so?' – pushes him to step up what started as paternalistic advice into urgent hustling. This Ophelia is dissident. She knows her own mind – and she knows Hamlet's. That's what drives her mad.

Her Ophelia breaks at the end of the play scene (3.2). For Vertinskaya, the break comes later, for Simmons, earlier, in the nunnery scene (3.1). Simmons enters the scene which is going to narrate her disintegration already disintegrated, for, by a trick of the deep-focus photography Olivier exploited so stunningly, she comes into focus so gradually that she looks like a spectre materializing into a body.[14] The camera proceeds to frame weird disembodiments. A hand shoots into a frame, arms appear across a shot. The camera articulates a profound uneasiness about whole-ness, about material substance, that keys a deconstructive reading of the scene. As Hamlet quizzes Ophelia, they move around a stone prie-dieu, which stands between them like a desecrated sacrament. She hears her mistake as soon as she answers 'At home my lord', for both of them know Polonius is behind the arras. As her betrayal catches in her throat, she reaches out her arms to Hamlet, but the shot cuts them off, making the appeal grotesque. Hamlet, savage, throws her on to her knees to resume her fake attitude of prayer and, as he starts up the stone stairs, her outstretched arms pursue him, straining for an embrace shoved viciously away. She is left prostrate and sobbing as again the film cuts away to watch Claudius and Polonius exchange verdicts. When the film cuts back to her after their exit, she is still reaching towards a Hamlet who is out of shot but who still controls our looking. The body that lies at the bottom of the stairs looks broken.

Vertinskaya's Ophelia survives the nunnery scene. But after Polonius's murder and the order for Hamlet's exile, the camera watches Ophelia's surreal shadow play upon a torch-lit window as Hamlet, in the courtyard below, mounts and rides for England. Kozintsev maps the trajectory of Ophelia's story with a visual metaphor exactly opposite to Olivier's. As Simmons goes mad, she comes apart, shedding her court dress and becoming a simple creature of nature so that madness is represented as prettiness and sweetness. Kozintsev turns this around. Scene by scene, the state imposes itself more oppressively upon Vertinskaya. Her hair, once natural, is stiffened and shaped over increasingly bizarre metal forms; her dress gets heavier, more rigidly constructed, weighed down by jewels, laced tight in bodices, thrust out by farthingales. These dresses not only claim Ophelia for the court, they signify state interference with her body. Her very breath is at the state's disposal. When the film cuts from the courtyard to the torch-lit interior, Ophelia is being dressed in mourning, her eyes closed and body swaying as if she were drugged. The attendant crows crowding round her lift over her head a metal frame, like the torturer's chains men were hanged in alive. Her breasts, her ribcage, her waist are strapped in metal. They fix a metal farthingale to it; over it they heave a black dress that it takes four of them to lift. Like a device whose clockwork has run down, Ophelia stands with her arms raised stiffly in front of her. One of the women pulls a voluminous black veil over her head and face, covering Ophelia like a wave. As if drowning, she reaches up, trying to find the surface. Positioned at a low angle which distorts the viewer's perspective, the camera magnifies the moment's grotesquerie, framing this ritual of investiture as a piece of bizarre theatre.

Abuse breaks Simmons' Ophelia; loss, Vertinskaya's. Bonham-Carter's Ophelia is broken by a kiss. Manhandled in a strategically cut nunnery scene (3.1) that is played in one of Elsinore's cavernous shadowed halls, she is left, small and desolate, picking up the pieces of the 'remembrances' Hamlet hurled away. Even the camera abandons her, moving further and further away into a high-angle shot that diminishes Ophelia to an afterthought against the flagstone floor. When she next appears, in the play scene, she sits rigid, at once tense and aloof, as the camera travels from the players tumbling and juggling with fire to the king's laughing face and to Gertrude, clapping delightedly. But the fire tossed from hand to hand seems more than a tumbler's trick or curtain raiser to *The Mousetrap*: it tropes Hamlet's strategy. The doublet he wears in this scene is diabolic red, and when he takes the chair next to Ophelia, she first turns away but then cannot resist him. Zeffirelli positions them both in head-shots, giving them private, if uncomfortable, space. Irritated by Hamlet's puerile double entendres that keep catching her out, Ophelia rebuffs him. When he mockingly asks, 'Do you think I meant country matters?', 'I think nothing' is a flat-toned capitulation of her thinking self. She is one who will think no more. The camera that earlier isolated her in long shot now achieves the same effect in close-up. Out of shot, the sound of the tumblers' revelry goes on, but Ophelia's face is a blank. Leaning in to her, Hamlet urges, 'get thee to a nunnery'.

The line comes like a fist in the face from the blind side. For of course, we're not expecting it; the nunnery scene's most notorious line should have come earlier, in the scene that takes its name from it. Placed here, the line effectively doubles Hamlet's abuse of Ophelia by pulling in the violence that, it turns out, was merely interrupted, not ended, in the 'remembrances' scene. Zeffirelli contrives to make us hear the famous 'missing' text twice: first when we automatically filled in the cut; now, when we hear it as if for the first time. This context gives Ophelia no room to manoeuvre. In the earlier scene she could at least move away; here, protocol pins her to her chair. The camera, again aligned with Hamlet, conspires with her tormentor, cutting out the laughing spectators who can be heard all around her to focus in on the looking that ties her gaze to his. 'I am myself indifferent honest,' he confesses, bitter with self-loathing; 'we are arrant knaves all . . . believe none of us.' Bonham-Carter's face registers nothing, as though she cannot integrate what she hears. What is the status of such instruction? Hard truth? Cynical fooling? What can be believed of one who discredits belief: 'believe none of us'? Suddenly the tabor clamours for her attention. Still caught in close-up, Ophelia blinks as if coming out of a trance and turns to watch the play. Hamlet says nothing more to her until, in the pandemonium once the king has risen, he seeks her out, leans in close and repeats 'believe none of us'; then, more softly, 'To a nunnery. Go – and quickly too.' Grinding his mouth into hers, then tossing off his next line lightly – 'Farewell' – he lets her go. The woman he leaves behind, still rooted to her chair, seems emptied out; her head twitches as if trying to shake something off; her eyes brim wide with tears, but they have lost understanding.

The shots that wedge Hamlet and Ophelia into claustrophobic intimacy make their intense psychodrama much more compelling even than the politics played out in front of them. On stage, a camped-up transvestite player queen, made up as Gertrude's double, boldly outstares the real Gertrude. Zeffirelli's changes serve ambiguously to 'enhance' Ophelia's role: she, not Horatio, gets to be Hamlet's 'buddy' at the end of the play scene. Still, Hamlet's 'farewell' sounds like the film's dismissal. It disposes of Ophelia's erotic claim to the prince to make way for the mother (who even now is expecting Hamlet in her bedroom) as though roughing up his girlfriend is only titillating foreplay to the serious sexual assault to come. But if Zeffirelli meant to motivate Ophelia's madness by his rejigging of the scene, to tie it to Hamlet as Kozintsev ties it to Polonius so that female subjectivity depends upon lovers and fathers, Bonham-Carter resists her director's strategy. She allows the spectator to read a different meaning in Ophelia's bewildered silence and the madness she maps across it. Her cerebral Ophelia goes mad not when she loses Hamlet but when words lose their meaning. She is the true philosopher in this Elsinore, and when knowledge fails, Ophelia is brain dead.

When she next appears this Ophelia looks as if she is climbing out of a tomb. First her fingertips emerge, curling over an edge of wet stone, then her head, her eyes level with the stone. There is nothing pretty about Bonham-Carter's mad Ophelia. She is a filthy ghost who tropes madness with pollution as she rises up to ask insolent questions – 'Where is the beauteous majesty of Denmark?'. Shuffling barefoot across Elsinore's ramparts she is repulsive, the materialization of repression unloosed: this is what raw libido looks like. The blond, boyish sentry she assaults (a remembered, displaced version of Hamlet's assault on her) tries to look away even as he has to stand to attention while she masturbates the leather belt that hangs over his groin. Mad, Ophelia is lewd. But she is also politically dangerous.

Claudius is visibly shaken by the joke that suddenly makes her laugh: 'My brother shall know of it.' When Laertes does catch up with her, she is sitting cross-legged on Gertrude's throne, sorting the bone fragments and straws that are her flowers. It is a mindless child who thrusts these new 'remembrances' into reluctant hands, who paces asylum-gaited, who puts her 'rue' behind her ear like a rose and pats her matted hair coquettishly. But this wrecked child has claimed the throne, usurping Gertrude, literalizing in her own person the metaphors of contamination that have been circulating around this throne from the beginning of the film. Bonham-Carter's mad Ophelia does more than embody these ideas. Squatting on Denmark's throne she locates them where they belong.

Vertinskaya's performance likewise projects politics. In madness, her Ophelia mechanically replays all her former scenes, only everything is out of sync, so when the music starts in her head she can't keep time – her movements are epileptic. As she starts up the stairs, bidding 'Good night, ladies', her hands move in slow motion to unfasten the heavy mourning dress she sheds as she goes. The dress is oppression, and when she next appears in a white smock, she is a free agent, her body's integrity symbolically reclaimed as her own. But un-dressed, she is also exposed. Kozintsev heightens the potential for multiple readings of her body by having Ophelia enter not to Laertes or to Claudius and Gertrude but to a hall full of soldiers mustered against Laertes' incursion. As she winds her way through them – fragile, female, sexualized, catatonic – Ophelia incites violence against the state, for in this context 'They bore him bare-fac'd on the bier' is not a song lyric but a line of bizarre political interrogation that invites the soldiers to judge the regime's policy in the matter of Polonius's funeral. When a soldier covers her in a blanket the gesture claims this alienated courtier for the people. When she picks her 'flowers' off the hearth and gives the twigs to the men, what is fragmenting is not just a mind but Claudius's whole political regime, responsible for making so many ghosts.

Even Jean Simmons, who earlier defined 'decorative' madness, becomes an Ophelia who, if only for a moment, has an insight, perhaps political, that frees her from the sham performances around her. It happens when she is making her final exit from the court, walking down the long corridor of receding arches. All at once her energy runs out and she slides down a stone pillar, crouching there to finish her song, offering her own answer to 'God a mercy on his soul' – 'And of all Christian souls'. Suddenly lucid, she looks back at the court as though ideas are crossing her mind for the first time. When she rises it is as though she has asked 'To be or not to be', answered 'not', and chosen what coward-conscienced Hamlet shirked. She is Strindberg's Miss Julie, and she knows what she is doing: breaking prison.

The camera follows her down the corridor, turns into her room and looks through her window. Then, as Gertrude begins 'There is a willow . . .' in voice-over, it cuts to the river, where Ophelia, singing and crowned in flowers, floats gently downstream, one arm trailing gracefully behind her, an animated version of Millais's Pre-Raphaelite *Ophelia*. She is colluding in her own apotheosis from mortal woman into muse, the figure that 'functions as a sign whose signified is masculine creativity'. For just as Millais's painting impresses its spectator more with its craft than its content, so Olivier's film foregrounds its own technical achievement as the real subject of this scene.[15] Like the painting, the film maintains a nice fictive separation between drowning and death: Millais's Ophelia lies with her eyes still open, her fingers still holding a posy; Olivier's disappears out of shot still singing. The camera lingers voyeuristically, licensing spectators to linger on the beautiful, pathetic spectacle, untroubled by any recognition that they are admiring a corpse. Ophelia's drowning is not the sight of Ophelia's death nor the site of any of the grotesquerie Shakespeare writes into Gertrude's report of it. Rather, annexed to Olivier's project, her drowning is the site where male ingenuity celebrates its own creativity. It exploits the woman's body as muse, but denies the body the death that would trouble and transform its signifying power.

Bonham-Carter's drowning is equally romanticized, and while it trafficks in more complicated images, those images still invite the reading of her death as 'comfortable'. This Ophelia's flight from Elsinore is coded as freedom; she runs down the green valley that was once the castle's defensive moat, away from the camera into long shot and the territory that earlier belonged to Gertrude. Barefoot, she perches on a wooden bridge over a stream and throws bright yellow gorse flowers into the blue water. The shot closes in on her face as Gertrude, in voice-over, tells the story of the drowning; then Ophelia's face dissolves into Gertrude's, and the momentary effect is like a horror film, as youth shrivels into age, and the faces morphing into each other produce the uncanny effect of being one, the same face. But the spectator is not allowed to dwell on this, or on any other disturbing thought, for 'death' cues a cut to a stone pool where, in distant long shot, Ophelia floats on her back. Avoiding any closer contemplation of the corpse, the camera rises from the pool to the sea and the sky beyond, wiping away the little death, subsuming it into a vision of eternity.

Only in Vertinskaya's performance is Ophelia's drowning disturbing. The camera scans her empty room, resting on the unicorn in the tapestry, as a gypsy violin reprises 'How should I your true love know?'. It cuts to a willow, a twisted spectre of death trailing its scraggling hair in thick water and, as it pans across the water, the music changes into the tinkling percussion Ophelia heard in her head. Her body floats on its back, submerged under six inches of water that acts like a magnifying glass to turn the grotesque scene into something bizarrely clinical, as though Ophelia has been prepared for autopsy. But then the film cuts to a seagull overhead, as though to recuperate her by evoking orthodox iconography which figures the bird as the soul and the seagull's free flight as a liberated Ophelia.[16] But the gesture is merely an ironic anodyne, for Hamlet, standing on a stone jetty, looks up and watches the seagull pass. He cannot know what he's looking at.

Snatched Bodies

In all three films, Ophelia's role is effectively over when she drowns. When the camera arrives at the grave, the bodies that interest it are men's; Ophelia gets only seconds of film time.[17] One effect of this near-exclusive focus on men is that, in these films, the scene at the grave feels stuck in a time warp, as if it were casting back to and endlessly repeating a Victorian *Hamlet*, the one fixed by Delacroix's classic image of the prince contemplating the skull. But if directors had revisited Shakespeare's playtext to re-read it with fresh eyes, to investigate its material and wonder about its theatrical strategies and scenic construction, they might have filmed Ophelia's funeral differently.

The theatrical elements Shakespeare deploys in 5.1 are extraordinary. First there is the physical rupture of the stage itself by the Gravedigger, who makes the grave gape by opening a trap in the floor that uncannily reveals what has been there all along, the 'prison house' with its harrowing 'secrets', not located at some distant address but always (already) underfoot. This absurdity matches the Gravedigger's absurd language-play, which ruptures other surfaces to reopen Ophelia's case by conducting a travesty inquest that, on the one hand, carnivalizes her death, making it slapstick tragedy, and on the other, constructs it as appalling transgression.[18] For it is the Gravedigger who makes Ophelia a suicide. Why does the play dispute Gertrude's story that Ophelia drowned 'mermaid-like', still chanting 'snatches of old lauds, / As one incapable of her own distress'? One obvious answer is that Ophelia-the-suicide is a much more problematic Ophelia than Ophelia-the-accident. In early modern culture, a 'crowner' – that is, a 'coroner' – who sat in a suicide case must declare for burial in unhallowed ground, at a crossroads, with the desecrated corpse laid in the earth face down, naked, covered in shards, a stake driven though the heart.[19] Ophelia-the-suicide, in short, makes trouble: when we look at *her* corpse, our looking is vexed.

But there's more trouble to come – the Gravedigger problematizes the very grave itself. In early modern England, the grave was mystified space, but a bogus grave in a stage floor, while it represented mystified space, was clearly no such thing. The Gravedigger is an agent of de-mystification – he sings at his work, cracks jokes, talks politics, makes the grave the site of live-lihood by outrageously disclosing what the Ghost's report represented as harrowingly undiscloseable.[20] At the same time, though, whenever he opens his mouth, the Gravedigger re-mystifies the grave with his utterly mystifying riddles:

Hamlet:	What man dost thou dig it for?
Gravedigger:	For no man, sir.
Hamlet:	What woman then?
Gravedigger:	For none neither.
Hamlet:	Who it to be buried in't?
Gravedigger:	One that was a woman, sir; but rest her soul, she's dead.

(5.1.126–131)

All this clowning around makes the grave a place of ambiguous rhetori-cal slippage, but more problematically, it fills up Ophelia's space with other matter. While it is happening, her funeral isn't happening. Why the deferral? How is Hamlet changed by being drawn into this 'interim' comic double act where he plays straight man to the Gravedigger in what amounts to a ritual of inverted burial? For what happens next is not that Ophelia is turned into her grave but that her grave is turned out instead. The Gravedigger's spade ousts skulls and bones as though resurrecting them in some loose-limbed, misdirected *danse macabre*. And at the end – there's Yorick! Why bring together the mad virgin and the mad-cap jester to share a grave?

The jester with his cap-and-bells crown and his bladder sceptre is, of course, the king's double. Where, once, Hamlet the ghost-king came from the grave to speculate on death and instruct 'revenge,' now Yorick, the jest-king, comes with other instructions, ventriloquized by yet another of the king's doubles, Hamlet, his son: 'Now get you to my lady's chamber and tell her, let her paint an inch thick, to this favour she must come.' Yorick's wisdom makes revenge superfluous. 'To this favour [we] must come' means we don't need to 'take arms' – taking our time will do. Claudius is going to die.

Yorick comes out of the grave to talk back to the king. But more than that, he comes out of the grave to speak up, one last time for Ophelia. Bizarrely, proleptically, Yorick is Ophelia's double, for 'to this favour she must come.' The skull makes the audience face up to death's horrors in a materially specific way that Hamlet's philosophizing has managed to avoid. Death, the prince learns from Yorick, stinks. The jester is a substitute who grounds ghastliness, displacing it from Ophelia *now*, for, newly-dead, her corpse still registers her sweetness, while casting imagination forward to Ophelia *then*, in the grave, 'instant old', no longer even a body but rotten flesh and jumbled bones. The words Hamlet puts into Yorick's mouth let Ophelia, strangely, speak for the last time – 'to this favour she must come.' Hamlet, holding the skull, thinks he holds the jester he loved; what he doesn't know is that, in this substitute, he holds Ophelia too. It is a bizarrely placed and displaced final love scene.

Only now, 200 lines into the scene, is Ophelia's body brought onstage to play dead, to perform the part of 'speaking property', an unsettled, unsettling signifier set inside 'maimed rites'. The body is legible, but in challenging spectators onstage and offstage to read it, the body invites multiple readings. Like Cordelia, when Ophelia plays dead, she plays up.

The funeral resolves nothing. It staggers through a sequence of disruptions that would be farcical if they were not so shocking, entering with such mangled ceremony that it is instantly legible as a suicide's. So much for the 'great command' that was supposed to 'o'er sway the order' and fix all that. Laertes bullies the priest; the priest devastates him in return. The corpse is finally lowered into the grave, and Gertrude scatters flowers on it, refashioning one sacrament into another, disclosing an alternative play, a woman's play not based on men's paranoid instruction ('Fear it, Ophelia, fear it'). It is a play that might have ended so differently: 'I thought thy bride-bed to have deck'd; 'I hop'd thou shouldst have been my Hamlet's wife'. Gertrude's transvestite flowers (recalling, perhaps, Ophelia's memory flowers) make this funeral look like a wrecked wedding.[21]

These grotesque deformations and disruptions are nothing less than sabotage, the relentless, incremental deritualizing of the ceremony that is meant to accommodate the living to death. The resistance written by means of this profanation reaches its climax when Laertes *'leapes into the graue'* (Q1 S.D.) on top of his dead sister, crying, 'Hold off the earth a while, / Till I have caught her once more in mine arms' as if he meant to ravish her from death.[22] The spectacle is more horrific even than the outrage. In his embrace, Ophelia rises from the grave. Reanimated (like the Ghost, like Yorick) she re-enters the field of play, her dead eyes gazing at the audience. And for this moment when she won't play dead, she embodies a subversion of each and every one of the patriarchal validations men in this play produce to glamorize death. But death isn't glamorous. It's hideous. Ophelia now – that's really what death looks like. Placed here, she anticipates the death of the hero that's fast approaching and proleptically deconstructs it, like Falstaff in *1 Henry IV* standing over dead Blount and shirking the 'grinning honour' the body tropes seconds before Hal enters to play out his fight to the death with Hotspur. Ophelia teaches the audience to read heroic death through the preliminary reading material that is its inversion.

Shakespeare raises Ophelia from the grave only momentarily. Hamlet upstages her, erupting with his self-conscious flourish, 'This is I, Hamlet the Dane', then he, too, *'leapes in after Laertes'* (Q1 S.D.), brother and lover grappling over the dead body ('Pluck them asunder'), trying to throttle each other ('take thy fingers from my throat'). Mocking Laertes as 'splenative and rash', coming 'here to whine', to 'prate', to 'mouth' and 'rant', Hamlet himself becomes the prater, mouther, ranter, outfacing himself in fustian swagger, a display that has all the dignity of Mark Antony's lurching progress up the monument hauled by Cleopatra and her girls. And that is the point – the ugliness, the awkwardness, the unseemliness. No sweetness, no flights of angels, no rest. The penetration of Ophelia's blank stare gets lost. Her manhandled body is dropped. After this, the funeral is dropped too. In Shakespeare's playtext, Ophelia never does get buried.

Turning back to the films, I find that they take on very little of this scene's ambiguity and generic instability, its moves between tragedy and farce. All three cut the Gravedigger's parody inquest and the debate about Ophelia's suicide as well as any mention of desecrated burial. They do, however, trouble the gravesite. Kozintsev's Gravedigger digs in a desolate length of dry ground among stones that lean drunkenly in the shadow of a one-armed cross; Zeffirelli buries Ophelia not in the castle's royal vaults but by the roadside out of Elsinore. All three films cut the bone juggling, although Kozintsev gets closest to its grim comedy when a skull, evidently under its own propulsion, comes shooting out of

Ophelia's fresh grave. Only Olivier's Hamlet registers the funeral as 'maimed rites'; only his Laertes menaces the priest. Kozintsev and Zeffirelli stop short even of putting Ophelia into the grave (the last shot of Bonham-Carter is on the bier beside the grave; of Vertinskaya, as the lid of her coffin is nailed down). All three films construct a version of Laertes' violation of the dead body, but only Olivier approximates Shakespeare's textual directions. From a distant long shot that takes Hamlet's point of view in the foreground, the spectator sees Laertes leap into the grave and raise Ophelia in an embrace, but then Hamlet steps out from among the gravestones across the line of vision. When he moves again Ophelia has been disposed of and Laertes is charging towards him. Almost as an afterthought the camera rests momentarily on Ophelia, then cranes away into distant long shot as the now-miniaturized body disappears into the grave. Kozintsev's version of this is much less decorous, but still does not get the effect the playtext bids for. His Ophelia lies in her coffin undisturbed while the camera follows Laertes. Cursing Hamlet, he hurls himself into her empty grave and flails on his back in the dirt, another child driven mad by Claudius's regime. None of these films consults the logic of the Q1 stage directions to see what

Plate 4 Ophelia rises from the grave. Jean Simmons and Terence Morgan in Olivier's 1948 *Hamlet*.
Source: Two Cities Films, 1948.

happens to the scene – and to the prince – if Hamlet leaps into the grave and grapples with Laertes over the body.

These heavily cut funeral scenes are by no means thoughtless; Kozintsev, indeed, politicizes his interpretation very acutely. When Hamlet lifts his eyes from Yorick's skull to see the funeral approaching, Kozintsev cuts to a strip of barren turf where ragged serfs stand watching the black parade toil across the plain, raising dust clouds. An advance rider on a black horse suddenly puts the spur in, riding down upon the little knot of peasants as if they needed dispersing, his horse's hooves rearing over their heads in a mindlessly excessive show of force. Still, Ophelia is desperately under-represented.

Because its technology has the power to frame, to focus, to edit, to give the spectator no option but to look at the ugly, the damaged, the dead, film has the potential to live more dangerously than theatre. But in all three *Hamlet*s, film is much more conservative, more idealizing than theatre. I have argued that Shakespeare's strategy in constructing the funeral scene as a sequence of contradictory points of view troubles any single reading of it. The theatre achieves this effect sequentially, as one idea literally displaces what went before (or not, if the first idea stubbornly refuses to go away). Film, though, might construct contradiction differently, using a vocabulary of image, frame and shot, manipulating distance and point of view. In the theatre, once Ophelia's corpse arrives on stage it is a material fact that the scene must reckon with: the body won't go away. But what these films do is avert the camera's eye from the body and, by taking the spectator with them, they erase the corpse.

Uniquely Zeffirelli does focus his camera on dead Ophelia, in two close-ups lasting two seconds. It is enough to suggest both titillation and taboo as Laertes draws the shroud from her face to invite our looking, which is also a violation. But our mixed emotions are instantly calmed by a spectacle of repose that requires no disturbed contemplation. Ophelia is pallid in death but beautiful, her hair combed of its matted tangles and bound in gold, the brooding intensity of her mad face smoothed by death. These shots, however, turn out not to be the film's real interest. They're intercut with close-ups of Laertes gazing down at her, and it is on his face that the camera dwells.

Obviously, these burial scenes are more interested in Hamlet than Ophelia. Kozintsev and Zeffirelli make him a pseudo-Odyssean hero coming home: one Hamlet strides through crowds of milling serfs, the other, like the Lone Ranger with his faithful Tonto, rides back into town. But none uses Hamlet's struggle with Laertes to interrogate male heroics because none considers that Shakespeare might be constructing

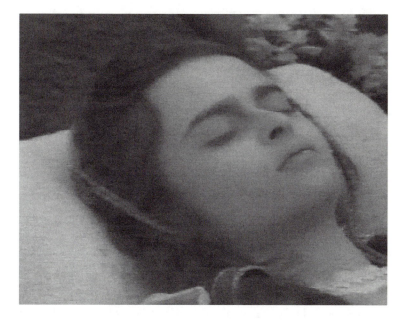

Plate 5 Dead Ophelia. Helena Bonham-Carter in Zeffirelli's 1990 *Hamlet.*
Source: Warner Bros., 1990.

this scene radically to deconstruct the hero – along the lines of Othello
foaming at the mouth, or Macbeth fumbling with his breastplate as he
bellows at the 'cream-faced loon', or Antony botching his suicide, or
Lear, crowned in weeds, hauling his boots off, moments seemingly
designed to make the hero absurd as a process of making him tragic. It
is, of course, in the moment of carnivalization, of absurdity, that male
heroics are most keenly interrogated in the tragedies, a moment that is
always felt as feminized. These films, however, eschew the female
grotesque to opt for the recuperation of Hamlet as hero and nice guy.
The kind who might leave Ophelia sobbing at the end of the nunnery
scene but who first breaks his exit, picks up a blonde curl and kisses it (so
Olivier). The kind who tells dead Ophelia, 'I lov'd you ever' (Kozintsev).
The kind who makes nostalgic gestures as music cues in sentiment
(Zeffirelli) – already leaving the grave, Hamlet turns back to stand over
Ophelia. Zeffirelli's camera studies his looking as he picks up a spray of
lilac, inhales its sweetness, then lays it on the body the camera ignores as,
instead, it watches him go. Wanting a hero, each film finds it inconceivable to imagine a Hamlet whose role pushes towards travesty,
buffoonery.

Full Bodies

Kate Winslet is cinema's latest Ophelia, in a film, directed by Kenneth Branagh, that claims to present a full-text *Hamlet*, including a full-text Ophelia and a full-text funeral.[23] If, then, the radical Ophelia I'm arguing for is somehow 'in' the text (and 'in' the text earlier films 'lost'), this is the film that should deliver her.[24] But it doesn't. Not least because Branagh writes supplementary texts on to this *Hamlet* that strip the possibility of radicalism, even of innovation, from Winslet's performance, to give us, finally, an interpretation of Ophelia that is depressingly predictable.

Winslet's Ophelia moves in an Elsinore that owes something to Olivier (Branagh's blond prince is an obvious *homage*), but more to Olivier in *The Prince and the Showgirl* than *Hamlet*. Branagh's Elsinore is Blenheim Palace on the outside, but inside, incomprehensibly Ruritanian, more kitsch than *belle époque*. Walled floor to ceiling with mirrors, the hall where most of the action is set becomes a self-regarding looking-glass chamber, where, it turns out, the mirrors anachronistically function as doors into through-the-looking-glass spaces. Improbably, Hamlet's apartments lie directly behind one of these doors; Ophelia's bedroom and later her padded cell, behind others. How prescient of old King Hamlet to have had this padded cell, straight out of a Victorian lunatic asylum, already installed on the premises. Even more anachronistically, one of the doors turns out to be a two-way mirror: the technology of the modern totalitarian state serves Claudius in 3.1 instead of an arras. Costumes in this Elsinore time travel between 1850 and 1945. The military dress uniforms of the first court scene suggest in their spruce artificiality a minor, turn-of-the-century Austro-Hungarian principality playing at toy soldiers; civilians – Laertes bound for Paris – look like prosperous Victorian bankers in cravats and pinstripes; the Gravediggers are Dickensian East Enders. And Winslet's flame-haired, Pre-Raphaelite Ophelia moves from Queen Victoria's Princess Alexandra as she might have been drawn by George du Maurier to William Holman Hunt's fallen woman in *The Awakening Conscience*.[25] Finally, though, Winslet's Ophelia belongs to Bram Stoker.

This four-hour *Hamlet* promises Shakespeare's uncut text but delivers rather more, especially for Ophelia. She gets all her 'original' lines but, in addition, a line (by Branagh?) that Shakespeare didn't write and a speech (originally Polonius's) that Shakespeare didn't give her.[26] And her performance is greatly expanded by a dozen or so invented scenes: the opening court wedding, a chase sequence that has her leaping from bed and racing down the corridors as soldiers search her room for the prince she's running to warn, a shot of her drowned – the actual drowning perhaps suggested by the violent hydrotherapy she's subjected to in her madness.

These inventions notwithstanding, Ophelia's narrative is most radically rewritten in a series of flashbacks, devised, Branagh claimed, to 'explain' the relationship between Hamlet and Ophelia. Each is triggered by a collision between paternal authority and erotic transgression, the memory of the lover who has already made it into Ophelia's bed. And each has implications for the coming funeral scene. The first occurs when Polonius takes his children into Elsinore's private chapel and sits them under the sign of the cross to deliver his paternal advice and blessing. After Laertes departs and Polonius, off camera, summons Ophelia to account for herself, unseen hands shove her roughly into a confession box. The camera, staring at her face, takes in the grille at the side, where Polonius utters his interrogation, priestlike. 'What is between you?' cues the flashback that covers – and contradicts – Ophelia's answer: 'He hath importun'd me with love / In honourable fashion.' While she says so, a flashback shows Hamlet naked in bed with her, grappling thighs and buttocks in vigorous love-making. Her account to her father is a palpable lie – this is no 'importun[ing] . . . In honourable fashion.' Her father's ultimatum, 'Look to't, I charge you', cues another flashback. Hamlet, asleep, holds her from behind in a post-coital embrace, but her eyes are open, so the line she speaks over this image, 'I shall obey, my Lord', is ambiguous. Which 'lord' does she intend to obey? What is most disturbing about these flashbacks is not their content but their technique. In them the camera does not record the love-making from Ophelia's point of view or memory; rather, it voyeuristically watches her having sex, and so performs upon her the classic move of denying her subjectivity in the process of objectifying her. But since these memories-in-flashback begin with Ophelia, since they present themselves as her memories and seem to simulate a first-person viewpoint, they effectively recruit her, willy-nilly, to the project of her own objectification.

Ophelia returns to this site of love-making twice more in later scenes. In 2.2 her father drags her before the king and queen and forces her to read out to them the contents of Hamlet's letter. Incoherent with humiliation, she chokes out her utterance, 'Doubt thou the stars are fire . . .'. A flashback shows the laughing lovers sitting up in bed playfully reading out loud these 'ill . . . numbers', but she can't continue after 'never doubt I love'; she crushes the letter into her father's hand and flees. Later, in 4.5, memory again triggers a flashback. Singing 'He is dead and gone, lady', Ophelia seems to be remembering Polonius, but when Hamlet, the lover who displaced the father, again takes over her consciousness, the song shifts into 'Tomorrow is Saint Valentine's day', and Ophelia's hands perform as brutal sex on her own body the past love-making which the flashback re-presents.

What mediates the 'information' produced in these flashbacks is that Polonius's authority turns out to be corrupt: the advice he gives his children is debased in his next scene, where he sprawls in a chair opposite Reynaldo, his truss exposed and his braces still down around trousers that have obviously been recently lowered for action. Polonius's apartments have the ambience of a gentleman's club when the cigars and port are being passed round, as he directs a monosyllabic Reynaldo to spy on Laertes in Paris, sleazily working out the degree of 'forgeries' – 'drinking, fencing, swearing', (and drabbing?) – that Laertes might be falsely accused of by way of verifying his virtue. But this father, who requires strict continence from son and daughter, is himself debauched. A whore lies in the curtained daybed behind him, and Polonius curtly motions her to leave. Minutes later, it is the space evacuated by the whore that Ophelia occupies when she bursts in to tell her father of a Hamlet 'loosed out of hell'. As he fulminates, she seeks the refuge of the parental bed and lies there in a foetal curl. Can she not – a sexually experienced woman – smell 'the rank sweat of an enseamed bed' on her father's sheets? Or is her place in this latest bed meant to write her 'whore'?

Branagh's flashback 'explanations' expose a serious illiteracy that serves to makes Ophelia's narrative incomprehensible and her text, nonsense, for Winslet's Ophelia must be either knave or fool – either sexually practised and a practised liar who makes a credulous dope of her grieving brother who still supposes her 'unpolluted flesh' deserves 'virgin crants'; or foolishly in thrall to a patriarchy whose hypocrisy she can't nose out even though it stinks to heaven. Either way, she ceases to represent a value different from Hamlet's mother or to embody a terrible ethical crisis when she is required to lie to Hamlet in 3.1: 'at home, my lord' is merely one of several untruths, not a shattering betrayal. This Ophelia ceases to signify as 'green girl', green either with inexperience's brave audacity that will defy 'adult' instruction in the play and credit Hamlet's 'tenders', or green with the sickness of virgin longing whose cure is consummation. It is impossible to determine whether Winslet's Ophelia goes mad in an excess of grief because she's deceived a father, now dead, killed by her lover, or because Hamlet, having bedded her, now rejects her. This second reading fits Ophelia into the logic of the St Valentine's Day song whose conclusion reiterates the misogynist stereotype – appetitive womankind, denied sex and so crazed, will 'naturally' join Brontë's mad Bertha in the attic. But since in this film sexuality and integrity, never mind innocence, seem unable to coexist, Winslet's Ophelia goes to her grave a fraud, evacuated of sincerity from her first exchange with her father to her brother's final obsequies.

So, given Branagh's busy flashbacks, is it significant that he declines to put one just where convention tells us to expect it? The tradition of *Hamlet* films, though they employ flashbacks nowhere else, is to show what happened in Ophelia's closet when Hamlet came to her 'unbrac'd', 'held her at arm's length', and fell 'to such perusal' of her face 'As a would draw it'. In a film that trains its spectators in the narrative satisfactions of the flashback, this craves explanation. Spectators want to know why Hamlet seeks out Ophelia in the wake of his encounter with his father's ghost; how she reacts, given her promise to her father to 'obey'; how what happens (or doesn't happen) in Ophelia's closet fuels the betrayals and violence of their next encounter. In Branagh's version, when Hamlet was last in Ophelia's closet, he was in her bed – *pace* the flashback. Coming again to her closet from seeing the ghost, is he seeking solace in sex? Does she deny him? We don't know, for Branagh, who explains everything else, withholds explanation here. Writing a gap into the Hamlet/Ophelia narrative, he cheats his spectators.

Denied explanation, what we see subsequently is an Ophelia that the film seems determined to punish excessively in ways that make her ugly, but decline, as in Zeffirelli's film, to refer that ugliness back on to her punishers. So the nunnery scene is merely a stagey *tour de force* in which Branagh's Hamlet drags Ophelia the length of the mirrored hall, flinging open then slamming the doors one after the other (he knows Claudius and Polonius are behind one of them), and finally shoving Ophelia's face up against the glass that happens to be Claudius's two-way mirror. Flattened, pushed out of shape, her face is grotesque. But what this moment might be saying about male violence – both the active violence of Hamlet and the passive violence of Polonius, who sets his daughter up as 'bait' to catch 'this carp of truth', a truth *about* male violence – is dismantled by Polonius's reaction. Never before scrupulous about abusing women's bodies or his children's credulity, Polonius is now represented as deeply caring of Ophelia. Trapped on the wrong side of the glass where he cannot reach his daughter, he still steps forward instinctively to intervene, and later he cradles her as she sobs in his arms. As in earlier film versions, Elsinore turns out to be populated by seriously nice guys – here, including Polonius.

Branagh's practice, in 1996, of writing Ophelia's sexuality in such a clichéd film idiom, making her something common, and marketable, may ultimately expose his need to appropriate and contain the role's far more elusive sexuality, Ophelia's virginity. This need is perhaps unconsciously expressed in the film's imagistic obsession with gates, doors, windows, openings of all sorts: the gaping mouth of the ghost in close-up; the mirrored doors; Fortinbras's ludicrously excessive forced entry; the gate hanging crazily off its hinges in the graveyard.[27] It is, I think,

Plate 6 'Hold off the earth awhile.' Laertes with Ophelia in the grave. Kate
Winslet and Michael Maloney in Kenneth Branagh's 1996 *Hamlet*.
Source: Castlerock Entertainment, 1996.

this sublimated but legible male desire to demystify female sexuality, to
possess and manage it, that gives access, finally, to Branagh's filming of
Ophelia's funeral.

He directs it like a Gothic scene out of Dickens, by torchlight, in
what is evidently a dubiously hallowed corner of London's Highgate
Cemetery where the shrubbery is overgrown and the iron railings
vandalised.[28] Exhuming the skulls, the Gravedigger arranges them
scientifically by size, then packs the jumble of bones into a Hessian
sack – evidently bound for the anatomy theatre, not the charnel house.
So when the crêpe-shrouded procession enters carrying the closed black
coffin to the grave, we are expecting Stoker's Van Helsing, not the
Danish court. The film passes briefly over the coffin but spends most of
its time cutting from (male) face to face, taking in the passionate agony
of Laertes making romantic sublimity of his sister's 'unpolluted flesh',
but focusing mostly on Hamlet's reaction. When the coffin is lowered
into the grave, Laertes gives an anguished cry, 'Hold off the earth
awhile . . . ', and leaps in after it, wrenching off the lid with his bare
hands and raising Ophelia to ghoulish resurrection.

Momentarily this film comes closer than any of its predecessors to
imagining what I think Shakespeare wrote as theatre, but it also throws

its achievement away. For it invokes a cliché that mediates shock and flattens audience response: it's the coffin lid that does it. For what we see in Laertes's melodramatic gesture is a replay of a classic trope of vampire films that locates Ophelia as the vampire bride. In the vampire movie the lid comes off the coffin so the stake can be driven through the heart of the erotically empowered, insatiable, un-dead vampire bride. This move thrills but also horrifies as it reclaims subjectivity for the object in the coffin, the corpse that is re-presented, ambiguously alive, as the bride who, appallingly, wears the signs of her appetite on her face. The man she loved in life must hammer the stake in, his action enforcing a spectacular readjustment of sexual politics as his phallic assertion of power (which claims for men the right, the responsibility, to control female sexuality and preserve women's innocence) transforms the predatory sexual woman back into that state of innocence; the conventional film dissolve watches her fangs shrink, her face soften. (This, of course, occludes anxieties that women may not be innocent.) Framing Ophelia as vampire bride in her funeral scene brings Branagh to a place where his Hamlet can, using the corpse as a proxy, symbolically lay to rest his fantasies about Gertrude's erratic sexuality, but also to a place where Branagh-the-prince can claim recuperative phallic control over the very sexual activity Branagh-the-director invented to make, in 1996, Ophelia 'real'.

In Branagh's film there is, of course, no staking. And this is where the

Plate 7 Ophelia's Gothic funeral in Kenneth Branagh's 1996 *Hamlet*.
Source: Castlerock Entertainment, 1996.

51

logic of the allusion breaks down totally, for the problem with this Ophelia is that she can't be staked. She cannot be 'redeemed' because the source of her pollution cannot be traced/admitted. She's not a virgin; she's not innocent. So is she held up here as a horror? Is this another instance of the film's (unconscious? conscious?) desire to punish Ophelia?

The image of Ophelia as Lucy Westenra is on our retina for a split second only, for Hamlet pulls focus. The camera turns to him; the grappling between brother and lover is removed from the grave, and the rest of the scene is about the men. So what happens to Ophelia? Before he leaves, and he is the last to go, Claudius tosses the Gravedigger a purse. But the Gravedigger does not reach for his spade to begin the process of filling in the grave. This Ophelia, we feel, may wind up with Yorick's skull on the anatomist's table.

I am not surprised by the editing of the funeral scene – the way, as in all the earlier films, Ophelia gets only seconds on camera. For after four hours, Branagh's *Hamlet* turns out to be the longest buddy film ever. All its big emotional moments are moments of male bonding, and its most serious intellectual and narrative contribution to our understanding of *Hamlet* – and it is a serious intellectual contribution – is its interrogation of bad buddies, the fathers in this film who, utterly undeserving, abuse their children with outrageous patriarchal claims on their autonomy and loyalty. One of those fathers is the repressive-yet-dissolute counsellor Polonius; another is the perhaps equally repressive-and-dissolute King Hamlet, the ghost who looks in his first apparition like a statue of a stony Czar Nicholas, who presents himself as a monster of devouring mouth and demonic eyes, and who ends literally toppled, like some has-been tinpot dictator of a failed regime, by the 'liberating' army of Fortinbras.

To see what performative meaning might have been written into the filming of Ophelia's funeral, I turn to the last minutes of Branagh's *Hamlet*. From a close-up on a dead face, the camera pulls slowly back into a wide angle long shot that situates the dead body as the focal point on a landscape that stretches, in the pull-back, to include mourners, ranks of soldiers, the whole of the palace façade. The focus fixes on the body, registering its concentration on the beautiful corpse, inviting spectators to meditate on the privileged meanings it proposes. This funeral, though, isn't Ophelia's. It's Hamlet's. And around this (final) celebration of the heroic male body circulates not a bit of irony.

A Body Restored

Can Ophelia's funeral be filmed differently? A new generation of film-makers, schooled not just in feminist readings of Shakespeare but in the everyday practices of feminist culture at large, and in the kind of digital effects pioneered in, for instance, *Titanic* (1997), might pursue film strategies learned from Quentin Tarantino and Baz Luhrmann. They might acknowledge the black comedic dissidence of Ophelia's performance narrative, and film this scene to rethink our cultural need to heroicize Hamlet. The sequence could be edited so that viewers speculated on the body of the woman and gazed into the dead eyes of the corpse.

A revisionist funeral scene might be keyed by Gertrude's 'There is a willow'. Her agitation, exposed in her compulsive iteration, marks her utterance as frenzy, not elegy, and herself perhaps as a Gertrude who is protesting too much (and therefore colluding in a cover-up), or trembling on madness. A camera that fixed on Gertrude's face as she spoke rather than cutting away to a representation of the drowning would register this speech as not nearly so much about Ophelia as about the messy political business Gertrude's narrative has to do in the court.

Later, as the Gravedigger dug and debated the coroner's verdict, his metaphoric reopening of the inquest might literally re-call the drowning, his account summoning a *revenant* Ophelia back to re-play first one, then another version of his conflicted narrative. 'The crowner hath sat on her, and finds it Christian burial' would cut to a representation of that scenario to frame the authorised version of events. Spectators would see an Ophelia, 'incapable of her own distress', slipping into the water that seemed to reach out for her, as an accidental drowning. But a discontinuity in editing that signalled a disturbance of looking would put the scene in quotation marks, registering it as one 'version' of events. As the Gravedigger's account continued in voice-over – 'It must be *se offendendo* . . . ' – a second cut would give spectators that other, troubled version of events, seeing Ophelia seek the water to drown herself 'in her own defence', a representation designed to invite spectators to worry over that malapropism, perhaps to read 'defence' as 'offence'. Or did the Gravedigger paradoxically get things right? Was drowning Ophelia's supreme act of self-'defence'? This appalling uncertainty would be Ophelia's legacy to the spectator in a film where editing did not privilege either sequence as what 'really' happened.

A film that wanted to rethink the heroic prince would make the Gravedigger more than a match for a Hamlet he reduced to a Polonius with put-downs like 'Cannot you tell that? Every fool can tell that . . . ' Their exchange – licensed by the Gravedigger's ironic failure to recognize the prince – would work to estrange Hamlet, not just to us, as spectators, but to himself. It would require him to start asking Lear's question, 'Who am I?' Why the non-recognition? Not because Hamlet was disguised (as in Olivier and Kozintsev), but quite simply because, from the

Gravedigger's standpoint shoulder-deep in the grave, authority is not – as Falstaff supposes – 'instinct'. His plebeian indifference would make Hamlet unprecedentedly self-conscious, demoting to a peripheral point of view the 'I' and 'eye' that obsess both Shakespeare's text and earlier film *Hamlet*s.

If a revisionist film wanted to look for it, there is uncanny recognition to be found in the grave when Yorick's skull is turfed out of it. Like Kozintsev's Gravedigger who answers Hamlet's desire to know the skull by rooting in the dirt to find a mouldering reminiscence of a sweeter time to set upon its grinning hollowness (the jester's cap-and-bells that instantly transforms it into Yorick) a later Gravedigger might unearth something that made the skull Ophelia, her linen chaplet, perhaps, that had somehow arrived in the grave before her. Retrieved from the dirt to bonnet the skull, the grave-wrecked linen would slip away when Hamlet took up the skull. He wouldn't recognize her.

Finally, from a long shot that took in the procession, a film that wanted to trouble the funeral could cut to mid-close-up to answer Hamlet's question, 'Who is this they follow?' by fixing on Ophelia, to show the corpse lying shrouded on an open bier, her face uncovered, the ugliness of her death painfully legible. Ophelia's skin, mottled blue like a fresh bruise, would look like wax; her jaw, pulled shut with a linen band, but her eyes wide open, the scene's most harrowing effect. Neither would the shroud conceal the abdominal distension that comes with death by drowning. Ophelia would look pregnant.[29]

Once it cut to the mid-close-up, this film would not move away from Ophelia's dead-eyed face. Laertes' wrangling with the priest, Gertrude's obsequies and Hamlet's vaunts would be heard as 'noises off' while the camera stared at the open eyes that stared back; digital technology post-*Titanic* knows how to deliver such effects. As unseen hands lowered the corpse into the grave, petals would fall on to the face. Suddenly, the image would blur as Laertes, off, cried 'Hold . . . !' and leaped on top of Ophelia to catch her 'once more' in his arms, struggling to raise the dead weight that pulled him down into the grave, his intrusion an obscenity. Slowly, seen over Laertes's shoulder, the body, stiff with rigor mortis, would rise, Ophelia's eyes staring at the camera whose sight-line was level with the grave. But when, off, Hamlet's voice cried out and his feet came in shot, his body filling the frame as he leaped into the grave, Laertes, exhausted, would drop Ophelia's dead weight into Hamlet's arms. The 'thing' would be between them as they strained for each other's throats. Suddenly feet would appear along the lip of the grave, responding to Claudius's bellowed commands. Hands would come into shot to reach down and haul the struggling, sweat-soaked men out of the grave by the scruff of their necks. Ophelia would lie as she fell, the blank eyes gazing upwards at the camera looking down while the scene rushed to its conclusion. Hamlet's strident protest 'I loved Ophelia . . . .' would come too late – more 'noises off'. Dirt from the Gravedigger's unseen spade would already be falling on Ophelia's face.

* * *

My longing for a film ending that disturbs conventional looking economies and simultaneously constructs and deconstructs Ophelia's funeral marks me, perhaps, as post-modernist, even post-feminist. But equally, it marks me as early modernist, for it's a desire that finds expression in Elizabethan practice. Christopher Marlowe wrote two endings to *Dr Faustus*, one, tragedy, the other, farce; Shakespeare declined to write for *The Taming of the Shrew* the ending that would fix it generically by closing its comic frame. Arguably, these unresolved endings result from textual corruption. Or perhaps, historically, textual corruption has been premised to explain their unresolved endings. Inarguably, though, Shakespeare wrote a post-modern ending on to *Troilus and Cressida*. Nothing is resolved: Hector dies, Cressida swerves, Troy stands, both sides claim victory, and the play's last speech defers the ending into an endless, receding future belonging to future generations, who will see this story feelingly because they are contaminated by its history. Pandarus bequeaths us our legacy, the diseases of Troy.

Among contemporary commercial film-makers it is only Baz Luhrmann in *Romeo + Juliet* who, so far, has probed Shakespeare's precocious post-modernism. His meta-filmic film uses 'looking' as a master metaphor to knowingly construct and anarchically deconstruct film's conventional looking economies. There are classic 'Hollywood' shots in this film that could come straight out of *Casablanca*; others spoof studio tradition and look like MTV send-ups. Luhrmann 'does' the ending twice, first as apotheosis, then as grunge.[30] Juliet lies 'dead' in a feast of light, on a high altar surrounded by flowers and candles in a kitsched-up cathedral where the central aisle is a runway of crosses lit up like tacky Blackpool illuminations. Waking, she reaches out to touch Romeo; he looks down, gasps – and knocks back the poison. She finds his gun, puts it to her temple and cocks the trigger. When the shot fires, the camera cuts away to see the scene from Christ's point of view on the cross over the altar, then cranes higher and higher, looking down on the scene below as an explosion of white light. A cut to outtakes that reprise the lovers' history yields to a low-angle shot that surrounds them, dead, in starburst patterns of candlelight that remember the fireworks at Capulet's ball. Fire dissolves into water: Romeo and Juliet are falling into the swimming pool, kissing, bubbles rushing like life around them. The image freezes. And then the death scene gets replayed. This time, on grainy, grey, low-resolution video footage. We're on the cathedral steps with the TV cameras watching body bags loaded into an ambulance. Another day's news. Another two for the morgue.

3

SHADOWING CLEOPATRA
Making whiteness strange

Think on me
That am with Phoebus' amorous pinches black . . .
Antony and Cleopatra (1.5.28–29)

'Cleopatra wasn't black'
John Caird, Director, *Antony and Cleopatra*, RSC, 1992

Othello represents a site through which the problem of the black
body in the white imaginary becomes visible, gets worked through.
Barbara Hodgdon, *The Shakespeare Trade*, 1998

Images

Four black-and-white production photographs lie side by side on the
library table. When they first turned up in the Royal Shakespeare
Company archives, they took me aback. The earliest captures a representation of race so embarrassingly crude that it put me in mind of Al
Jolson singing 'Swanee' in *The Jazz Singer*. It's an image that works a
cruel retrospective exposure upon the post-war, post-imperial cultural
moment in Britain that produced it. The only way I (whose racial consciousness reached adolescence in the summer of 1969, post-Kennedy,
post-Martin Luther King, forced into thought by black power and stu-
dent protest) could read this image without aversion was historically, as
a witness of 'the way we were'. Later, though, dozens of similar images
from subsequent productions emerged from the archives. Seeing in them
newer versions of what I'd taken to be a redundant racial representation
continuously re-inserted into contemporary performance, I realized I
wasn't looking at 'history' but at politics – a politics of performance.

The production photograph is, of course, an odd sort of document,
both a record and a non-record, for it violates two basic conditions of theatrical activity: that performance happens continuously, across time, and
that performance is ephemeral. It's not supposed to last.[1] The photograph

delivers up performance to a later generation of spectators who see things differently. It is essentially distorting: it freezes single moments as if they were frames edited out of film footage, uncannily (for its conceit is suspended animation) capturing theatre's moving images and holding them in stasis. On the one hand, this allows us to pore over them, scrutinizing intensely; on the other, privileging those shots and what they select coerces, even over-determines, our looking. In the case of the four photographs lying on the table, though, such coercion is remedial. These photographs interrupt what performance blurs, stop us in our tracks.

All show Cleopatra and her 'girls'. The first dates from 1953. Peggy Ashcroft's Cleopatra appears on the Shakespeare Memorial Theatre stage, regal in chin-high profile on her sunburst throne, her snake-clasp necklace winding round her throat, her features scored in the exaggerated stage make-up of the period, extending her hand to Caesar's messenger. Behind her stand Iras and Charmian, and to the right, another of her train, all in 'Egyptian' costume, with black wigs and heavily kohled eyes. The fourth girl, seated at the edge of the frame, backed right up against the proscenium arch as though she's peripheral to the scene, is the one who arrests my gaze. She is black – not a black actor, but an actor (Diane Chadwick)

Plate 8 Cleopatra receives Caesar's messenger. Peggy Ashcroft and her court in Glen Byam Shaw's 1953 *Antony and Cleopatra*.
Source: Angus McBean photograph. Courtesy of The Shakespeare Centre Library, The Shakespeare Birthplace Trust, Stratford-upon-Avon. (The original print was torn by McBean to indicate it was not to be used.)

Plate 9 'Times, O times!' Cleopatra and her court. Janet Suzman in Trevor
  Nunn's 1972 *Antony and Cleopatra*.
Source: Reg Wilson photograph. Courtesy of The Shakespeare Centre Library, The
Shakespeare Birthplace Trust, Stratford-upon-Avon.

blacked up so heavily that the stage lights bounce off the cosmetic surface.
Upstage, another blackface Sambo, Mardian in a turban, holds back a curtain, looking in on the scene, blandly voyeuristic. In the second (1972),
Janet Suzman, flanked by her women, kneels arms outstretched on a
bed-sized cushion under an undulating canopy, remembering Antony.
Behind her an 'authentic' pharaonic court – hairless eunuchs, superfluous
kings, musicians, messengers, attendants with papyrus-leaf fans – play
rapt audience to her theatre of memories. All are tawny. Her messenger is
black. In 1982, Helen Mirren and her girls, again remembering 'Times,
O, times!', roll, laughing, in a sensuously tangled heap on the floor.
Charmian's blonde hair is plaited in piccaninny cornrows. Iras is black. In
1992, the three women crouch together, arms encircled, rocking, their

faces ugly in grief. Antony is dead, and they are 'for the dark'. Charmian is black. What links these images is the black body that shadows Cleopatra. Only once has Cleopatra herself been played black at the RSC and then, by default, not design. For one night only, in November 1992, in a production directed by John Caird, Claire Benedict (cast to play Charmian and to understudy the lead) went on for Cleopatra in one pre-view performance.

But as the photographs show, if black bodies don't play Cleopatra, they constantly play her sidekicks and servants, like the black boy in the Veronese-inspired opening of the 1981 BBC *Antony and Cleopatra* who tugs at Cleopatra's hounds, or the black Charmian opposite Vanessa Redgrave (Riverside, 1995) and the black Iras (again) opposite Helen Mirren (National Theatre, 1998). In Britain, only on the fringe, in non-mainstream companies like Talawa (Dona Croll, 1991), Northern Broadsides (Ishia Benison, 1995) and the English Stage Company (Cathy Tyson, 1998) is Cleopatra ever black. Elsewhere, though, the practice of annexing blackness to Cleopatra's whiteness turns out to have a history in the theatre traceable in production photographs to the beginning of the century. A blackface

Plate 10 'We are for the dark.' Cleopatra and her girls. Clare Higgins, Claire Benedict, Susie Lee Hayward in John Caird's 1992 *Antony and Cleopatra.*
Source: Malcolm Davies photograph. Courtesy of The Shakespeare Centre Library, The Shakespeare Birthplace Trust, Stratford-upon-Avon.

Alexas appeared in Oscar Asche's *Antony* tour of Australia and South Africa (1912–13) with Lily Brayton as Cleopatra, a blackface Alexas (1935) and Mardian (1945) appeared at the Memorial Theatre in Stratford.

In 1906, both Mardian and Eros blacked up. A photograph of that early production, Beerbohm Tree's extravaganza at His Majesty's Theatre, shows Cleopatra (Constance Collier) dead in a monument whose interior is written with hieroglyphics. These recall Hathor's temple at Dendera, to put on view her 'Ptolemaic' ancestors. All, in this representation, are black: the ancestral figures in the wall friezes, the animal-headed statues supporting her throne. This traffic in images conducted with narratives they ghost but never fully embody intensifies elsewhere, in the lavish souvenir *Play Pictorial* magazine compiled from Tree's production. In it, half-profile portraits of Collier illustrate the designer's concept of Cleopatra as 'neither Greek nor Roman, but Semitic', her 'authentic' semitism indicated not by colour (Collier's Cleopatra is white) but by the shape of her nose.[2] Elsewhere in the *Pictorial*, however, the two illustrations that frame Mrs Jameson's notes on 'Shakespeare's Cleopatra' (for Jameson, 'the real historical Cleopatra') work against Collier's pallid semitism to capture Cleopatra's image for blackness. One is a *faux*-hieroglyphic, drawn in profile like Collier's Cleopatra and, like Collier, crowned as Isis. But this 'real' Egyptian Cleopatra is black. So are her 'real' attendants, whose lithographic portrait appears lower down on the same page, bracketing Jameson's text. These five men (what Coleridge would have called 'veritable negroes') are dressed as noble savages (or wild animals), in gold collars, wrist and ankle bracelets, with leopard skins belted around their torsos, sitting stiff, gazing straight at the camera, the directness of their black looks arresting attention.[3] Uncaptioned, unlocated in any context of Tree's production, the photograph has a shocking immediacy, for it asserts itself at a different level of representation from the hieroglyphic line drawing. It does so less in its content – though it is disturbing enough to figure exotic princes as captive slaves – than in the way it withholds black identity while conspicuously inserting into Beerbohm Tree's theatre authentic (in excess of his Mardian's faked) black presence.

By practising annexation, white theatre, it turns out, is simply reproducing the practices of white culture at large. In paintings, drawings and etchings from Tiepolo and Trevisani to Gérôme, Alma Tadema, Etty and Sandys, black figures crouch at Cleopatra's white feet; black figures pour her wine, hold her mirror, steer her barge, play her music and stare down at her from wall paintings.[4] What these representations have in common with the production photographs is their artists' sense of the theatrical. The canvas or mural is a crowded *mise-en-scène* packed with extras swelling the epic narrative, which Tadema locates boldly in the foreground, as on a forestage; Tiepolo frames it with a *trompe l'oeil* proscenium arch, registering the narrative as self-conscious artifice, a performance. What is distinctive, and what sensationalizes performative practice, is that while both media represent blackness, theatre of the period employs white bodies to represent the representation.

Films repeat the same trope, but employ 'real negroes': when Claudette Colbert salutes Caesar in de Mille's 1934 *Cleopatra* the shot captures the half-naked black slave standing behind her. When Elizabeth Taylor in Mankewicz's 1963 kitsch epic *Cleopatra* undoes her Roman salute with a wink, again, the shot frames behind her one of the 'cast of thousands' massed in her black retinue.[5] Indeed, this representational trope seems to have been in place for as long as white culture has been imagining Cleopatra white. Even the frontispiece to the 1680 *Secret History of the Most Renowned Queen Elizabeth and the Earl of Essex*, which imagines Elizabeth, in the foreground, as Cleopatra kneeling before Essex/Antony, puts in the walled Roman garden behind them a black body caught in the act of looking.[6]

But if Cleopatra is never black in white culture, in black New York, black LA or black London, another Cleopatra leads an Other-cultural life that cites her history differently. She's the brand name on the beauty products black Joe Trace hustles door-to-door through 1920s Harlem in Toni Morrison's *Jazz*; the name Lorraine Hansbury gives to the black consciousness Beneatha discovers in 1950s *Raisin in the Sun*; the name the female Bond spin-off takes (along with her hip boots and .45) in the 1973 blaxploitation film, *Cleopatra Jones*; the name of the 1999 chart-topping black girl group from Manchester (who read Shakespeare, they said, backstage); the working name of the 'Fantasy Facilitator' who bills herself as 'a traditional independent Female Supremacist' at a Y2K web-site address whose logo features hieroglyphics, pyramids and the sphinx. Cleo Laine sings soul versions of Shakespeare's Sonnets: Cleopatra in the 'real' world of mass, not elite, culture is a black woman.[7]

This survey of exclusion, marginalization, and annexation helps me position my thinking on blackness – the black body, the trope of blackness – as a preliminary to exploring blackness in *Antony and Cleopatra* on the post-war British stage. I want to argue that Shakespeare wrote a black narrative at the centre of *Antony and Cleopatra*, a narrative marked by racial self-reference as explicit as Othello's. I 'am with Phoebus' amorous pinches black,' says the Egyptian, and the Moor, 'I am black.' This black narrative may have as little to do with 'real' Egyptian history as Richard Gloucester's hunchback has to do with 'real' English history, but it works, like Gloucester's, performatively, and draws upon the theatre's same logic of semiotic exchange.

Cleopatra's blackness has meaning in itself, but signifies beyond her single body to raise the ante in a play that turns out to stage a contest not just between Alexandria and Rome, east and west, male and female, Caesar and Cleopatra, but black and white, an imperial sweepstakes whose winner will write the future history of the world. Given that the theatre has regularly avoided this black narrative, the 'coincidences' of photographic representation I identified earlier document a project of denial in the white cultural imaginary whose effects are both ideological and theatrical, like stripping Othello of blackness, denial that distorts not just the performative but the discursive body.[8] To map this avoidance, I revisit the RSC's archives to read as case studies three post-war productions that tell this story of black appropriation and exclusion across fifty years.

Thinking Black

I begin, though, with yet another photograph, this one of Helen Mirren in Adrian Noble's chamber-play *Antony and Cleopatra* (1982), set in the RSC's bare black-box theatre, The Other Place. Mirren faces the camera, kneeling, in a gauze shift that is tied at one shoulder and clings to her

Plate 11 Cleopatra observed by Iras – 'the black body behind'. Helen Mirren and Josette Simon in Adrian Noble's 1982 *Antony and Cleopatra*.
Source: Joe Cocks photograph. Courtesy of The Shakespeare Centre Library, The Shakespeare Birthplace Trust, Stratford-upon-Avon.

figure; her arms are stretched wide, her fists balled. Her head, thrown back, casts her blonde, Garbo-style hair off her face. Her eyes are closed. It's a study in whiteness: Mirren's body photographs in high definition against a dense blackness, a picture of rapture, of radiance. But it's also a picture that defines white Cleopatra against a dark Other. Behind one of Mirren's arms another face is just visible in the photograph: Iras, played by Josette Simon, who is black. I have shown this photograph to students, professional Shakespeareans and archivists who've looked at it dozens of times. They don't see the black body.

Because the black face is both there and not there, because the image both constructs whiteness as based on blackness yet triumphantly fore-grounds itself, this photograph offers an emblem for my search for black Cleopatra. This search traps me in the paradox Richard Dyer explores so brilliantly in *White*: to talk about black representation that registers only in absence or exclusion, I have to talk about white Cleopatra. Talking 'white', though, my project is to make whiteness strange, not by focus-ing on white representation, as Dyer does, but rather on what we might think of as white practice, the way hegemonic white culture casually, 'nat-urally', inserts blackness into white representation as a strategy for defining itself. For as Dyer observes, 'at the level of representation, whites remain . . . dependent on non-whites for their sense of self'.[9] As my brief history of *Antony and Cleopatra* in performance so far has shown, reading blackness on to a text which the post-war contemporary theatre has 'naturally' constructed white, evidently serves some perma-nent white cultural interest. What does blackness signify that white representation wants to appropriate?

To address that, I need to theorize and historicize white representation of blackness (or rather, blacknesses) for white culture in Britain made something different of blackness in each of the years (1953, 1972 and 1992) I'm interested in. Equally, white culture in Britain, coerced by the civil rights and black consciousness movements in the USA, the post-war transition to self-government in India and Africa, and Britain's reassessments of its own colonialist/imperialist past, has, since 1953, been required to pay more urgent attention to recovering black history and learning to read its white narratives iconoclastically. In particular, it has had to reconsider the part black history has been required to play in the white imaginary, particularly in revisionist re-writings like Edward Said's *Orientalism*, that have forced western culture to rethink its historic understanding of how the West constructed the East as an Other that made sense of itself. But if blackness needs to be historicized, so does cul-tural theory, otherwise we apply it anachronistically. *Orientalism*, published in 1978, examined ideas in ways undreamt of in 1953 and, twenty-five years later, helped to dismantle cultural orthodoxies that were the bricks and mortar of political policy in Elizabeth II's coronation year. It appeared too late to be of use to Trevor Nunn directing *Antony and Cleopatra* in 1972, but by 1992, it was mainstream. How could any director ignore it?

If Otherness can only be understood historically, it is nevertheless clear that some of what Herodotus 'knew' about blackness in the fifth century BC persists as common 'knowledge' in contemporary urban society. As Wole Soyinka has wryly observed, 'We all have our prejudices, of course, but some of these prejudices are the result of experience.'[10] From this history that persists, then, it is possible to map a well-trodden *terra cognita* of blackness as a rough guide to the images, racial dynamics and cultural assumptions *Antony and Cleopatra* trafficks in, a map whose grid points – what blackness signifies – coincide with the play's major concerns: identity, sexuality and imperialism.

Race and racism as familiarly conceptualized and practised in contemporary London or Los Angeles are comparatively recent cultural inventions, introduced in the eighteenth and elaborated over the nineteenth century,[11] but there seems never to have been a time when blackness did not signify ethically or symbolically. As an idea its intellectual history begins in Egypt, where its earliest surviving records are wall paintings. One from 1200 BC depicts Queen Ahrus-Nofretari, crowned as Isis, holding her sistrum and mnet, her body conspicuously feminized, her skin painted deepest black, the colour of Nile silt. This body tropes fertility even as the figure constellates ideas of blackness, the sensual female and fecundity that are going to resonate for 3,000 years. Seven centuries later, Herodotus made similar connections. He knew the Egyptians as a black people and was fascinated by the idea of a land so fertile that it brought forth abundance effortlessly, copiously; a land permissive of easy indolence. Ever the imperturbable scholar, he recorded in academic detail the rituals that magically rehearsed Egyptian fertility, but, as we shall see, grew quite flustered when it came to documenting the Egyptian bacchanals, a female carnival of phallic licentiousness. It wasn't until the third century AD that blackness was 'blackened'. Origen, writing, significantly enough, from Alexandria, used darkness as a spiritual idea to allegorize Egyptian religious error against the light of Christian belief, instantiating dualistic thinking that produced the black/white binary western culture still cites, to trope not just morality and ethics but aesthetics and politics.

As Dyer argues, race is always about bodies, and white identity is bound up in precise body specifications: the 'white' body is a 'hard, lean body', a 'trained' and 'dieted' body held upright in an erect posture, its movements 'tight rather than loose', its domestic arrangements and eating manners demonstrating 'abstinence' in relation to appetites. It is a civilized body, a rational, ordered body, a Western body. By the logic of binary thinking, the black body is Eastern: loose, sensuous, irrational, primitive, 'natural' – a lazy, lascivious body whose failure of abstinence figures savagery or incontinent sexuality. Inside the white body white identity is animated by white 'spirit': energy, discipline, spiritual eleva- tion, intellect; in sum, 'enterprise' and 'will', 'a central value in western culture', traceable to Plato. 'Will,' writes Dyer, 'is literally mapped on to the world in terms of those who have it and those who don't, the ruler and the ruled, the coloniser and the colonised.' Moreover, this spiritual quality of enterprise is deterministic: it qualifies white bodies to lead humanity, direct destiny, conquer and construct dynasties, cities and empires.

Such ideas converge to rationalize racism as imperialism, what Dyer calls the 'will to power of the white race'.[12] Race operates as a spatial dynamic. One of the qualities that marks the 'native' as uncivilized is that he has no (white) concept of boundaries or borders: his space is 'the wild'. The white man maps human intervention on to the landscape: fixing borders, establishing limits, identifying frontiers and pushing them further and further back. Clearly, the fiction writer works as actively in this project as the geographer and cartographer. In terms of Africa, the white imperial imaginary fantasizes a dark continent (not just of the map but of the mind) that tropes the white man's dark imaginings, which he projects on to the black – 'obscurities of his own unconscious', says Dominic Mannoni, that he 'would rather not penetrate'. Hence, 'the image of Africa remains the negative reflection, the shadow, of the British self-image'.[13] When the 'dark continent' is represented as a seductive woman whose 'dark' interiors white imperialism penetrates and searches even as it combats the 'dark' forces native there; when Freudian psycho- analytic discourse picks up a similar trope to make female sexuality an imagined 'dark continent': we are seeing an ancient triad of ideas – ideas represented in the Ahrus-Nofretari wall painting – reconfigured by obses- sive white male anxiety.

These anxieties reach identity crisis when whiteness comes to repro- ducing itself, for whiteness can only preserve racial purity by mating with whiteness. But sex, figured as desire or as mechanical practice, isn't 'white'. It's 'dark'. And it's inimical to white 'spirit' – the control white minds must exercise over white bodies. In the dramas that test their white masculinity, men must resist and struggle to master the dark drive towards sex, must project sexuality on to blackness as a means, writes Dyer, 'to represent yet dissociate themselves from their own desires'. This observation is certainly relevant to *Antony and Cleopatra*, for 'dark desires are part of the story of whiteness': they constitute the desires that whiteness must struggle against, for the whiteness of white men resides in the tragic quality of succumbing to darkness, or the heroism of resisting it. But here's another twist, what might be called (after Cleopatra's eunuch) the 'Mardian factor'. For 'Not to be sexually driven is liable to cast a question mark over a man's masculinity' – darkness 'is a sign of his true masculinity, just as his ability to control it is a sign of his whiteness'. Living in a perpetual state of anxiety, the white man is always at risk from one side or the other, his 'masculinity "tainting" his whiteness or his whiteness emasculating him'.[14]

I hear a synopsis of *Antony and Cleopatra* in this analysis. The play offers no one 'whiter' than the anti-sensualist, utterly sterile, imperialist Octavius; no one 'darker' than the constantly 'becoming' Cleopatra whose 'infinite variety', like the Nile's, can't be mapped, contained, bounded. Antony is most his white, western self when, beaten from Modena, he crosses the frozen Alps, enduring famine, his body hardened to adversity, a 'white' narrative which, projected from Octavius's memory (or fantasy?), serves Roman political discourse. A companion projection wants to 'negrify' Antony, to imagine the lean, hard body softened with 'lascivious wassails' and inexhaustible erotic indulgence:

> Salt Cleopatra, soften thy waned lip!
> Let witchcraft join with beauty, lust with both;
> Tie up the libertine in a field of feasts;
> Keep his brain fuming. Epicurean cooks
> Sharpen with cloyless sauce his appetite
> That sleep and feeding may prorogue his honour . . .
> (2.1.21–26)

The 'East' where 'pleasure lies' operates a forcefield of attraction and repulsion: the 'space' – Cleopatra's body? – that is Egypt is the space of darkness ('desire', 'dotage', 'lust', 'sport', 'appetite'), where Antony vacillates between Orient and Occident, duty and desire, bastard children and 'lawful' issue, space and empire, magnanimity and calculation, extravagance and measure, black and white, Cleopatra and Octavia.[15]

The story Shakespeare's play has to tell of male identity, female sexuality, imperial conquest and the triumph of the West and western 'whiteness', makes a different kind of performative sense if Cleopatra is played as Shakespeare wrote her, black. But even where Cleopatra has been captured for whiteness, performance makes her whiteness strange by its fascinated association with bodies that are black.

Performances

Whiting Out Betty: 1953

Thirty-five years after she played Cleopatra, Peggy Ashcroft remembered the production – directed by Glen Byam Shaw and designed by Motley – for her biographer, Michael Billington, who'd been a mere schoolboy when he saw her 1953 performance. 'Wisely,' he writes, Ashcroft 'and her director decided to banish the serpent-of-old-Nile cliché and not present the audience with some bedizened harlot resembling Betty savagely deprived of Wilson and Keppel in the old music-hall sand-dance.' Her thinking about the role, Ashcroft reported, 'was much influenced by a picture in the old Temple edition that showed Cleopatra to be a Macedonian Greek, like Alexander, without a trace of Egyptian blood.'[16]

Clichés, of course, are elusive property, one generation's common demotic, the next generation's impenetrable code. What 'serpent-of-old-Nile cliché'? And who was Betty, that Byam Shaw should banish her? Betty bears thinking about. For she, with her alternative, the bizarrely juxtaposed 'Temple edition . . . . Greek', turns out not just to have been Ashcroft's starting point but a trope for the production's ambiguous cultural work, its capture of Cleopatra for Shakespeare and for high 'white' culture.

Stratford's 1953 production was Byam Shaw's second attempt at *Antony and Cleopatra* and his second with Margaret Harris of Motley's design team. His first was a production he started planning as therapy at the end of the war, recovering in a British military hospital bed in the Far East, where, for him, pleasure did *not* lie. Back in London, theatre entrepreneur Binkie Beaumont offered to produce whatever Byam Shaw wanted to direct, and then became the victim of his own 'rather camp little joke' when, having facetiously offered Edith Evans the chance, at fifty-eight, to play Cleopatra for a second time, she accepted.[17] Opening at the Picadilly Theatre in December 1946, that production read *Antony and Cleopatra* as an Elizabethan play. Pseudo-Elizabethan costume design put Egyptians and Romans alike in doublet and hose; the permanent set jutted forward like a flattened and enclosed Elizabethan 'heavens', with a tower on top for the monument. Most conspicuously, Evans' Cleopatra ghosted an English narrative that visually remembered the fag-end of female rule in a moribund Tudor dynasty, when 'infinite variety' read as querulousness and power as petulance. Her costumes were via Tiepolo, but her red wig marked her as Queen Elizabeth I.[18] In production photographs she looks like a raddled 'Queen Betty', *c.* March 1603.

As this 'Betty' closed, another opened, ten minutes walk up Regent Street at the Palladium: a 'two shows daily' revue that featured, topping the bill, 'Wilson, Keppel & Betty' with their long-running (466 performances) music hall sand dance routine, 'Do the Egyptian'.[19] For the estimated 800,000 theatre-goers who saw it, Wilson, Keppel & Betty – not William Shakespeare – defined the 'Egyptian'. These two Bettys – parody queen and music hall quean – may have been on Byam Shaw's mind when, in 1953, he returned to the play with Peggy Ashcroft (having scrapped everything from 1946 except a restyled red wig). Undoubtedly, however, the more potent representation was the one that circulated as 'common' theatrical currency in the post-war cultural economy. Low-brow Betty as 'bedizened harlot' dominated the cultural imaginary – and survived in reviewers' memories.

The alternative – at least for Ashcroft – was a Cleopatra from 'the old Temple edition' of the play, published the year before she was born (1906, the same year as Constance Collier's Cleopatra), a Cleopatra 'without a trace of Egyptian blood'. The face that gazes out of that Temple frontispiece is captioned 'Cleopatra: From a bust in the British Museum'. But if you went to the British Museum looking for Egypt's queen in the Department of Egyptian Antiquities you wouldn't find her. For this Cleopatra isn't Egyptian but Graeco-Roman.[20] She's certainly no low-brow Betty: three generations of experts mistook her for royalty. And no wonder: her nose is patrician; her hair, dressed ingeniously in exact ring curls laid in rows across her head and bunched to hang from the crown; her eyes, frank (from what we can see of them, for the sculpture has been turned, in the Temple reproduction, to look, not insignificantly, westward out of the frame). She is matronly, rather severe: a headmistress or an alderman's wife. Cut in marble, 'Cleopatra' is Pierian white. Cleopatra's whiteness, adopted by Byam Shaw and Ashcroft as her most conspicuous physical signature, consciously summoned absence (that 'trace of Egyptian blood') in order to exclude it. Critics saw what was erased, describing Ashcroft's Cleopatra as 'without tincture of the East, a whitely wanton . . . ghost pallid'; 'snowy skinned'; 'as English as Lily Langtry'.[21]

There were compelling cultural reasons, in 1953, for 'whiting' Cleopatra, detaching her from her low (English) music hall and (dark) eastern connections. In this coronation year, white queens were on the national agenda in a post-war, post-imperial, scaled-down Britain that had been working to reimagine itself inside boundaries certainly diminished in terms of geography but not of the imaginary. In redrawing this shrunken world map according to cultural co-ordinates, post-war British theatre played a crucial part; Britain's new-model imperialism would depend more on cultural than political exports. Anthony Quayle, Enobarbus in Byam Shaw's first *Antony* (and, like him, a war hero) was now installed as Artistic Director of the Memorial Theatre and, in his second season in Stratford, in the process of revolutionizing the company and transforming Shakespeare into Britain's most potent cultural icon. Two years earlier, he had hit upon the idea of a history cycle – a Shakespeare tetralogy from *Richard II* to *Henry V* performed not just in repertoire but in sequence – to contribute to the Festival of Britain, and to the newly emerging narrative of the nation. By 1952, when Quayle commissioned Byam Shaw to direct *Antony and Cleopatra*, Stratford was being hailed as Britain's (unofficial) national theatre, its 'reputation gained since the war' making it 'the leading Shakespeare playhouse in the world.'[22]

In February 1952, Elizabeth Windsor came to the throne. Her definitively English family name was, of course, a recent acquisition, invented by her grandfather in the middle of the previous world war to shed 'foreignness'. The coronation on 2 June came within weeks of *Antony and Cleopatra*'s opening and, that night, the Memorial Theatre put the new queen on stage, holding the *Richard III* interval curtain to broadcast her coronation speech from the stage. As it did so, it acknowledged the traffic it was directing between real and imaginary things by begging the indulgence of 'patriotic patrons': the demon king, it assured them, would not contaminate this historic moment, for he would not be crowned until *after* the interval. Elsewhere, the media made connections, actual and symbolic, between this Elizabeth and the first. Pathé news reported that, 'Like that great Queen Elizabeth I', Elizabeth II 'was to be crowned as a sovereign', while the national press proclaimed a new, second Elizabethan Age. Citing the original Elizabethans was less a nostalgic reflex than an optimistic trope of recovery, mobilizing a national myth of abundance, a golden age of intellectual, spiritual and cultural energy, of expansion, achievement and acquisition, on which to map present austerities. Wartime rationing would not finally be lifted for another year.

Meanwhile, visitors from around the world, but particularly from the Commonwealth's so-called 'White Dominions' of Australasia, came in droves to celebrate not just the coronation but the latest victory of West over East. Japan's Emperor Hirohito sent his nineteen-year-old son, newly named heir to the throne and, like England's Elizabeth, another of the new generation, to represent his Hiroshima-burnt-out Empire of the Sun, only recently restored to national sovereignty. At the Shakespeare birthday celebrations in Stratford on 28 April, with *Antony and Cleopatra* the birthday play, Japan's flag was raised for the first time in Britain since the war. Stratford's mayor told reporters it was time 'to turn over a new page in our relations with the Japanese',[23] a project made easier by Prince Akihito's fully 'westernized' appearance as the model of a model English gentleman, almost a dapper Wales to Ashcroft's Lily. Newspapers reported approvingly that he stepped off the London train in grey tweed, trilby and yellow gloves, and they itemized an itinerary for the state visit that was not quite a Roman triumph, but near enough: the British Museum, Oxford and Cambridge Universities, the Bank of England, Lloyd's, Lord's, aircraft, automotive and shipbuilding firms – and *Antony and Cleopatra* at the Shakespeare Memorial Theatre – institutions that articulated British supremacy in materially authoritative terms.

Reviewing Ashcroft's 'whitely' Cleopatra, critics picked up the racialist terms of the performance's self-invention but, ironically, misread them. Failing to see Cleopatra as Greek (Macedonian or otherwise), they saw her as 'English', 'as English as Lily Langtry'; indeed, 'too English'.[24] Certainly, Ashcroft's excessive Englishness claimed Cleopatra – 'royal Egypt' – for high British culture, but for reviewers it likewise troped a lack. Ashcroft couldn't find Cleopatra-the-gipsy, Cleopatra of low art and low cunning, Cleopatra-as-Betty: 'patrons of the "deepies"', commented the *Wolverhampton Express*, 'would probably expect more for their money'.[25] *Time and Tide*, disappointed, noticed a 'certain lack of sheer sensuous abandon and raillery' in her Cleopatra. 'We miss the sluttish and unpredictable gipsy,' said *The Spectator*, while Philip Hope-Wallace asked, 'Is it such a hard part? Or is the trouble that the kind of English actresses who attempt Shakespeare usually have not the temperament, simply?'[26] The logic operating here moves from race ('whitely') to nation ('English') to nature – 'temperament' serving as a 1950s euphemism for libido. English 'girls' were too 'white'. And from certain angles, so was 'Shakespeare' (who figures as a conflicted double signifier lashing high-art status to low-art practice). The kind of actress Shakespeare needs to pull off a Cleopatra, Hope-Wallace implied, was one he was going to find hanging out with Wilson, Keppel & Betty round the back of the Palladium, not with the 'Hons' in the tea room at Fortnum & Mason. As *The Spectator* reminded readers, Cleopatra 'only dazzles us at close range'; 'Shakespeare never allows us to forget' that, from a distance, 'like a more recent ruler of her country' (*The Spectator* is thinking of the ubiquitously burlesqued King Farouk), she is 'a music hall joke'.[27]

In a review headlined 'Cleopatra From Sloane Square', Kenneth Tynan, just down from Oxford and settling into the role Michael Redgrave, Ashcroft's Antony, had recently assigned him as 'next casting for the *enfant terrible* of the English theatre',[28] took these ideas even further:

There is only one role in *Antony and Cleopatra* . . . which English actresses are naturally equipped to play. This is Octavia, Caesar's docile sister: the girl 'of a holy, cold and still conversation' whom Mark Antony marries and instantly deserts: and if Shakespeare had done the modern thing and written a domestic tragedy about her disillusionment, generations of English ingénues would by now have triumphed in it. But alas! he took as his heroine an inordinate trollop, thereby ensuring that we should never see the part perfectly performed – unless, by some chance, a Frenchwoman should come and play it for us. The great sluts of world drama, from Clytemnestra to Anna Christie, have always puzzled our girls; and an English Cleopatra is a contradiction in terms.[29]

Tynan's review offers a snapshot of cultural discourse in 1953 Britain: racism, nationalism, misogyny and paternalism map transparently on to each other as he aligns Englishness with western Octavia, naturalizes frigidity to 'our girls', and assigns sluttishness to a foreign Other. (Though if Tynan were headed for the Mediterranean to locate this Other he was reckoning – as we shall see, perhaps with good reason – on travelling only as far east as the *Côte d'Azur*.) Marking Cleopatra as 'inordinate', Tynan makes her excessiveness sexual, 'puzzle[ing]' to her cerebral English sisters. For them, tragedy is a kitchen sink experience – marital 'disillusionment' – not carnal, not epic, not devastating of political and emotional worlds. So in Tynan, racisms collapse into each other as the binaries that conventionally hierarchize British cultural elitism – high/low, English/foreign, continent/inordinate and, implicitly, white/black – are mobilized in the business of performance criticism, but disconcertingly inverted. That is, the great performance of Cleopatra requires the bad ('inordinate', 'French', 'slut', metaphorically, black) woman to perform her, while the very categories that mark English cultural elitism and racial supremacy produce theatrical defect. For Tynan, Ashcroft failed at Cleopatra as she succeeded at Peggy, and she would have needed to be, by Tynan's logic, a very bad Peggy indeed to make a good Cleopatra. As 'bad', perhaps, as the celebrated 'French' Josephine Baker whom Matisse had just painted as *La Nègresse* (1952), thereby elevating into a European icon the black American ex-pat who'd arrived as *l'art nègre* swept Paris, resexualizing the 1920s Parisian *monde* and, along with other black imports (jazz, cakewalks, gospel, *revues nègres*) had coloured 'the intelligence of modern man . . . *nègre*'.[30] When Tynan imagined Cleopatra French, the woman he had in mind came out of this cultural *monde*, a *monde* reviewers in 'white' England didn't want to visit even as Antony-style tourists. Their 'whitely' Ashcroft remained for them mythologized as the best of all possible good girls, the 'loveliest Cordelia of her period'.[31]

And yet, they wanted Betty too. Astonishingly, Ashcroft had to hand material that just might have given them Betty – or a version of her they weren't expecting. For the same Temple edition that inspired her 'whitely' Cleopatra contains another Cleopatra, one whose representation exceeds the marble matron as extravagantly as Bakhtin's grotesque carnival body exceeds the classically closed body. One page over, on the edition's title page, set inside a florid frame that might have been designed by William Morris or Charles Voysey and looking *eastwards*, her back perpetually turned on the white marble Cleopatra, is a very different representation, neither a Hellenic patrician nor a music hall Betty. Drawn like a hieroglyphic in profile, flanked by papyrus flowers, wearing the ibis headdress and jewelled collar of Isis, and holding the asp curled voluptuously around her wrist, she is exotic, abundant, 'quickening', sensual, hot. This other Cleopatra is royal, Egyptian – and black.

Two prototypes, one of them putting squarely in view a black representation. Choosing to 'white' Cleopatra, it is inconceivable that, at some level of artistic instinct or cultural consciousness, Ashcroft wasn't denying the other, black representation. Of all actors on the British stage, she must have known what was at stake here, for as a twenty-three-year old in 1930, she had played Desdemona to Paul Robeson's Othello at the Savoy, a performance impossible on any stage in the USA and one that even in England activated racist comment. She heard audiences gasp when Robeson kissed her and remembered being bewildered, then appalled, when she learned he was not welcome at the Savoy Hotel. 'Rather unpleasant letters', whose racism ran along the same axis that polarizes Alexandria and Rome were delivered to Ashcroft at the stage door: 'East is East and West is West, and no more theatres where you play for me after this'.[32] Was 'whiting' Cleopatra – banishing Betty – the price Ashcroft paid for recuperating Cleopatra from music hall travesty?

Yet, despite reviewers' emphasis on whiteness, both Ashcroft's performance and Byam Shaw's production did contain traces of 'colour'. Ashcroft lowered her voice half an octave for the part, darkening her vocal register as Olivier would to play Othello in 1964, and adopted a 'flamboyant' red wig that quoted Edith Evans's from 1946, but with a world of difference. Gathered into a lashing pony tail ('jaunty Chelsea', said Tynan)[33] this wig invoked (black) 'sass'. Repudiating the culture of the faded Queen Elizabeth, Ashcroft wore costumes that 'made the women in the audience gasp'. She was a 'queen who braved a clash with bright orange and purple robes', designed by Motley, who imagined

Egypt as an Other-coloured nation and backed the near-empty stage with a cyclorama that turned Egypt gold, blue, purple, magenta, orange – an exotic Eastern palette that literally shocked western aesthetic sensibilities.[34] Rome, by contrast, was grainy-grey, as drab as post-war Britain. Most spectacularly of all (and here I return to the photograph that began my thinking), this production never really banished low-art Betty but simply moved her to the side of the stage, in the process supplementing, exaggerating her conventional white repertoire of low-cultural reference by colouring her black; in short, registering her symbolic function explicitly, a Betty in blackface. The photograph shows Diane Chadwick attending her queen yet peripheral to her audience, wearing the blackness that slides off Ashcroft's Cleopatra almost like a snakeskin. As the photograph documents, blackness is not excluded from this production; rather, it is invented for representation, an excessive artificial blackness whose very artifice draws attention to a whole range of signifiers.

Looking at the photograph forty-five years later, it is difficult to see Chadwick's 'black' Egyptian as anything but a crude proxy for ideas the production wanted banished from the space of the white royal body, but wanted circulated nonetheless, ideas that 'puzzled our [white] girls' but were 'natural' to the 'inordinate' black body – and that could be inserted via Cleopatra's mute attendant. Quite possibly, though, the actual 'meaning' of Chadwick's black is both more and less arresting. For to the middle-class, middle-England audience who patronized Stratford's post-war theatre in 1953 *it meant nothing* – at least, nothing that the political consciousness could read. For colour, while superficially legible when visible, was not yet politically inscribed in Britain, certainly not interrogated, and in any case was notional, not actual. 'Whitely' London, never mind the provinces, unlike Paris, had not, for the vast majority of the population, encountered black people. West Indians, 'imported' only five years earlier to supply Britain's crippling post-war labour shortage, were a novelty, and consideration of 'other races' was not only generalized, a comfortable mental habit residual from colonialism, but sited 'out there somewhere' on a map of empire that distanced the Other at a safe remove while locating white superiority so definitively in England that it did not even have to be discussed. England was colour blind because whiteness alone defined the collective racial unconscious. In these terms, 'race' was an unformulated question because 'difference' did not exist, and blackness was illegible because invisible. Where it was represented, as on Byam Shaw's stage, it served as set dressing, part of the furniture, décor that extended Motley's designs beyond exotic fans and feathered headdresses into exotic material bodies.[35] Looking back, the fact that

Chadwick's black meant nothing, precisely constitutes the political meaning of 'race' in 1953.

Yet, however tentatively, I want to suggest something more: that Chadwick's black body unconsciously marked out a reserved space, a space held in abeyance for theatre's future consideration. She occupied a 'watch this space' space. Barbara Hodgdon has acutely observed that white culture uses *Othello* – a play that twins *Antony and Cleopatra* – to perform particular white cultural work. '*Othello*,' she writes, 'represents a site through which the problem of the black body in the white imaginary becomes visible, gets worked through.'[36] I want to suggest that *Antony and Cleopatra* performs similar white cultural work, that it represents a site where the black body in the white imaginary *reserves* visibility, and where the work gets deferred. For all their hankering after 'foreign', non-whitely, non-English Cleopatras, not one reviewer in 1953 noticed the black body beside her or considered what empty space, in their desiring imaginary for this play, it might fill.

Racial Evasions: 1972

Almost twenty years later, and two weeks before Stratford's next *Antony and Cleopatra* opened in August 1972, Trevor Nunn was fretting. Not about his production but about politics, the theatre, and that late 1960s buzz word, 'relevance'. Anglo-American youth culture found radical politics on the streets in the summer of 1968 – for them, all art was political. Establishment culture responded by closing eyes, ears (and ranks) to revolution: Politics and Art were separate, and neither, radical. How should someone like Nunn mediate this dichotomy? Did Shakespeare belong to politics? Where were the dissident early 1960s political energies of Nunn's predecessors, young Peter Hall and Peter Brook, to be channelled, now that Shakespeare's company in Stratford was both 'royal' and subsidized?

On the face of it, the 1972 season, which brought together *Coriolanus, Julius Caesar, Antony and Cleopatra* and *Titus Andronicus* to be played in repertoire in chronological, not compositional, sequence – so that Shakespeare's earliest tragedy came last, his last, first – looked 'political'. Structurally, it looked like the kind of season Anthony Quayle had put together in his 1951 history cycle or Peter Hall in his 1963 Wars of the Roses. But where Hall fiercely politicized his cycle as the story of 'England' by using the plays to examine the machinery of power politics, Trevor Nunn's Roman season seemed evasive of politics. These plays were about 'civilization', not politics, about – as RSC in-house publicity put it – 'the birth, achievement, and collapse of a civilisation'.[37]

Nunn may have been experiencing something of a political identity crisis. He still looked like Che Guevara, but, at thirty-two, he'd hit the wrong side of youth culture's 'generation gap' and, as Artistic Director of the RSC, he was running a theatre whose directorate may have been leftish but whose governors were solidly Establishment. In April, members of his company, led by Buzz Goodbody, Nunn's feisty assistant, the first woman to direct at the RSC, sabotaged the Shakespeare birthday celebrations by staging a street demonstration against political repression in Greece. In total contrast, in July, a reviewer applauded Nunn for making 'no attempt to use Shakespeare's plays to put across a political message which isn't in the text.'[38]

If only the sort of trenchant cultural analysis Terence Hawkes would be writing in the 1990s had been available in 1972, Nunn might have found it easier to frame the debate between politics and theatre, for Hawkes would have confirmed Nunn's worries that 'Art and Politics' are 'not just opposites' in British culture, but 'the organizing epicentres of two quite contrary discourses' separated by 'an unbreachable wall'. To propose any common ground 'is almost to sanction some illicit act of transgression in which a grubby "Politics" may be "dragged" across a threshold to sully the otherwise sacrosanct shrine of Art' or worse, Shakespeare 'be "dragged into politics".'[39] Still, while Hawkes' critique is an accurate enough analysis of the debate in 1952 and 1992, it would have told only half the story in 1972. In the wake of that extraordinary, revolutionary year – 1968 – when censorship was abolished and Nunn, a twenty-eight-year-old, took over from Peter Hall as Artistic Director after only three years at the RSC, the relationship between Art and Politics was up for grabs. 'Illicit acts', 'transgressions', and cross-overs between 'sacrosanct' Art and 'grubby' Politics (or was it 'grubby' Art and 'sacrosanct' Politics?) were explored in theatres like the Royal Court by anti-Establishment playwrights and directors like David Hare, Howard Brenton and John McGrath. Art and Politics were cut free from their traditional opposition and were attracted, not dragged, towards a common centre which, for a time, it seemed possible they could mutually occupy. Ironically, had Nunn been more committed to finding common ground for Art and Politics, he might have prevented the scenario Hawkes was resigned to twenty years later.

As it was in 1972, Nunn's views, as reported in the *Coventry Evening Telegraph*, were so conflicted as to be incoherent. 'I frequently fret,' he told the interviewer, 'about the dichotomy I feel between the kind of theatre company which morally and politically I have been impelled to form and the kind of company the Royal Shakespeare Company must be.' On the one hand, he insisted, 'Shakespeare is not a propagandist'.

On the other, because Shakespeare 'does challenge us to examine our social and political views', a director has to read a Shakespeare play 'as if it is completely new and has just dropped through your letter box that morning. That means looking at it in the context of all that is happening in the world around you.' But, he insisted, 'You must use the most thorough scholarship.' He doesn't elaborate, but presumably scholarship that would privilege authorial 'intentions' and 'authenticity' over contemporary cultural engagement. It was this 'original' play, retrieved by scholarly practice and *ipso facto* conservative, which meant, for Nunn, that 'it isn't possible for the Royal Shakespeare Company to be a revolutionary company or a Maoist company or a Marxist company, because its house dramatist won't respond to that.' Here Nunn seems to take a deep breath before his bizarre double-think, built on double negatives, concludes by both advocating and repudiating politics: 'But sometimes I have to stop myself from taking an intransigent position. Because Northern Ireland and Vietnam and the American elections are there it's not enough to say "I care about all that but they have nothing to do with my work." That is the worst kind of English liberalism.'[40]

I am especially interested in how this interview frames a material context for Nunn's *Antony and Cleopatra* and how it discloses his ideological strategy for dealing with that material. Quite simply, if Northern Ireland, Vietnam and the US presidential elections were on Nunn's mind so, too, was their evasion. For, producing them as 'matter' that would be pertinent if *Antony and Cleopatra* were a new play he then deletes them (it isn't, so they aren't). Significantly, this same pattern of evoking what was to be evaded turned up later on stage. It is, then, worth recalling what Nunn had on his mind as he rehearsed a play whose topics were war, empire, sex and betrayal.

In Ireland, the previous twelve months had produced the worst catalogue of disasters in the Troubles to date: the first shootings of British soldiers by the IRA in Ulster in early 1971; the contentious internment without trial policy imposed in response that summer; the Derry protest in January 1972 that ended on Bloody Sunday with thirteen dead; direct rule imposed within weeks. At heart, the Troubles were about British imperialism; the rhetoric was framed in the language of political discourse – nationalism, separatism, republicanism, unionism. Unofficially, however, a racist discourse was at work, for the British not only saw the Irish as their native Other, but had brought the Irish to see themselves as Europe's 'niggers'.[41]

By the summer of 1972 the racist profile of America's non-war in Vietnam was, after ten ignominious years, indisputably visible: the US military-industrial complex was white; so were the generals. But the draftees from America's urban ghettoes were black, and the enemy, 'gooks'. In Paris, delegates to the Peace Conference debated the shape of the conference table; in London, RSC actors protested against American imperialism outside the US embassy; in Washington, Nixon campaigned for re-election, his aides spin-doctoring the Watergate break-in that July. There followed lies, cover-ups, betrayal, the disgrace of the presidency, and ultimately, months later, Nixon's resignation.

Meanwhile, the miners' strike, called in January, brought daily power cuts across Britain; by spring, when a national state of emergency was declared, work on the complete technical refit of the RSC stage got further and further behind schedule. Pressure on labour relations, already in crisis, took a racist spin in August when Uganda expelled 40,000 resident British Commonwealth Asians, refugee victims of imperialism who flooded into Britain, swelling a 'black' tide already flowing out of India in the wake of the 1971 Bangladeshi wars. Enoch Powell's infamous 'rivers of blood' speech reverberated in public utterance as one-culture, white-culture Britain contemplated a multicultural future.

There was also another item on the agenda – feminism. By 1972 Germaine Greer's *The Female Eunuch* (1970), borrowing black militancy's core trope, the castrated 'nigger', the 'nigger' eunuch, as its discursive starting point to analogize female suppression, was reaching a popular audience and raising women's consciousness across the culture. Greer's analysis of sexual politics and her radical social – and marital – programme made claims for women not just for equal employment and pay but for equality of aspiration, spirit, selfhood. Feminists challenged male supremacists as aggressively as immigration challenged white supremacists.

With the map of cultural Britain heaving and bucking underfoot, the opening of the fabulous King Tutankhamun exhibition at the British Museum in March 1972 served, as Elizabeth's coronation had twenty years earlier, to provide cultural focus and a respite from controversy. Coming to London fifty years after Howard Carter and Lord Carnarvon, intrepid sons of empire, had opened the pharaoh's tomb, the exhibition nostalgically recalled that moment of penetration, possession, plunder. As mile-long queues lapped the British Museum, Egyptomania ran wild in everything from fashion to television documentaries to a commemorative 3p stamp. The sensation produced by the exhibition felt like an exhilarating aftershock from the age of empire, stirring memories of Egypt as a British protectorate, as dependent upon London as it was upon Rome at *Antony and Cleopatra*'s close. Meanwhile, Trevor Nunn was in rehearsals. How much of what was in the news travelled into his production? Tutankhamun, obviously. The production's stunning opening spectacle quoted the exhibition directly, reproducing in theatrical terms the experience of walking into the dark gallery where King Tut's gold sarcophagus lay. Nunn began with a full-company tableau: Cleopatra resplendent as Isis; Antony as Ra; their children, gold-robed, flanked by priests as jackal-headed Anubis and Horus, the hawk; musicians, bare-torsoed attendants, bald eunuchs. Such in-your-face glitz announced Alexandria's theatricality – 'the full MGM spectacle'; 'a sweep of great canopy . . . golden bird head-dresses, tinkling cymbals'; 'heavy with gold . . . decorated with blue scarabs' – while asserting authenticity. 'The costumes looked . . . borrowed direct from the British Museum'; 'Cleopatra's court has an authentic glitter that seems appropriate in the year of the Tutankhamun Exhibition.'[42] Cannily, the souvenir pro-gramme invited double reading across this same theatrical/historical binary, setting out side-by-side character portraits of Antony and Cleopatra 'In History' and 'In Shakespeare'.[43] And in another 'portrait', this one textual, the programme historicized as 'authentic' the extrava-gant theatricality of the self-styled 'Illimitable Livers' by quoting Plutarch's father's eye-witness accounts of fabulous banquets, jests, com-petitive games of sex and dressing up. These tales illustrated one kind of insatiable appetite by recounting the famous story of Cleopatra winning a wager that she could outdo Antony in culinary extravagance by knock-ing back a priceless pearl she'd dissolved in vinegar; another, by reproducing a 'Fragment of a bowl made at about the time Antony and Cleopatra lived' that showed a naked couple athletically copulating.

Reviewers saw – clearly – that Nunn's production was about new-style sexual politics and – more dimly (because more dangerously?) – that it was about gender identity, exchange, fantasy, fluidity. Greer ghosted Janet Suzman's 'rather masculine' Cleopatra, 'the Ptolemaic equivalent of your modern emancipated woman' whom you'd 'expect to catch [. . .] reading *The Female Eunuch*,' not 'dallying with male ones'. Her 'touch of masculinity' made her 'an Egyptian Elizabeth I' or, in 'this age of Women's Lib', a 'gypsy tomboy' in 'unregal attitudes' who 'flopp[ed] around like a hoyden, legs wide apart'.[44] (Apparently, the constitutional 'sluttishness' reviewers read in the role in 1953 they re-read, twenty years later, as 'liberated' femininity.) Again, the programme framed spec-tators' viewing. A two-page spread laid out Antony's 'character' like a centrefold, illustrating it with images from a sarcophagus relief showing a riotous procession of goat-footed, priapic followers attending the char-iot of (sprawling) Dionysus, one of Antony's avatars. Opposite, stood another, Hercules, in a full-page reproduction of a statue carved in Augustan Rome, a statue not representing him as the 'Herculean Roman'; rather, as Hercules made over by Omphale, in drag. His right arm, raised above his head, holds a distaff, not his club. His woman's chiton, falling in folds that outline the penis, has slipped off one shoulder, teasing the gaze to look below it for the breast that isn't there, while the delicate hem is raised titillatingly at one side, revealing – a nasty shock to punish our voyeurism – the massy naked leg beneath. The face under the headscarf has a beard. Where, in 1906, Beerbohm Tree's *Play Pictorial* portraits quoted allusions to Hercules to image Antony as the chisel-jawed, blue-eyed imperialist, Nunn's 'pictorial' proposed him as a happy (hapless?) transvestite, and 'Women's Lib' proposed the contemporary politics for locating that transformation.

What reviewers didn't see, or didn't acknowledge, was that this production was also about race. While they noticed Cleopatra's 'shiny, brown eunuchs' (Nightingale), 'negro eunuchs' (Lewis), 'genuine dark-skinned servants' (Chapman), they perceived them as set decoration.[45] Even the (Communist) *Morning Star* bunked politics, ignoring what its own metaphor put conspicuouly in view when, having called Egypt 'prolific and sumptuous . . . a world alien to Rome in every way', it declined to unpack 'alien' as troping racial Otherness.[46] Nobody mentioned visible difference or the difference it made that Rome was white and Egypt, black – except, of course, for Cleopatra, described as 'dusky', even 'dark', in adjectives describing not her skin but her emotions. Reviewers read Suzman white, even as several, referring to her as 'the South African actress' made her literally the foreigner, and hinted, echoing Tynan on Ashcroft, that it would take a 'triumphantly wanton' foreign woman 'to break through the barrier of innate gentility that has separated so many of our girls from the essence of the character': alas, however, even Suzman 'does not quite make it'.[47] Reviewers, that is, read her 'white' in spite of the work the programme was (again) doing in the plot synopsis, titled 'Contest for the World', to construct Cleopatra not just as racially Other but as powerfully racially Other: 'hated in Rome, and feared as the queen of the East, an older, richer, more mysterious and still potentially greater civilization'. Her rivalry with Rome, 'the ultimate contest . . . between West and East', ending at Actium, ended in blunt hegemony: 'the West had won'. One page over, the programme split castlist down the same geo-racial axis, 'East' on one page, 'West' on the other.

In spite of all this pointing, not one reviewer mentioned the obvious: that Trevor Nunn's *Antony and Cleopatra* was packed with black bodies, more black bodies than reviewers had ever before seen on the RSC stage. Eight black actors were cast across the Roman tetralogy that season in a fifty-strong company. Moreover, Nunn required the entire 'white' Egyptian court, from Cleopatra, Iras and Charmian to Mardian and his *corps de castrati*, to make up tawny. The company used so much body make-up that Guerlain cosmetics were credited separately in a programme note. This 'Felliniesque' 'whirl of voluptuous opulences' contrasted, for Michael Billington, with Rome's 'cold calculation and white knees',[48] presided over by an ascetic Caesar (Corin Redgrave), the archetype of 'whiteness'. His clenched, unbending body was impervious to appetite or instinct, his face drained of colour, his ambitions inscribed on the wall-sized map that backed his summit meeting in Rome, a plan of the yet-to-be-conquered empire, each territory's border precisely marked.

Why the universal colour blindness? Why the failure in review discourse to register Egypt as a 'coloured' court or to measure the threat an older, 'black' Egypt, an Egypt mysteriously 'wrinkled deep in time', posed to a white-kneed, boy-Caesared, pre-imperial Rome? Wasn't the 'authentic' black representation on Nunn's stage ('genuine darkskinned servants') doubly legible, historically and currently, since it pertained to the ancient world and to today's politics? Didn't blackness contest white, imperial hegemony, in Rome and Britain, in Egypt, India, Asia, Africa and Ireland?

To answer, I have to circle back to my reading of Trevor Nunn's political evasions. In terms of raw numbers, Nunn's casting policy was progressive: black actors in the late 1990s remember his early period at the RSC as the golden age of inter-racial casting. It was also theatrically shrewd. Responding to Britain's multiculturalism and to the sheer statistical facts of Britain's new racial demographics, Nunn put black actors on the stage, and on the payroll. But politically, he went on to betray the progressiveness of his own initiative, evading the racial issues those black actors materially evoked, for his casting didn't unsettle a single racial stereotype. Rather, it merely reproduced predictable contemporary stereotypes, and worse, represented them as historically 'authentic': black actors played servants and messengers in *Antony*; plebs in *Caesar*; Volsce barbarians in *Coriolanus*. Black performance was required to stage its own invisibility. No wonder reviewers missed it.

No wonder, either, that they missed the production's black Cleopatra, who turns out to have been Nunn's supreme evasion. For she never appeared on stage. She's in the souvenir programme, though (just as she was, ironically, in Beerbohm Tree's 1906 souvenir *Play Pictorial*) but not in the programme's text. Her character profile in the text, 'Cleopatra: In History', seems uncannily to quote Peggy Ashcroft disclaiming darkness: 'Cleopatra had no Egyptian blood – she was a Macedonian Greek, like Alexander.' The image placed alongside this text, however, sensationally contradicts that claim to white origins, reproducing, from 'a bas-relief carved at the time of Cleopatra in the temple at Deir el Bahri, Egypt', a representation of the 'real' Cleopatra. This 'real' Cleopatra is black.

'Passing' Cleopatra White: 1992

The same sense of *déjà vu* that links Nunn's production to Ashcroft's also connects it to John Caird's, for when Caird met his full *Antony and Cleopatra* company for the first read-through of the play in the autumn of 1992, he seemed to be reading from Nunn's programme notes. For openers, he said he wanted to 'get something straight right from the beginning': 'Cleopatra wasn't black. She was a Macedonian Greek. Like Alexander. She didn't have any Egyptian blood.'

Claire Benedict – cast to play Charmian – remembers Caird's opening shot verbatim because 'it was so bizarre'; 'it came out of nowhere'. Cleopatra wasn't black? Who said she was? Only John Caird, denying it. Benedict didn't think to wonder what Caird was protecting with his 'rather hysterical' disclaimer, for she was too busy deciphering what she took to be his coded message: 'I was the only black actor in the rehearsal room. Clearly, I wasn't meant to be playing Cleopatra. I was only her understudy.' Then Benedict exchanged looks with Clare Higgins, 'And I could see her thinking, "I'm not a Macedonian Greek, so who's John got to play Cleopatra?".'[49]

Benedict, of course, was wrong. Caird's comments did come from somewhere besides her specific black present and presence. They came from history, and they ghosted conversations with Shakespeare's text that Benedict knew nothing about. Undoubtedly, Caird's original instinct in quoting Trevor Nunn was to authenticate the politics of his own representational strategies. It's a pity, then, that, instantiating 'what Cleopatra was', he muddied things by opening up his actors' collective imaginary to what they hadn't seriously considered before – 'what Cleopatra wasn't'.

When Nunn echoes Ashcroft it feels uncanny; when Caird echoes Nunn, it reads like homework perhaps because, having started life at the RSC a decade earlier as Nunn's assistant director, Caird here was still the swot parroting the master. For starters, he cast Nunn's Antony in the title role. But twenty years on, Richard Johnson's Herculean Roman had deteriorated into self-parody, an 'ageing lecherous slob'; an 'elderly party who radiates the sexual magnetism of a retired magistrate'.[50] Next, Caird borrowed Nunn's spectacular opening tableau but relocated it, putting his 'breathtaking and faintly ludicrous' 'Egyptian parade' just before the interval.[51] Finally, he quoted the *trompe l'oeil* effect of Nunn's monument scene but reversed it: Nunn's rose hydraulically, monumentally, out of the stage; Caird's – bizarrely – lowered the monument to stage level. Costumes, props, even Cleopatra's eunuchs looked like makeovers raided from Nunn's production wardrobe.

Caird borrowed elsewhere, too. From earlier productions: raiding the heart-stopping moment from 1982 when Cleopatra (Helen Mirren), preparing for death, knelt on the floor in front of a basin and simply washed her face; Higgins, in 1992, tugged off her latest wig to reveal herself 'no more but e'en a woman'. From music hall: 'the opening set looks like *son et lumière* at the Sphinx,' said Malcolm Rutherford under the headline 'Oh! what a carry on up the Nile'.[52] From film, specifically *Gone With The Wind*: 'at the end, the lovers are miraculously resurrected, and embrace in silhouette against a stormy tourquoise sky.'[53] From tradition: Higgins' Cleopatra embodied 'infinite variety' by changing wigs 'more often than she changes her mind' but finally settled – after the interval – for a frazzled version of the red wig that connected her back, via Judi Dench (National, 1987), Vanessa Redgrave (Haymarket, 1986), Glenda Jackson (RSC, 1978) to Ashcroft, Evans, and, ultimately, Elizabeth I.[54]

If race – 'Cleopatra wasn't black' – was Caird's point of entry into this text, more recent theatre history accounts for his defensiveness. In the late 1980s the RSC was in trouble. An overview of the 1989/90 season from the always generous Peter Holland calls the work 'disappointing, as if the company had run out of ideas and energy: directional clichés and excesses substituted for real reinvestigation of the texts; glib concepts dominated without offering illuminating rediscoveries.'[55] By 1992, the company's best work was not being generated from the centre but bought in from outside by the Artistic Director, Adrian Noble, whose most nakedly Thatcherite PR stunt was that season's collaboration on *Hamlet* with Kenneth Branagh (a dry-run for his full-text *Hamlet* film). With the company's body and soul evidently deep in hock to the accountants – and corporate sponsors – the voice of the RSC ventriloquized market forces: 'The RSC,' Noble admitted, had 'lost' – some said sold – 'the right to fail'.[56] With it went the company's right, its duty as a maker of contemporary cultural meaning, to take risks, to be controversial, dissident, oppositional, avant-garde. The RSC had to play safe. So the most interesting work – innovative, radical and mainstream work – went on elsewhere. In, for example, Yvonne Brewster's all-black Talawa Theatre Company.

When Talawa's touring production of *Antony and Cleopatra* hit London in May 1991 Shakespeare hit the headlines. 'Theatrical history is currently being made,' said Michael Billington, in this 'first British Shakespeare production to combine a black company and a black director.'[57] Dona Croll, Cleopatra, was 'the first black woman to play the temptress of the Nile' on the British stage.

These two theatrical 'firsts' looked alike, but in fact staked out vastly different political territory for performance. An all-black production proved, wrote Billington, 'that Shakespeare is universal property and

that we have a sizeable corps of black actors who speak verse with ring-
ing authority' (or, wrote Rick Jones, it proved 'the petty racism that
forces a company like Talawa TC into existence in the first place'). But
playing Antony black, Jeffrey Kissoon made no claim for a black Antony.
Playing Cleopatra black, Dona Croll did.

Interviewed before the London opening, Yvonne Brewster was quite
clear. 'Cleo' was a part Shakespeare wrote 'for a non-white woman', and
Brewster compared the 'backstage battle to establish' Cleopatra as 'a black
woman's part' to the 'British theatre's blindness to Othello's blackness',
asking rhetorically, 'why is it so difficult to imagine a black man *as* a black
man?'[58] Croll, too, was convinced of Cleopatra's blackness. She knew
Cleopatra's father was Macedonian. But she pointed out that Cleopatra
also had a mother – racial original unknown, but possibly Egyptian –
which could account for Cleopatra's well-documented ethnic consciousness. She was the first and only Ptolemy to learn to speak Egyptian, and she
embraced Egyptian religion – facts Nunn's 1972 programme noted but did
not examine, along with her patriotic 'devotion' to a country her father
'had been willing to sell out to Rome'. Blackness literally mattered to
Croll: it belonged, she said, to Cleopatra's 'earthiness and movement'.
'European actors' – white actors? – were physically disabled, 'not very
good at using their bodies', but Croll's 'African side' equipped her to 'do
these things'. Here Croll collapses the distinction of 'things' into racial categories that neatly remap black/white stereotyping to reverse it: 'White
actresses play her as a sexy queen. I play the politics and power. Any
woman who runs a country, turns it round from famine to feast and
seduces Roman emperors is not a blonde bimbo. She is somewhere
between Maya Angelou and Tina Turner.' Croll's words recall Tynan's, pit-
ting 'our girls' against those Others. Now, however, all the signposts are
reading back to front, Othering black English Cleopatra as jive-American.[59]

By a happy coincidence, the same day Croll's Cleopatra arrived in
London, so did Lucy Hughes-Hallett's: *Cleopatra: Histories, Dreams
and Distortions* is a cultural history that accounts for the 'imaginary' as
well as for the 'real' Cleopatra in representation. Before 1800, European
writers and artists, writes Hughes-Hallett, 'were seldom preoccupied
with her foreignness'. Some of them 'puzzled over the conundrum presented by her complexion', but her colour was a 'problem' that remained
'insoluble': no historical description survived to determine it. As a
Macedonian, 'she may have been quite fair', but 'a few Western inter-
preters were haunted by the possibility that, as a north African queen, she
might have been as black as Othello the Moor'. One was Shakespeare's
contemporary, the playwright Robert Greene, whose 1589 Antony was
'enamoured of the black Egyptian Cleopatra'.[60]

Hughes-Hallett did not argue Cleopatra's blackness (in history) nor did she track blackness (in the theatre) through Shakespeare's text, but she still helped support Croll's confidence in black representation by unpacking the cultural process by which Cleopatra, over the course of 'a thousand years', was whitewashed, 'represented by western artists as being western' and 'always described by writers according to their own canons of beauty' – that is, 'blue-eyed and blonde'.[61] The key term was 'beauty'. Cleopatra, in western culture, had to be white, for her 'reputation for beauty, though unsupported by any historical evidence, was unassailable' and that made her 'a light-skinned European lady', since beauty, as distinct from sexual magnetism, was 'the prerogative of social and ethnic élites'.[62]

Importantly, Hughes-Hallett put into the popular domain a version of Edward Said's revisionist cultural history, *Orientalism* (1978), and Martin Bernal's two-volume *Black Athena* (1987, 1991), books that dropped like bombshells on Anglo-American academia. Between them, they exposed the historiography of western culture as white racist mythography. Bernal had been, he wrote, 'staggered' to discover that the dominant 'Aryan model' of historiography, 'far from being as old as the Greeks themselves', was developed 'only in the 1840s and 50s', and that, far from fictionalizing, the ancient Greeks, Herodotus among them, knew what they were talking about when they wrote that Greek culture originated in black Egypt.[63] Like Bernal, Said looked to nineteenth century formulations to begin unpacking the system of ideas troped in that word 'Orientalism', which Europe had always found so useful in organizing its thinking about itself. And like Bernal, his analysis read race, power, and (western) cultural hegemony as intersecting discourses. Significantly, the inventory of racial traits attached to Orientalism – luxury, sensuousness, barbarity, exoticism, effeminacy, lassitude, abundance, irrationality, infantilism, voluptuousness and depravity – reads like a repertoire of 'blackness'.[64]

After Said and Bernal – and the popularizing of Hughes-Hallett – Cleopatra could no longer be 'naturally' assimilated by European orientalist fantasy, could no longer 'pass'. Her past representation on the British stage from Tree onwards had to be re-read through the imperialist presumptions and projects they revealed, and her future representation, if it referred itself to 'what Cleopatra *was*' would, at some level, have to take on Said and Bernal.

Certainly, young black actors like Dona Croll were ready to force the issue. She saw her performance as a cultural intervention, wanting it to unsettle white attitudes, to be read politically, 'to cast a dark shadow over the whole Eurocentric portrayal of human history'. 'There is an unwillingness,' Croll told the *Guardian*, 'on the part of Europeans to acknowledge the contribution of Africa. The fable of the white Cleopatra is just another way of bleaching out history, cutting the nose off the sphinx [as Napoleon was supposed to have done, objecting to its Negroid broadness]'. Her Cleopatra began the process of reading history black to make whiteness strange.

What she couldn't do, in Talawa's all-black production, was to charge Egyptian blackness with the ultimate signifying power Shakespeare assigns it, its racial difference from Rome. For that, she needed a white Antony, a white Octavius: only with white opposition in place would the black/white binary that maps what is really at stake in Shakespeare's text become visible in performance to show that where Shakespeare's Battle of Actium ends, Said's Orientalism begins.

From Talawa's position on the fringe of cultural production in Britain, one of Yvonne Brewster's hopes was that her casting of Croll would agitate expectations at the centre: 'No one ever thought of a black Cleo before.' Now, 'the next time they go to cast her [at the RSC, the National], that image will sweep across their brains. It might just be the beginning.'[65] As it turned out, what occurred was a 'beginning', but not the one Brewster had in mind, for whatever images swept across the collective brains of the RSC's casting department, they were discarded or repressed. John Caird cast Cleopatra white, Charmian black. That is, he reproduced casting practices dating back to the turn of the century to preserve, for Shakespeare's Royal Theatre, the space of white cultural iconicity even as he imperialistically annexed to it the darkness it both desired and disclaimed. What was new, however, was that white casting of Cleopatra was no longer tacit, no longer 'natural'. It could only be instantiated by denial, denial of black history, denial of black representation – 'Cleopatra wasn't black.' Flushed out by Bernal, Said, Hughes-Hallett, Croll and Brewster, Caird had to articulate the racism earlier directors could evade: Cleopatra's 'passing' narrative turned into Caird's 'outing' narrative. And whereas Nunn's evasion was made tolerable because he at least proposed political discourse, Caird's denial was a betrayal that evacuated the space of the political altogether as if, having quoted Nunn, his work (twenty years later) was done. What he produced in his echo-chamber *Antony and Cleopatra* was a theatre of decadence, an MGM spectacle of theme park nostalgia preoccupied, like so much in Thatcherite Britain, with the surfaces of things. Caird's glitz, unlike Nunn's (which could be read against King Tut at the British Museum as setting up, if only incipiently, the terms of an orientalist debate between white man's fantasies and real material things), was legible only in terms of Saatchi and Saatchi advertising hype.

What accounts for Caird's vehement denial of black Cleopatra? One answer comes from the Thatcherite marketing strategies displayed across the forty pages of his *Antony and Cleopatra* souvenir programme. Fifteen pages cover the production from plot synopsis to critical 'obituaries'. The rest bulges with advertising, advertising that shows 'Shakespeare plc' aggressively in business promoting the RSC promoting its promoters: Royal Insurance, Jaguar, Mercury, British Gas, AT&T all have spreads in the programme.[66] Given the sponsorship tie-ups with big business and individuals alike evidenced in this marketing publicity, could Caird afford to do something so unsettling to mass white cultural expectations as, in Barbara Hodgdon's phrase, disowning 'dominant cultural imaginaries of desire' by casting their white icon black?

Meanwhile, another production, scheduled to play opposite *Antony and Cleopatra* that season, was cast. Terry Hands, directing, and Tony Sher, in the lead, auditioned Claire Benedict, Caird's Cleopatra under-study, for *Tamburlaine*, to play another Egyptian royal, Zenocrate, daughter of Egypt's 'sultan' (that is, pharaoh), and not in the company's main house but in the smaller (marginal?) Swan. As Marlowe's epic tale of sex, war, empire and betrayal has it, Zenocrate, taken captive by Tamburlaine, captivates him Cleopatra-like.[67] If anyone noticed that Egyptian queens were playing on alternate nights in playhouses standing side by side, they might have made something of the coincidence that cultural-outsider Marlowe's queen was black, insider Shakespeare's was one of 'our' girls, (lily) white.

Recovering Blackness

Authentic Marks

At the end of 1998 actors, it seemed, were queuing up to play Shakespeare's Egyptian queen. First in line was Antony Sher, who, interviewed between rehearsals for *The Winter's Tale* at the RSC, con-fessed to *The Independent* that 'the Shakespeare role he still most want[ed] to play on stage [was] Cleopatra'. So he'd asked the RSC for the part in the production planned for 1999. Adrian Noble turned him down; he 'said he'd be lynched by about a dozen leading actresses'. Here the interview makes an interesting lateral switch; Sher moves from cross-sex casting on to cross-*race* casting, almost in mid-sentence as though unconsciously revealing that categories of race and gender were collapsed in his thinking. About cross-sex casting, he'd been diplomatic, only implying, by setting his sights on Cleopatra, that it was time to end women actors' monopoly on women's roles. About cross-race casting, however, he was outspoken. 'The bar on white actors playing Othello' had to end. It was, Sher said, 'a terri-ble shame that all the great actors aren't given their Othello. It's tragic, and it's ludicrous.' And he asks rhetorically, 'Why should I, who's not heterosexual, be allowed to play Leontes?'[68] (Kate Chedgzoy's shrewdly sophisticated *Shakespeare's Queer Children* gives Sher his answer.[69])

Within a week, Sher's fantasy casting, uncannily, materialized elsewhere. The *Guardian* reported – not insignificantly, on the 'Home News' not the 'Arts' page – that Mark Rylance, Artistic Director of Shakespeare's Globe, was to play Cleopatra in the theatre's next season: 'handing the role of the Queen of the Nile to a man is one of several recent examples of cross-casting, although it is more often in the reverse direction with women taking roles written for men. But while many cross-casting experiments are carried out in the name of quota filling, granting employment to actresses, or simply to satisfy curiosity, the Globe's decision has been taken in the name of authenticity.'[70]

What did the Globe mean by 'authenticity'? The *Guardian* told us: 'All Shakespeare's plays were originally written for and performed by men, although the female parts were played by boys.' 'By contrast', the article noted, Rylance 'is 37'. So no 'boy' then? But if no 'boy', what happens to 'authenticity'?

That, of course, is one trouble with 'authentic Shakespeare'. As W.B. Worthen has comprehensively shown, it's a spurious idea, doomed to self-annulling compromise the moment it's announced as a production concept. Worse, it's a theatrically stagnating idea, for by staking so much on a nostalgic return to privileged early modern origins (an 'authentic' text and 'authentic' performance practices) it ignores theatre's primary business – in Worthen's phrase – of 'interpreting ourselves to ourselves'.[71] Even so, the chimera of 'authenticity' dogs the British theatre: at the RSC, the Royal National Theatre, the Old and Young Vics and the Globe, directors of Shakespeare trot out 'authenticity' to legitimate whatever – particularly whatever 'dangerous innovation' – needs authorizing. In this way, the shock of the new – say, a male Cleopatra – is naturalized and validated as a return to the old, the authentic.

Sitting in the RSC archives over those same weeks in December when the *Guardian* and *Independent* articles were appearing, I found them dismaying in another way, because I was uncovering Cleopatra's hidden history and growing convinced that 'next casting' of Cleopatra had to play her as Shakespeare wrote her. But once (white, male, gay) actors of Antony Sher's stature and box office clout and Mark Rylance's (white, male) Globe-al authority set about claiming Cleopatra, the chances of recovering her blackness, of reversing the cultural hijack of the role, receded to vanishing point. The argument for recovery, then, grows more urgent. Let us, for one thing, be under no illusion that arguing 'authenticity' is harmless antiquarianism. Rather, it's a tactic of legitimation whose end is political, for it leaves Shakespeare in the sole possession of white male actors, gay or straight, Shakespeare's only 'authentic' players. What this means is that at a time when Shakespeare in Britain is being opened up pluralistically in companies like Talawa, Northern Broadsides, Cheek by Jowl and the English Shakespeare Company to cross-race, cross-gender, cross-class and cross-cultural casting (and viewing), Shakespeare is likewise being claimed as the exclusive property of 'authorized' Shakespeare playhouses like the Globe and the RST: 'our Bill', it seems, must be located at the 'centre'. Although I will return to this issue, for now, I have to align with the 'devil's party' to argue tactically. For if Cleopatra's 'tawny front' stands a chance of being reinvented in mainstream representation, arguing her 'authenticity' is the imperative strategy for recovery: I have to legitimate my shocking 'new' black Cleopatra as a return to the 'old'. What marks of blackness, circulating in source texts, might Shakespeare have picked up to lay down in his playtext? To address the question of an authentic black Cleopatra, I want to situate Cleopatra's blackness historically, attempting what Terence Hawkes calls 'the insertion of texts into their material context' to reanimate the '"conversation" that accompanies and finally constitutes the construction of cultural meaning'.[72] That is, I want to remember some of the issues that circulated around the play's Jacobean moment of production, to see *Antony and Cleopatra* as a companion play to *Othello* and to Ben Jonson's *Masque of Blackness* and Cleopatra not just as a nostalgic homage to Elizabeth, a queen of 'infinite variety', but a tribute to yet another 'wrangling queen', Anna of Denmark.

Black Marks

For Joyce Green MacDonald, writing in 1995, Cleopatra is so obviously written black that 'the casting of white Cleopatras constitutes a denial of representation'. But just a year earlier Lynda E. Boose saw her 'only by the remotest suggestion represented as being Negro'.[73] Shakespeare might have made things easier for us; he might have imaged Cleopatra's blackness in *Antony and Cleopatra* as obsessively as *Othello* does the Moor's. What is there to mark her black beyond two scripted references to her 'tawny front' and her cheeks, sunburnt black 'with Phoebus' amorous pinches'? Most insistently, her name. For Cleopatra is 'Egypt', 'Egyptian', aphetically, a 'gipsy', and gipsies, popularly thought to come from Egypt and first appearing in England at the beginning of the sixteenth century, were, to English eyes 'black'. Almost immediately, white Albion wanted them excluded; a 1514 order 'agaynste people callynge themselves Egypcyans' ordained 'that no such persons be suffred to come within this realme'.[74] Certainly, Shakespeare always imagines his gipsies black: wherever they're cited (in the text, never appearing on stage, and always as women), the point of their insertion is to contrast the 'black' with the 'fair', the white. So Mercutio in *Romeo and Juliet* proposes 'Cleopatra a gypsy' as the mock-hyperbolic term of disparagement set against Romeo's peerlessly fair 'lady' (2.3.37). And Theseus in *A Midsummer Night's Dream* sees it as a symptom of lovers' frenzy to see 'Helen's beauty in the brow of Egypt' (5.1.11); their 'shaping fantasies' can turn bushes into bears, loathsome into fair, black into white, Helen (always 'white-armed' in Chapman's 1598 translation, as in Homer's original *Iliads*) into gipsy. Gipsies traditionally trafficked in the black arts: consider Cleopatra's fortune-telling Soothsayer in Alexandria or the charmed provenance of Othello's handkerchief, given by 'an Egyptian to my mother' (3.4.53). Through such linkages, racial darkness covers dark practices that trope dark sexuality: the Soothsayer's clients seek information about their future erotic history; the handkerchief that makes the hand that holds it 'amiable' magically 'subdue[s]' the lover's 'spirits' 'Entirely to her love' (3.4.57–58).

Cleopatra inhabits this scheme. She of the 'tawny front', which tropes her 'gipsy's lust', is by turns 'Egypt', 'great Egypt', 'royal Egypt', then 'foul Egyptian', 'false soul of Egypt'; a 'right gipsy' who, like a black devil, has, says Antony, 'Beguiled me to the very heart of loss' (4.12.28–29). 'Beguiled', 'heart', and 'loss' all carry double valence as images of sexualized black magic (potency undone as impotency) and of damnation. When Antony calls Cleopatra 'spell', 'charm', 'witch', 'spot', 'triple-turned whore', it is her metaphoric blackness, doubling back upon her dark sexuality, that is being imaged. But her literal blackness is also imaged in the allusive imagery of lines like 'Salt Cleopatra, soften thy waned lip!' where 'salt' certainly means 'lecherous' but also 'preserved', like fish laid down in barrels, gone hard and withered black. 'Waned' also moves imaginatively into black territory – the waned moon's dark sky – and travels towards the ideas clustered around Octavia (cold, chaste, pale as the moon) eclipsed by hot, sunburnt Cleopatra.

Fifteen years after *Antony and Cleopatra*, in his 1621 masque, *The Gipsies Metamorphosed*, Ben Jonson would assemble in one text all the elements that square the quadrilateral equation connecting Cleopatra, Egypt, gipsies, and blackness. In Jonson's conceit, the '*Ægiptians* . . . nation' masses for its 'yearelie . . . musters' (however improbably) in Derbyshire. 'Queene *Cleopatra*' is called 'The *Gipsyes* Grand-matra', and the gipsy children, 'fiue Princes of *Ægipt*', are the 'ofspringe of *Ptolomee*, begotten vppon se*ver*all *Cleopatra*'s in theire seuerall Counties'. When, at the end, the gipsies are finally metamorphosed, the Epilogue glances at that old apothegm about 'washing the Ethiope white' to demystify the magic transformation:

> . . . least it proue like wonder to the sight,
> To see a *Gipsie* (as an *Æthiop*) white,
> Knowe, that what dide o*ur* faces was an oyntment
> Made and laid on by Mr *woolfs* appoinntment,
> The Courtes *Lycanthropos*: yet without spell*es*
> By a meere Barbor, and no magicke ell*es*,
> It was fetcht of w*i*th water and a ball;
> And, to o*ur* transformation, this was all . . .
>
> (1479–1486)

Their tawny faces were cosmetic blackface, theatre 'slap'.

A black gipsy Cleopatra would have come to Shakespeare via popular theology and folk custom: the medieval mummers plays traditionally made the King of Egypt by some bizarre quirk of paternity both the father of St George and black.[75] Blackness was popularly supposed to have been fathered in the world by Cham, one of Noah's three sons, whose illicit copulation on the Ark produced an illicit son, marked as indelibly as Cain. So Noah's sons, tasked with repopulating the world after the Flood, went out in three directions, into Europe, Asia and Africa (the same partitioning the Roman triumvir maps on to the world in *Antony and Cleopatra*, assigning the regions this time to Julius Caesar's 'sons', Octavius, Antony and Lepidus). Chus, born black as punishment for his father's disobedience, became the original parent of the black African Moors. It followed, typologically, that those black races would be represented at the birth of Christ by one of the Magi. So, as early as the eighth century, the third king, Balthasar, was, according to the Venerable Bede, represented black: 'Tertius, fuscus, integre barbatus, Balthazar nomine, habens tunicam rubeam.'[76] Typologically, the Epiphany was anticipated in the Old Testament visit of the Queen of Sheba to Solomon: like the 'black and comely' beloved of the 'Song of Songs', she was represented black. So, too, were Marlowe's African Dido, Queen of Carthage, Tamburlaine's Zenocrate, daughter of the Egyptian 'soldan', and Zenobia, Queen of Palmyra, who claimed descent from Cleopatra and whose 'history' was played by Lord Strange's Men (Shakespeare probably one of the company) at Philip Henslowe's Rose playhouse on 9 March 1592. Here then is a line of black player queens anticipating Shakespeare's Egyptian.[77]

In court performance, too, Egypt was represented black. A 'masking' before Henry VIII in 1510 presented six ladies, 'their heads rouled in pleasauntes and typpers lyke the Egipcians, embroudered with gold. Their faces, neckes, armes and handes, covered with fyne plesaunce blacke [a lawn-like cloth] . . . so that the same ladies seemed to be nigrost [sic] or blacke Mores.'[78] A hundred years later, Ben Jonson would elaborate another court masque (which I turn to later), Egyptian in inspiration, danced by twelve court ladies – only this time, they would wear their blackness on the flesh.

The one place where Shakespeare wouldn't have found Cleopatra black was in North's translation of Plutarch's *Life of Marcus Antonius*, his closest source for *Antony and Cleopatra*, for Plutarch imagines Cleopatra as a Ptolemaic Greek, never as 'Egypt'; indeed, he rarely imagines her in Egypt, most of his 'big scenes' being set remote from Alexandria (Parthia, Cilicia, Cydnus, Actium). Plutarch's Cleopatra spends as much time in Athens as Alexandria, while in Shakespeare, no matter what the map says, the onstage space Cleopatra occupies always feels like Egypt. Plutarch's Egyptians, though, are most their Shakespearean selves when they are in Antony's company, not Cleopatra's, drinking and gourmandizing, going in disguise, 'ambl[ing] up and down the streets' with him as he 'would peer into poor men's windows and their shops, and scold and brawl with them within the house', inclinations that make Antony the true 'Oriental' of Plutarch's story.[79]

Significantly, however, Shakespeare would have found Egyptian blackness in another Greek historian, Herodotus, whose *Famous Hystory* of Egypt was translated into English by Barnaby Riche and published by Thomas Marshe in 1584.[80] For Herodotus, it was climate, the fact that Egypt was a 'lande . . . continually voyde of rayne', that accounted for 'the blacknesse and swartnesse of the people, couloured by the vehement heat and scorching of the sunne' (f. 75). On the basis of skin colour, he observed that 'The people colchi spro*n*g of the Aegyptians' for 'both people are in cou*n*tenance a like black, in hayre a like fryzled' (f. 96). And he marvelled at a country that 'hath more strange wonders then any nation in the world', not least its cultural practice of gender reversal:

> In this countrey the women followe the trade of merchandize in buying and selling: also victualing and all kind of sale and chapmandry, whereas contrarywise the men remayne at home, and play the good huswives in spinning and weaving and such like duties . . . . Women make water standing, and men crouching downe and cowring to the ground. (f. 78v)

According to Herodotus as Riche translates him, 'the flower' of 'beauty' among the 'wom[e]n of Aegypt' is 'a fayre browne blew, tanned and burnt by the fyery beames of the sunne' (f .85v) – an image Shakespeare may recall when Cleopatra offers the messenger her 'bluest veins to kiss'

(2.5.29). (Egyptian beauty regimes were famous in Rome as 'sovereign remedies', evidently, for curing blackness. Ovid in *Ars Amatoria* advised those 'that are more swarthy' to 'have recourse to the aid of the Pharian fish', that is, the Egyptian crocodile, whose intestines and dung, according to Pliny, were used by Roman women as a cosmetic to lighten dark complexions. The crocodile, it seems, constituted the original recipe for 'blanching the Ethiope'.[81]) Marvelling at Egypt, however, Herodotus still found the country's Bacchic rituals lewd. To celebrate the feast of Bacchus, whom they associated with Egyptian, not Grecian, Hercules (f. 81), the women of Egypt out-did the Greek custom of wearing 'about their neckes the similitude of a mans yard named Phallum, wrought and carved of figtree' – a significant choice in a country that troped figs with carnality and obscene jokes: 'I love long life better than figs,' says Shakespeare's Charmian (1.2.34). The Egyptians, by contrast, flaunted immodesty, devising not just phallic objects but priapic machines:

> small images of two cubites long, which by meanes of certayne strings and coardes they cause to mooue and stirre as if they had sence and were living . . . making the yard of the image (which is as bigge as all the bodye besides) to daunce and play in abhominable wise. Fast before these marcheth a piper, at whose heeles the women followe incontinent with sundry psalmes & sonets to ye god Bacchus.

Recounting Egyptian worship, Greek Herodotus seems struck suddenly with a 'Roman thought' worthy of Octavius:

> For what cause that one member of the picture is made too big for the proportion & frame of ye body, and also why, that, only of all the body is made to moove, as they refused to tell us for religion, so we desired not to heare for modesty. (f. 83)

Most significantly of all, in Herodotus Shakespeare would have found a supplement to Plutarch's Egypt, a black nation managed by women whose frank sexuality caused grown men to blush: 'mine eares glowed to heare it', admits Herodotus, recording one final 'indecency' (f. 82v).

If, searched for 'black marks', Shakespeare's playtext ultimately appears short on them, that absence might be accounted for by the fact that unlike *Othello*, *Antony and Cleopatra* pairs racial transgression with gender transgression, and the more potent in mobilizing white male anxiety (as both Lynda E. Boose and Joyce MacDonald argue) is gender. Gynophobia masks, even cancels, xenophobia.[82] First, then,

Shakespeare's Romans fear Cleopatra as a 'strumpet' capable of transforming their general from 'Mars' to 'fool' to phallic puppet to mechanical sex aid, the 'bellows and fan' to cool 'a gipsy's lust'; second, as 'tawny front' (1.1.4–9). Of course, another explanation lies in the fact that Cleopatra's blackness is performative – constantly and conspicuously on view in the theatre. It hardly needs textual marking. Moreover, I want to suggest that the performative space Shakespeare's Jacobean Cleopatra was entering was already marked, and so sensationally that it needed no additional indexing. Cleopatra was not the first black queen to illuminate the English court of 'fair Albion' with darkness.

Black Masques and Foreign Queens

Did *Antony and Cleopatra* – finished by Shakespeare in late 1606 or early 1607 – play at court? Emrys Jones, calling it the 'most courtly of Shakespeare's tragedies', thinks it did, though no record survives, unless it's hidden among the nine unnamed plays listed in the Revels accounts as having been performed by the King's Men at court between Christmas and Shrovetide that season. This absence of information is all the more maddening since, in the previous two years, the Revels clerk had obligingly entered titles opposite payments, among them, *Othello,* 'The Moor of Venis'.[83]

Paul Yachnin thinks so too, arguing the play's political topicality in 1606–1607 and reading Cleopatra as Shakespeare's nostalgic tribute to Queen Elizabeth, a tribute that functions also as a critique.[84] The 'old woman' troped cultural ideals that died with her (at least rhetorically), ideals of courtly 'libertas' and magnificence, retrospectively rejuvenated in Cleopatra to set against the 'measured', mercantile King James, the self-styled 'Augustus' who, ascending the English throne in 1603, consciously constructed himself as the new 'Caesar' presiding over the new empire, 'Britain'.[85] He ordered his coronation medal to be inscribed 'IAC : I : BRIT : CAE : AVG : HAE : CAESARUM CAE.D.D.' – 'James I, Caesar Augustus of Britain, Caesar the heir of the Caesars'.

Mapping one queen of 'infinite variety' on to another may indeed have served Shakespeare's original strategies of representation in 1606 – unsurprising, perhaps, only three years after Elizabeth's death, when, on the twentieth-century stage, the trope has survived with astonishing persistence, from Dorothy Massingham (1931) dying improbably in Egyptian headdress over Tudor coronation robes to Vanessa Redgrave (1995) in Elizabethan starched ruff and farthingale. Even at her most hieroglyphic, twentieth-century Cleopatras are Elizabeth to reviewers: Janet Suzman was deemed 'an Egyptian Elizabeth I' in 1972; Glenda

Jackson, famous to television audiences as *Elizabeth R* in 1972, was 'still Elizabeth I' under pharaonic headdress in 1978. Only Helen Mirren (1982) among recent mainstream Cleopatras escaped Elizabeth, but at the cost of being twinned with another royal, Elizabeth (II's) anti-type. Mirren's 'freshness', wrote one reviewer, 'could compete with the charming naivety of Princess Diana, racing from one emotional whirlpool to another like a barefoot Egyptian nymph'.[86]

In 1606, Cleopatra may very well have stood nostalgic Elizabeth to James's aspirant Augustus. But I want to assemble a different set of historical conjunctures to speculate that she remembers another, equally intractable queen, much closer to home in the Jacobean court: Anna of Denmark, James's consort and Elizabeth's successor as Queen of England. I am not arguing derivation or even direct relationship so much as observing the circulation of ideas and their influence in court culture and among players and playwrights. As Yachnin reminds us, the London literary community in 1606 was tight-knit; theatres knew what the competition was up to. And beyond that, court news circulated freely, almost, it seems, instantly. John Chamberlain heard daily in St Paul's what was busying the shakers and makers in Whitehall, and passed it on to correspondents in the country, on the Continent, in diplomatic bags and by private carrier.

First, some dates. The Revels Office on 21 January 1605 noted payment to 'the K's players' for 'A play in the Banketinge house att whithall called The Moor of Venis' on 'the first of Nouembar' 1604.[87] Within weeks, as Chamberlain wrote on 18 December, the Revels Office was casting about for more entertainment to occupy the King. He'd returned from his hunting lodge at Royston only days earlier 'but [was] so far from beinge wearie or satisfied with those sportes, that presently after the holy dayes he makes reckening to be there again . . . In the meane time here is great provision for cockpit to entertaine him at home; and of maskes and revells against the mariage of Sir Phillip Harbert and the Lady Susan Vere . . . on St. Johns day.' Also, the four-year old Prince Charles was to be created Duke of York, and Anna was devising 'a great maske' to follow the ceremony on Twelfth Night 'for which there was 3,000 li delivered a moneth ago' – in mid-November. Chamberlain finishes with court gossip: 'Yt is generally held and spoken that the Quene is quicke with childe.'[88]

Anna, now thirty, was indeed 'quicke', her seventh pregnancy since the birth of Prince Henry in 1594. After Candlemas, she would retire from court until her confinement in April. The 'great maske' she'd commissioned employed the wordwright, Ben Jonson, and the showman, Inigo Jones, with whom he was collaborating for the first time. What she had in mind for this entertainment was recounted in Jonson's preface to the 350–line printed text of 'these solemnities', the *Masque of Blackness*:

> Pliny, Solinus, Ptolemy, and of late Leo the African remember unto us a river in Aethiopia famous by the name of Niger, of which the people were called *Nigritae*, now Negroes, and are the blackest nation of the world. This river taketh spring out of a certain lake, eastward, and after a long race falleth into the western ocean. Hence, because it was her majesty's will to have them blackamores at first, the invention was derived by me, and presented thus.

The conceit of *Blackness* is straightforward. Niger, 'in form and colour of an Ethiop, his hair and rare beard curled', tells Oceanus, 'presented in a human form, the colour of his flesh blue', his troubles. His daughters (described in Jonson's note as 'the masquers, . . . twelve nymphs, Negroes') thought their black was beautiful until they learned from 'some few / Poor brainsick men, styled poets' that, before hapless Phaeton ran amuck with his father's chariot and burnt the peoples of the equator black, 'Ethiops were as fair / As other dames.' (It is this myth of origins that Cleopatra remembers as her personal history, though she cuts the reckless boy and goes straight to the father/god Phoebus, whose 'amorous pinches' made her 'black'.) Disconsolate, the daughters have come in search of beauty's 'fairness', which, they've been promised in a vision, they'll find in a land whose name ends in '*tania*' and whose ruler, a sun, paradoxically reverses Apollo's programme. Because 'His light sciential is' and 'past mere nature' this sun is one 'Whose beams shine day and night, and are of force / To blanch an Ethiop, and revive a Cor's', that is, a corpse.[89] In *Britannia* they find their whitening agent, the sun king James. The masquers, thus introduced, come forth and dance – the main business of the masque and the night's extensive activity – then retire, the conceit closing (in the absence of the kind of quick-change transformation Jonson's 'meere Barbor' would perform with some 'water and a ball' in 1621), with instructions in a year-long blanching regime.

The masque's political flattery of James is transparent. And the consternation generated – in one spectator – by the masquers' appearance is both documented and often quoted. The queen and eleven of her chief female courtiers were dressed, said Jonson, 'alike in all . . . , their hair thick and curled upright in tresses, like pyramids . . . .the ornament . . . orient pearl, best setting off from the black.'[90] Dudley Carleton, writing the following morning, thought the 'apparel rich, but too light and curtisan-like'. Worse, Anna hadn't followed court convention in representing blackness with vizards or stocking masks; she and her women blacked up cosmetically, like common players – like Burbage in *Othello* at court in November. Carleton thought 'Theyr black faces, and hands which were painted and bare vp to the elbowes' a 'very loathsome sight',[91] and in a later account, written to the violently anti-Spanish Ralph Winwood, elaborated the repulsiveness of the night's revels:

> Their Apparell was rich, but too light and Curtizan-like for such great ones. Instead of Vizzards, their Faces, and Armes up to the Elbows, were painted black, which was Disguise suffi-cient, for they were hard to be known; *but it became them nothing so well as their red and white, and you cannot imagine a more ugly Sight, then a Troop of lean-cheek'd Moors* [original ital-ics]. The Spanish . . . Ambassador . . . was taken out to dance, and footed it like a lusty old Gallant with his Country woman. He took out the Queen, and forgot not to kiss her Hand, though there was Danger it would have left a mark on his lips.[92]

Carleton – the arch court sophisticate – sounds more amused than scandalized.[93] By contrast, the Venetian ambassador found the masque 'very beautiful and sumptuous'. And a third writer, not a witness, nev-ertheless passed on observations to 'discerne the humor of the time': 'a sumptuous shew . . . some dozen Ladyes all paynted like blackamores face and neck bare . . . strangely attired in Barbaresque mantells to the halfe legge . . . .It cost the K. betweene 4. and 5000 li to execute the Q. fancye.'[94] This was extravagance on the grand scale, on a par, perhaps, with Cleopatra's banquets (and just as vulnerable to exaggeration). Incidentally, the observers and their range of reactions predict another trio of spectators: Philo, Enobarbus and Agrippa (who, no eyewitness either, still comments upon Cydnus).

What interests me in Anna's masque is the traffic the performance con-ducts between images of blackness and images of Egypt, traced in Jonson's text and Inigo Jones's costume designs, one of which survives. It illustrates a 'Daughter of Niger' and confirms Jonson's directions so that Egypt allusively ghosts *Blackness* in stray visual details and marginal glosses that keep bringing it back into view. So, for example, the mas-quers' hair was dressed 'like pyramids' and they carried fans inscribed with 'a mute hieroglyphic', chosen, wrote Jonson, 'as . . . applying to that original doctrine of sculpture which the Egyptians are said first to have brought from the Ethiopians.' Æthiopia appeared '*in a silver throne made in figures of a* pyramis' [original italics], figuring the moon, whose horns, derived from Io and familiar in iconic representations of

Diana/Chastity/Elizabeth the Virgin Queen, originated with Isis. And 'Niger', of course, was another name for the Nile.

Given that the masque's conceit was hardly innovative, why did Anna commission *Blackness* then? Is it possible that Will Shakespeare's *Othello*, so recently at court, cued 'her majesty's will' and taught her to 'think black'? If so, she perhaps caught at the conceit because it troped for her a discursive network of ideas connected not to race but to religion.[95] I, however, am more interested in wondering not what provoked *Blackness* but what *Blackness* provoked. Did it teach Shakespeare to 'think black' in *Antony and Cleopatra*? London society, those, like Chamberlain, who exchanged daily 'news upon the Rialto', knew of Anna's blackface the morning after the performance. The players on the South Bank may have known about it in advance, given Jonson's open migration between the court and the public playhouses. By the end of the week, all London could have known, for according to Carleton, writing the following day, there was already 'a pamflet in press' that promised the full story.[96]

In Anna's *Masque of Blackness* Shakespeare would have encountered material to reshape in *Antony and Cleopatra*: the core narrative, a black queen from the East, identified with a river who tropes not just her nation but her bounteous influence, who challenges white imperial authority. *Blackness* asks whether the sun king, another Augustus, can bring the 'stranger' into conformity with his 'fair' rule by whiting out her difference, or whether she will elude effacement at the end. If Shakespeare remembered Elizabeth in Cleopatra ('her militancy, . . . her fiery temper, her fondness for travel in a river-barge, her wit, her immense charm')[97] he might equally have remembered Anna in *Blackness* in Cleopatra: her breathtaking extravagance, her astuteness in politicizing spectacle, her subversive wit, her rages and political relentlessness, her volatile relationship with the king, her stunts, played out on her own body, whose effect was to *épater les bourgeois* (and *le roi*), her female 'government' (Anna established at Somerset, later Denmark, House a female court, an alternative, even competitive household to the king's), her vulnerability to erotic betrayal and her machiavellian manoeuvres for making the best of it.[98] And, what found no example in Elizabeth, her fertility, her generative bounty. Like Cleopatra in Shakespeare's text, if not on his stage, Anna was surrounded by children, their usefulness as political counters ballasting their privilege, and their futures proving as mixed as Caesarion's, Alexander's, and the rest.

It is the queen's maternal abundance, figuring as a trope of 'government', that puts Anna, as much as Elizabeth, in the place of opposition to James, unsettling his aspirations to 'measured' Augustan rule. I want to elaborate on this claim by bringing to bear Janet Adelman's acute reading of 'scarcity' and 'bounty' as the organizing metaphors that key the 'new psychic economy' Shakespeare imagines in *Antony and Cleopatra*. Shakespeare's Rome under Octavius institutionalizes scarcity as the basis of male selfhood, such that heroism equals deprivation. (Its definitive trial, starvation in a winter landscape, is narrated in the retreat from Modena.) Scarcity, writes Adelman, 'is the sign of the state from which the female has been excised.'[99] Egypt is Rome's opposite: Nile's slime quickens, priests bless Cleopatra 'when she's riggish', and progeny evidence an erotic history across three Roman administrations. Abundance offers itself in feasting ('Eight wild boars roasted whole at a breakfast'); in service ('superfluous kings for messengers'); in imagination ('I dreamt there was an emperor Antony'); in reputation ('For his bounty / There was no winter in't'). Cleopatra *is* bounty. Essentially abundant in herself, the agent of every one of Alexandria's scenes of extravagance, she dreams an Antony who is abundant in bounty, a vision that defeats any triumph of the 'scarce bearded' 'boy' Caesar by making that triumph 'paltry'. In short, Shakespeare's play constructs Caesar's political agenda of scarcity along the same lines as James's self-promulgated Augustan 'measured' rule. In this scheme, Anna figures as the feminized sign of 'bounty', Cleopatra to James's Octavius Caesar, with 'Britannia' as Antony, poised between two self-constructions.

Ironically, of course, James's 'measured' rule was more of a fantasy than the Antony Cleopatra dreams. Newly installed king in fabulously wealthy England (compared to 'paltry' Scotland), he began in Cleopatra-mode, distributing favours and largesse 'as yf,' wrote Chamberlain, 'this world wold last ever'. 'These bountiful beginnings raise all mens . . . hopes, inso much that not only protestants, but papists and puritanes, and the very poets with theyre ydle pamflets promise themselves great part in his favor: so that to satisfie or please all *hic labor hoc opus est*: and wold be more then a mans worke.'[100] So it proved.

Within a year Whitehall was looking for economies, deliberating 'about ordering the houshold and bringing yt to the French fashion of bourd-wages', efforts frustrated by a king who, knowing that 'monie go low in the exchequer', airily wrote off the staggering debts of several wayward favourites. By 1610, London customs had dropped to £14,000 per annum, the king raising revenue by selling titles; baronetcies were going for £10,000. 'We have many banckrupts daylie,' groaned Chamberlain, as a commission 'to devise and project the best means for monie' began deliberations in August 1612. Only six months later, however, Princess Elizabeth's marriage was celebrated in an 'excesse of braverie' and 'dasell';

she wore a coronet valued at a million crowns, while one of her retinue was arrayed in 'a gowne that cost fifty pound a yard the embrodering'. Unsurprisingly, the royal coffers were empty in April and the king had to be rescued by the very favourite he'd fattened on largesse, Robert Carr, soon to be created Duke of Somerset, who, 'seeing the world . . . at theyre witts end for monie, . . . sent for some of the officers of the receyt, and geving them a key of a chest bid them take what they found there . . . 22,000 li in gold'. But in September, bankruptcy again loomed and 'all the ingeniers and projecters are put to theyre shifts how to supplie the present need without sale of land'. The king had no money to pay his post-men in December, but still meant 'to bestow 10,000 li in jewels' on Frances Howard's marriage to Somerset at Christmas.[101]

And so it continued, James's 'measure' producing 'scarcity' bred of irresponsible 'bounty' – his 'extreem cost' making 'us all poore'. Queen Anna died in March 1616. The exchequer was too poor to bury her: 'they are driven to shifts for monie, and talke of melting the Quenes golden plate . . . the commissioners for her jewells . . . offer to sell or pawne divers of them'. After the funeral, finally conducted in May, 'the King came to Greenwich' to take possession of Anna's estate. He was reckoned to be vastly enriched by her death: jewels valued at £400,000, plate, £90,000, 'redy coine 80,000 Jacobus peeces', 124 whole pieces of cloth of gold and silver, 'besides other silkes, linnen . . . hangings, bedding and furniture . . . beyond any Prince in Europe'. The following morning, 'the Quenes trunckes and cabinets with jewells were brought . . . in fowre carts, and delivered by inventorie'. 'The King perused them all.' And immediately began converting Anna's bounty into Augustan scarcity, bestowing 'some reasonable portion' on his latest favourite, the Duke of Buckingham, to whom he'd already given Anna's residence, Denmark House.[102] Had he, or his councillors responsible for arranging his credit, I wonder, read enough Augustan history to know that, when news reached Rome that the treasure chests of Alexandria were conquered, the standard rate of interest dropped from 12 per cent to 4 per cent?[103]

* * *

I want, finally, to move forward from this recovery of early modern blackness and performativity, to contemporary performance, to conclude with a final pair of photographs, a two-minute video clip, and two questions that travel back to the beginning of this essay to interrogate my own preoccupations. Does it matter whether Shakespeare wrote Cleopatra black? What difference does it make?

Blackness matters first, I think, to the structure of political meaning in the play. A black African queen who expertly manipulates a body politics that sensationalizes and sexualizes darkness even as she inhabits it, turning the fantasies that shape the desiring white imaginary back upon themselves as a strategy for evading imperial white-out, such a Cleopatra embodies the most potent sources of threat imaginable to the white male project of establishing a Roman empire. 'Her "blacke" skin,' writes Joyce MacDonald, 'and her powerful sexuality together work to define the nature of the political challenge she presents to Rome's designs in Egypt.'[104] Her blackness, registering difference from Rome and continuously representing the politics of that difference, registers, too, the ultimate futility of Rome's project to conquer Egypt. Even if Rome leads Cleopatra in triumph, stages her to the view, presents her greatness 'boy[ed]' by 'some squeaking Cleopatra', Rome cannot absorb Egypt into its imperial system and remain itself. Her blackness is unassimilable. The 'Ethiope', as at the end of Anna's *Blackness,* is not 'blanched' but remains imperviously itself, and where the white mates with the black, as Aaron in *Titus Andronicus* delightedly gloats, holding up to staggered Rome white Tamora's 'coal-black calf', whiteness is erased, darkness dominates, the secret narrative that is meant to stay repressed surfaces to take over the story, to take white out. And here's a neat irony. Octavius cannot win, either, by resisting Cleopatra's blackness. For insofar as he disdains Cleopatra and (unlike 'Oriental' Antony, the white man who 'tragically' gives way to his dark desires) remains ascetically and 'heroically' impervious to her seduction, he dooms Rome to a different form of white-out. Caesar's 'scarcity' is sterility, yielding racial extinction.[105]

But Cleopatra's blackness matters, too, to the subsequent politics of representation on the contemporary stage. Until white spectators encounter images of blackness where we don't expect them, we won't be impelled to examine white, hegemonic cultural assumptions or dismantle structures of spectatorship that have naturalized 'white looking'. To be sure, in the fifty years since Ashcroft's Cleopatra, we have disowned certain white practices – we've made some whiteness strange. Consider my final photographs, a pair that captures the same moment in *Othello* at the RSC in 1979, first in rehearsal, then in performance, with Donald Sinden playing the Moor opposite Suzanne Bertish's Desdemona. How strange the white man in rehearsal clothes looks, blacked up for performance in Jacobean doublet, the imperfect make-up around his eyes giving him the startled expression, ironically, of a raccoon. How strange, how unimaginable this theatre practice looks to us now, as distant and redundant, twenty years on, as Victorian gaslights.[106] Urgently, though,

a

b

we must disown other white practices and learn to open up the space of performance to other narratives of desire, other cultural imaginaries. Anna's *Masque of Blackness* and Shakespeare's *Antony and Cleopatra* did that work, I believe, in their time; recovering blackness, *Antony and Cleopatra* can do it in our time too. To show the way, as a sort of cultural audition piece, I offer a moment of radical viewing as instruction towards further performance, a two-minute clip from the 1999 Oscar award ceremonies in Los Angeles showing 'Queen Elizabeth' arriving on the platform to introduce 'her' film, *Shakespeare in Love*. Every jewel, every fold of ruff and farthingale is authentically in place, but the face under the white, plaster-thick cosmetic surface is unmistakeably black, and the voice emanating from the 'Elizabethan' body is just as unmistakeably Whoopi Goldberg's, raucously announcing, in a 'bad-ass' American accent, 'I am the African Queen!' So Goldberg puts Cleopatra finally in view as a palimpsest of white performance, embodied black – she is, of course, impersonating not just Judi Dench's film Elizabeth but Dench's stage Cleopatra too – a fusion of high and low, black and white, that does not erase but rather foregrounds these contradictory categories and, in a moment of high-camp celebration, works to explode them.

Plate 12 'I am the African Queen!' Whoopi Goldberg as Queen Elizabeth, 1999 Oscar Awards, Los Angeles (a). Judi Dench as Queen Elizabeth in John Madden's 1998 *Shakespeare in Love*(b).
Source: Miramax Films/Universal Pictures, 1998.

4

DESIGNS ON SHAKESPEARE

Troilus's sleeve, Cressida's glove, Helen's placket

Soft, here comes sleeve . . . Hold thy
whore, Grecian! Now for thy whore,
Trojan! Now the sleeve, now the sleeve!
Troilus and Cressida (5.4.18, 24–25)

In the past, critics reviewed actors; more recently, directors. Today one reviews the designer.

Ralph Berry, *On Directing Shakespeare*, 1989

Modern dress is one thing. Fancy dress another. With modern dress we know where we are. With fancy dress we might be anywhere, which means anything goes.

Eric Shorter, the *Birmingham Post*, 13 November 1987

The designer, like the writer and director, may flatter or disturb the dreams of spectators.

Michael Ratcliffe, *British Theatre Design*, 1998

All art is political.

Michael Bogdanov, *The Times Literary Supplement*, 28 April 1995

Designs on Bodies

I can date with some precision the moment I learned what a designer does in the theatre: twenty past seven, 11 July 1977, the opening night of the Royal Shakespeare Company's revival of Terry Hands' *Henry V*. Until then, the stage was bare, like a rehearsal room, the actors in rehearsal gear. But when the French Ambassador entered, an aristo in court costume, the under-dressed English began to shift uneasily, bristling at the stranger's hauteur, the arrogance with which he introduced into their visual poverty the Dauphin's elaborate gift, a gilded coffer that opened to present a curious 'engine', a mechanical hand flourishing – a tennis ball. King Harry's crooked, boyish smile froze.

'This mock of his / Hath turned his balls to gunstones,' he announced dryly. It was then that the scene exploded. From the flies dropped a massive canopy; it caught the air with a roar like flame seeking oxygen and billowed open to hang over the action, a gorgeous, terrible mush-room cloud that literalized imperial ambition and made politics explicit. Blazoned in red, blue, gold, in lions rampant and fleur de lys, it represented, materially, the arms of France and England, and held out to the aspiring conqueror's reach the 'crowns imperial . . . / Promis'd to Harry and his followers.' 'Now sits Expectation in the air,' crowed the Chorus. The canopy reified Expectation. Later (like Expectation) it fell, covering the stage in a vast expanse of grey canvas underbelly, the mud of Agincourt – adventurism turned bleakly unheroic-side out. Camped centre stage and longing for the dawn that would bring the battle, the effete French lounged in a circle of light, stroking their plumed crests and high-gloss armour while, around them, in the shadows, the wretched English in filthy battle fatigues, St George crosses faded to the colour of dried blood, hugged the canvas mud and tried to sleep.

Abdul Farrah's canopy showed me, in one spectacular moment, how designers translate Shakespeare into visual language, how they reimagine him in material terms. Their business is to *wright* the play, like Prospero in partnership with Snug the joiner, fashioning for the poet's 'airy nothings' a 'local habitation and a name' that invents a physical world and locates the play in it among functional objects. Designers see words. They structure the audience's looking: closing down or opening up the scenic aperture; blocking the view or giving access to seeing; framing the scene; ordering or distorting perspective; creating visual parallelisms or superimpositions; foregrounding; distancing. They offer a repertoire of visual images to make Shakespeare's text legible in performance. In 1983, for example, the RSC's *Measure for Measure* (designed by Bob Crowley) opened in front of a full-length ormolu mirror where 'seemers' narcissistically played to their own appearances; in 1991 (Maria Bjornson), *Measure* was set in Freud's Vienna, in a room with an analyst's couch; in 1978 (Christopher Morley), in Hogarth's Gin Alley, beneath an icon of blind Justice armed with sword and scales; in 1987 (Mark Thompson), in Thatcher's Soho, among rent boys and kerb crawlers cruising a set that looked like the gents' loo off Leicester Square.[1] A designer's images work intellectually and emotion-ally – and always, politically. In the RSC's 1987 *Merchant*, designed by Kit Surrey, Venice from one angle was the epitome of High Renaissance art and culture – a gold and lapis lazuli mosaic of a Madonna and Child adorned one wall. From another, it was a slum defaced by racist graffiti – down the opposite wall dripped a Star of David daubed in yellow paint.

Designers, working in space, make the stage a world, a notional 'wooden-O' that can be dressed as a claustrophobic 'cockpit' or 'the vasty fields of France' to replicate reality or to burst reality expressionistically apart. When spectators walked into the theatre for *As You Like It* designed by Ultz in 1989 they saw on stage an exact copy of the RST foyer. When the globe that hung over the heath Anthony Ward designed for *King Lear* in 1993 split, bizarrely recalling the Fool's proverbial egg and spilling out the sands of time into a Beckettian heap, spectators saw Dover pre-playing *Happy Days*. Hamlet roamed an open-plan Elsinore in striped pyjamas in 1989 (Antony McDonald); in 1997 he retreated to a cramped attic boxroom littered with half-read books and crusted milk bottles (Mark Thompson). In 1985 Celia and Rosalind trudged into banishment pulling over their shoulders out of the centre of a cold winter sun lengths of parachute silk that, spreading out behind them, sculpted Arden into an expressionist landscape frozen white (Bob Crowley).

In all these examples, the style of the design powerfully mediated the production's meaning. Designers who locate Shakespeare in a period (his, ours, or something in between) construct a 'whole' world, one that, by conceit, simulates reality, is authentic, consistent, self-contained; one of the great satisfactions of period design is its attention to detail. So, for example, Timothy O'Brien put *The Merry Wives* (1975) in a densely realized Elizabethan world, against a replica Windsor skyline, *c.* 1593, where social gradation was measured in depths of ruffs and widths of farthingales. Ten years later, Bill Dudley's *Wives* (1986) belonged to 1953, the second Elizabethan age: 'Mrs' Ford and 'Mrs' Quickly wore pedal pushers and sat under hairdryers in a beauty salon paved with linoleum. The young turks in Alison Chitty's *Romeo and Juliet* (1991) were Renaissance bravos who swaggered in doublet and hose and surrendered rapiers at Capulet's door; Verona's punks in 1987 (Chris Dyer) carried flick knives and cruised on roller skates. Modern dress makes Shakespeare our contemporary, tells us that comedy and tragedy are today's news in the *Guardian,* the *Daily Mail* or *The Sun*. Period dress requires us to historicize, to see the story in a past that is a 'foreign country' where 'they do things differently'.[2] One strategy sets the designer to work almost as an archivist; Bill Dudley copied table tombs from the Beauchamp Chapel for *Richard III* (1984). The other sees him as a comparativist or translator, looking for the apt visual analogy or parallel world that will locate the production in a place or time that the audience recognizes, that makes sense of the play's issues and approximates its original rules of engagement, its social organization, caste system (particularly its gender hierarchy), its political rivalries, its religious and ethnic antagonisms: John Napier set *Much Ado* in the British Raj (1977); Ralph Koltai, *All's Well* in the Crimea (1981); Rae Smith, *Henry VI* in Bosnia (1994).

Since the 1960s the design style that has come to dominate at the RSC as designers have moved away from consistency and scenic decoration toward non-illusion is what the theatre critic Michael Billington calls 'eclecticism', design for a post-modern stage that works by pastiche to deconstruct the notion of the self-contained playworld. Eclectic design mixes fantasy with realism, nostalgia with the avant-garde; the play becomes a palimpsest of its previous productions. Disintegrationist by temperament, eclecticism takes pleasure in fissures: a fault line cracked the Fool's face in *Lear*, 1982 (Crowley); a red gag slashed his mouth in 1993 (Ward). *Troilus and Cressida* in 1985 (Koltai) occupied a shelled mansion in ante-bellum Virginia or perhaps Chekhov's Crimea; a samovar and a ticker-tape machine sat on a table, a battered honky-tonk piano took refuge under a wide staircase that swept up in a curve designed for a culture used to making grand entrances. But exploding shells had shuddered the window frame to a crazy angle and, below, the mosaic floor was split; here was a culture literally coming apart at the seams.

For actors, designers construct a play space that is also a work room, furnishing it with 'stuff' for performance, with costumes that are working gear but also an intimate scaffold for building a character. They use bodies as material and write meanings on to them; serious work in costume design is significant design, never merely 'fancy dress'. Thus, Portia, dressed in the costume Shelagh Keegan designed for her mourning (1993), was a woman trapped in the claustrophobic conditions of her father's will, dragging miles of heavy black velvet around like chains, hardly able to breathe for the corseting. No one could get near her – the skirt was so massive it stood her suitors at bay. When Desdemona suddenly appeared in the Venetian council in the dress Alexander Reid (1985) designed for her first entrance, she was not Brabantio's daughter, his 'jewel', but, staggeringly, a 'wheeling stranger' – a Moorish bride. Queen Margaret's costume changes across the *Henry VI* trilogy (designed by Farrah, 1977) mapped her personal, and political, metamorphosis from lissom girl, in figure-hugging velvet, stepping fastidiously through smoke and battlefield carnage, to harridan hag, her body made over in chain mail moulded to her curves and monstering her sexuality. In the theatre, costume is the most conspicuously charged material for writing a politics of the body, the boldest and at the same time the most nuanced, and for women's roles particularly, the most problematic, for costume determines the discursive space a role occupies and how the audience reads it.

The first designer of Shakespeare was, of course, Shakespeare himself. Like his subsequent designers who follow 'the oblique imperatives of [his] dialogue',[3] Shakespeare began with the material of the body, making that material signify in radical ways from the skin up: from Othello's blackness and Edgar's nakedness; from Coriolanus's scars, those wounds that map Rome's triumph on his martial body; from Richard's (and Caliban's) deformity; from Falstaff's corpulence. Making the body signify, he required his audience to read it, and never just one way. The fat knight's mountain of flesh, for example, is both Good Cheer and Gluttony, Common-wealth and Riot, his great belly troping him both as 'cannibal' (consuming not just 'some' but 'all') and 'female'. For Falstaff, whose 'womb undoes me', is the 'sow that hath over-whelmed all her litter', a travesty Doll Tearsheet 'pregnant' with a cushion up her skirt, a Mother England devouring her offspring, daub-ing her lips 'with her own children's blood'. Set against him are the kingdom's Slenders and Shallows; coming after him, the Fangs and Snares who, embodying Lenten leanness, bring in the new regime's ascetic reformation, the end of carnival.

The body as Shakespeare writes it demands to be read as 'thing itself' (like Poor Tom, naked on Lear's heath) or as inscription: 'Was this fair paper, this most goodly book / Made to write 'whore' upon?' (4.2.73–74) asks Othello of Desdemona, defaced – as he thinks – with pornographer's graffiti. Trying to read bodies, King Duncan laments human inscrutability: 'There's no art to know the mind's construction in the face' (1.4.11–12). So does Leontes. Unable to decipher his wife's gravid belly, he turns to his son's face instead: 'They say it is a copy out of mine . . . /Art thou my calf?' (1.2.124, 129). On Shakespeare's stage, 'Look there, look there!' draws attention time and again to the body, to its multiple signification; to its plural or contradictory interpretation; or maybe to its indecipherability. Everywhere in Shakespeare the body is politic: Cressida's 'foot speaks' (but in what language?); so does Juliet's. Menenius's belly smiles. Phebe's eyes wound. Bottom's head wisely con-firms him an ass. Or perhaps not. For these bodies contest those interpretations fixed upon them as soon as they are constructed. Without question, though, bodies reproduce: twins double-cross their plays, and children 'print off' their parents, Polixenes and Hermione standing before Leontes a second time copied in Florizel and Perdita.

Putting costumes on bodies, Shakespeare, like every early modern play-wrighter, had to hand a semiotics of dress regulated by cultural practice and legal constraint in the Tudor sumptuary laws, a code, item-ized in the mind-numbingly 'tedious brief' style of a Polonius, whose object was to illustrate each scrupulous gradation of social hierarchy by assigning every cloth, every buckle, every stocking (silk, woollen, worsted) its right sartorial station in life. So, beginning at the top, the statute of 1597 commanded 'that None shall weare in his Apparell':

Cloth of gold or siluer tissued, Silke of colour Purple,
vnder the degree of an Earle, except Knights of the Garter
in their purple Mantels onley.

Cloth of gold or siluer, tincelled Sattin, Silke or cloth
imbrodered with Pearle, Gold, or Siluer, woollen Cloth
made out of the Realme, vnder the degree of a Baron,
except Knights of the Garter, Privey Counsellors to
The Queenes Maiestie.

Veluet in gownes, cloakes, Coates, or other vppermost
Garments, embroderies with silke, Netherstocks of
silke, Under the degree of a Knight, except
Gentlemen in ordinarie Office, attending vpon her
Maiestie in her house or chamber; Such as haue bin
imploied in Ambassage to foreine Princes. The sonne
and heire apparant of a knight. Captaines in her
maiesties pay: and such as may dispend CC. li [£200]
by the yeere for terme of life in possession aboue all
charges.

Sattin, Damaske, Grogeran, Taffata in Hose, Doublet,
Under the degree of a Gentleman bearing Armes . . . And
such as may dispend xx. li [£20] by the yeere . . .[4]

The one clause in this frequently reissued proclamation that was never amended was the one fixing the bottom rung on the social ladder: 'no Seruyngman in husbandrye, or Jurneymen in handycraftes, takyng wages, shall weare in his doublet any other thyng than fustyan, Canuas, leather or Woolen cloth.'

Theoretically, at least, this statute meant that a person's rank, profession, family, position of precedence in that family (the heir to a title being allowed a dagger forbidden to his younger brother), even annual disposable income were displayed in the cut, cloth, colour, insignia and ornamentation of his gown, a sign system legible on the street and on the stage. How convenient for the play-wrighter that such a visual shorthand be common parlance. We know from the company accounts in Philip Henslowe's *Diary* how lavishly the players spent on costumes.

The sum of £6 was their standard payment to a playwright for a new 'book', but they regularly disbursed many times that amount to dress a play in costumes that designed expectation: 'cottes for gyantes' in *Brutus*; 'a grey gowne for gryssell' in *Patient Grissell*; £20 for 'taffataes & sattyns' for *The Seven Wise Masters*; 'A canves sewt & Lame skenes' for *The Black Dog of Newgate*; £2 10s 'for mackynge of crownes' for *Mahomet*; £21 for 'ij pylle velluet of carnardyn' (plus another £17 'for tynsell & tyffeney & lynynge & other thing*es*) for *Cardinal Wolsey*; 'blacke buckrome to macke a sewte for a fyer drack' (a dragon) in *Tom Strowde*.[5]

Like bodies, costumes on Shakespeare's stage were legible, freighted with significance that is both iconic and performative. Osric's hat, Shylock's gabardine, Caesar's assassinated gown, Macbeth's armour, the popinjay's snuff box daffed in Hotspur's sweating face, Coriolanus's 'gown of humility' (or rather, his 'wolvish toge' that bizarrely reverses the fable to make him the scapegoated sacrificial lamb in wolf's clothing) all work as much theatrically as discursively. 'Apparel oft proclaims the man', but just as 'oft', interrogates him, for if a man is what he wears, a change of clothes is a change of role, of identity. 'Which is the justice, which is the thief' when clothes can lie, when clothes – onstage, always – are 'usurp'd attire', a cover-up? Who is the hypocrite in *Hamlet*, the sable-suited prince, obstinately affecting condolence, or Claudius, the spruce bridegroom? How are the politics of gender exposed in Rosalind's transvestism, or the politics of marriage in Kate's wrecked wedding dress? And what about the politics of politics as England's crown goes the rounds as fashion accessory to a string of self-promoting 'wannabe' kings: it's fashioned in paper for dogged York; in 'brass impregnable' for Richard II. But it's always hollow. It can be bored through 'with a little pin' by antic King Death.

Costume writes an entire level of theatrical meaning for Shakespeare. In *Lear*, for example, the king's costume changes demonstrate a life coming apart and mark the stages of his transformation with a savage, ironic visual commentary. Grief is finally re-dressed at the end when Lear wakes in new robes, but the effect only alienates comfort. 'Oh reason not the need,' the child-changed father cried before the storm broke over his head. But in that storm, Lear learns to reason the need inflicted by deprivation. In Act 1, he asked, facetiously, 'Doth any here know me?' That question of knowing by reading externals is a serious one, though, for what is a king when regiment is gone? Having metaphorically stripped his daughter to her smock and banished Kent from all he possesses in scene 1, Lear's journey is towards equivalent self-exposure, a literal process of stripping away ('What need you five and twenty, ten, or five?'; 'What need one?') that razes Lear's likeness to King Lear as implacably as Kent defaces Kent to play the servant Caius or Edgar ruins Edgar to travesty sanity in the savage grotesquerie of naked, mad Tom. The costume changes of *King Lear* materialize a terrifying spectacle when Authority, reduced to 'unaccommodated man', stands naked in the storm, teeth chattering. 'Is man no more than this?' wonders the grief-wilded king. But is authority no more than this? That's what the play-stricken audience has to wonder as it is required to look at a king whose crown is 'idle weeds', whose chief courtier is a squint-eyed Cupid blinded by love. Shakespeare's design for this play constantly projects ways of seeing that teach a radical politics. Given such a vocabulary of costume, how is it possible to leave *King Lear* with an ideology of authority intact?

As a designer, Shakespeare made costume work both literally and figuratively: to identify and decorate, but also to dismantle (as in 'undress', 'expose') and so, by theatrical seeing, to dismantle (as in 'take apart') cultural practice. Costumes tell stories in Shakespeare's performance text that were never written into his playtext. Consider Vienna's duke in *Measure for Measure*, interested to see 'what our seemers be', becoming a 'seemer' himself. He puts on a friar's habit and so 'passes' in disguise for four acts of the play as the unselfconscious embodiment of the hypocrisies he's discovering are endemic to his regime; his costume tells a complicated story in continuous visual dialogue with the lines the friar/duke speaks.

Or consider Cressida and her change of clothes. Like Romeo and Juliet, but with a world of difference (for starters, in this warped world, Pandarus plays the Nurse), Troilus and Cressida spend one night together (4.2). Early, while the morning is still cold, Troilus makes to leave since 'night will hide our joys no longer,' urging Cressida 'To bed, to bed . . . I prithee now, to bed.'[6] Troilus fusses, 'You will catch cold and curse me.' Is Cressida in her nightgown?[7] She answers his concern with anxiety, 'Are you a-weary of me?'; 'I might have still held off, / And then you would have tarried.' The intimacy of her un-dress, however, mocks as vain her strategy of holding off. In bustles Pandarus, as always, salacious and officious ('How now, how now, how go maidenheads?'), feigning incomprehension as he pointedly asks Cressida to her face, 'where's my Cousin Cressid?' For last night's Cressida, virgin Cressida, is gone. Cressida's changed. It's a profound point, made grossly. Two virgins went to bed together the night before. This morning, only one of them is physically inscribed with the act they mutually consummated. Cressida is changed, and Pandarus's joke enjoys the cultural discrepancy his mockery depends upon: Cressida's 'privates' are somehow publicly legible. She is now irreversibly – and what's more, to the practised eye, visibly – the 'deed's creature'.

A knock at the gates interrupts Pandarus's banter; the lovers withdraw, but Troilus (alone) re-enters to hear Aeneas's message about the hostage exchange, Cressida for Antenor. 'Is it so concluded?' asks the prince. ''Twill be his death . . . he cannot bear it' – that's as Pandarus sees it. But the phlegmatic Troilus who left with Aeneas didn't seem inclined to 'go mad or die'. Not so Cressida. When she finally prises the news from her uncle, demanding 'What's the matter?' four times in twelve lines clotted with Pandarus's wailing *non sequiturs* that nicely make her the 'fault' ('I knew thou wouldst be his death'), she vows 'I will not go', 'I will not uncle':

> O you gods divine,
> Make Cressid's name the very crown of falsehood
> If ever she leave Troilus! . . . I will not go from Troy.
> (4.2.99–112)

Shakespeare takes Cressida off stage for twelve lines (4.3). When she returns, in 4.4, she is changed. She is dressed for going. She has her gloves: she gives one to Troilus at line 70. Her costume tells a story the lines withhold. The lovers swear constancy. The clothes dismantle constancy. The lovers exchange tokens, giving what they have to hand in the extremity of the moment, suddenly – Troilus, his (heraldic) sleeve, Cressida, her glove.[8] These piecemeal tokens of absent bodies are loaded with the promise of metaphor, for hands pledge hearts, and chivalric arms defend female honour. But in signifying the (absent) body part, these tokens are likewise cruelly ironic, for they are, literally, emptied out of meaning. The sleeve comes without the arm, the glove, without the hand; material has become the body's proxy.

Four scenes hence (5.2), Troilus's sleeve will change hands yet again when Cressida hands it over to Diomedes to pledge a new vow, 'token for the surety of it'. What is this 'it' Diomedes wants sworn? 'It' remains unuttered, but Troilus, looking on in 5.2, sees Cressida first offer the sleeve – his pledge (had she nothing else to commit perfidy with?) – then take it back. She takes back, too, the faith-breaking vow she's just sworn to Diomedes, only to lose it again to his 'snatch' and surrender languidly to the bargain with him that the sleeve signifies. 'It' as Troilus sees 'it' is betrayal – 'False, false, false.'

After this, Cressida writes herself out of the story. She sends a letter back to Troy and Troilus the next morning (5.3). What does it say? Like the 'it' of the night before, the message is undisclosed. Troilus reads it silently – 'Words, words, mere words, no matter from the heart' – then tears the paper and throws the pieces to the promiscuous 'wind . . . there turn and change together'. Meanwhile the sleeve that Diomedes flaunts in his helmet taunting the Trojan who owned it to combat, is no longer 'the thing itself' but reconstituted, by Thersites, into a trope – 'Hold thy whore' – and synecdoche for Diomedes: 'Here comes sleeve.' Women are excluded entirely from the exchange of meaning the token now tropes, for the testosterone-driven combat for the doubly evacuated sleeve is about male bonding in death's *paso doble*.

Designs on Shakespeare

To see how Shakespeare's subsequent designers interpret Shakespeare, I want to use *Troilus and Cressida* as a case study, for this is a play whose crises are written as moments that are peculiarly sensitive to design decisions. Moreover, *Troilus and Cressida*, uniquely in the canon, is a twentieth-century Shakespeare play. (Its performance history begins post-war. Post-Vietnam, though, there have been eight RSC productions.[9]) This means that in a very immediate sense, the play is our invention and the theatre images we have to think it through are modern ones. It's no wonder that we use *Troilus and Cressida* discursively to reflect ourselves to ourselves; its take on heroic Homeric epic is tuned to our own disillusioned, dissident post-modernism. Michael Billington calls it 'a cynic's Iliad'[10] peopled, says Paul Taylor, with 'big shots' on both sides who 'fail, with embarrassing frequency, even to recognize the opposition VIPs' – no wonder, though, since 'there is a farcical discrepancy between the glamorous "press" these figures have received in legend and the collection of machiavels, geriatrics, sulking narcissists and slippery self-deceivers the play actually presents.'[11] For Benedict Nightingale, it's 'a play for an anxious generation in a pluralist society', 'bewildering, offensive, or ridiculous' to 'past ages', but to us, 'only too lucid',[12] its bleak reductivism and corrosive comedy immediately familiar to a culture that invented 'smart bombs' and 'post-traumatic stress syndrome', that laughs at Scarfe and Doonesbury and transmits HIV.

It's not just the debunking of heroes and romantic idealism we recognize. It's the politicking, the ethical relativism in a world void of absolute values, the indeterminacy of actions in a doldrum-ed narrative that seems to be all middle, where the muddled, unresolved ending has both sides claiming victory in a war where everybody loses. The play stages the end of heroics: Troilus, metamorphosed overnight from mooning calf to murderous thug; Hector, pursuing golden fantasies, troped in golden armour, rotten at the core; Achilles, roused from lolling in his tent clapping Patroclus's cheap theatricals to slaughter Hector ignominiously. Productions since 1960 have gazed unflinchingly at the deglamorized death of heroism in this play. We can watch that impassively.

But what about the death of fidelity? That's a different story, for we're much less certain of Shakespeare's take on love and faith in this play, the way idealism, and worse, both wonder and pleasure, are stripped from what (under greenwood trees in the Forest of Arden or behind box hedges in walled gardens in Illyria) were wooing and wedding games, but here are commodified exchanges of variously valued merchandise managed by variously situated 'broker-lackey[s]' – upmarket Paris, hustler Pandarus. In this commodities marketplace which speculates on futures and residuals and doubles as a battlefield, Helen may be 'A pearl / Whose price hath launch'd above a thousand ships, / And turn'd crown'd kings to merchants' (2.2.82–84). She may, that is, be worth a Cressida, 'a pearl', says Troilus, whose 'bed is India . . . / Ourself the merchant' (1.2.100, 103). Or she may be, as Hector argues, 'not worth what she doth cost the keeping', no more 'dear' than 'Every tithe soul 'mongst many thousand dismes' (2.2.52, 19) slaughtered in war's body brokering. Maybe, like them, she's only so much dead meat or 'carrion', a carcass in the flesh trade for 'every scruple' of whose 'contaminated . . . weight / A Trojan hath been slain' (4.1.72–73). Troping love and war is no surprise in Shakespeare. What's different here is that the combatants, all of them, are mercenaries, and vows are not eternal pledges but interim bargains on the look-out for better deals.

This discrepancy interests me. The same productions that pull no punches when Achilles betrays Hector duck, weave, and back-pedal when Cressida betrays Troilus. (Notice that men who betray men in Shakespeare are called traitors – that's politics; women who betray men, though, aren't traitors, they're called whores.[13]) Cressida's betrayal makes directors nervous. There's no model for it elsewhere in Shakespeare to teach them how to play it, and no performance history for reference. In the event, taking a route via stereotype and cliché, they 'design' their way out of their confusion.

One recourse is to reconstruct Cressida's betrayal as something else. That was John Barton's strategy in 1968. The costumes Timothy O'Brien designed for Helen Mirren offered Cressida as a voluptuary from the start: her breasts were seductively displayed to every 'ticklish reader' in a dress that clung to her thighs and, in the 'morning after' scene, her naked body was unwound from the bedsheet she wore instead of a nightgown. She was a slapper; Troilus, a twerp not to have noticed, so what she did couldn't be construed as betrayal. It was 'natural'. Another recourse is to motivate it, via, for example, the poignant story Tom Piper's design told around Cressida's suitcase in 1998. Dragged kicking and screaming towards the hostage exchange, Cressida managed to tear her suitcase out of Pandarus's grip, wrench it open, and hurl her clothes defiantly to the ground. Then, appalled, bereft, she dumbly watched Troilus stumbling to retrieve her scattered bras and cardigans, fold up her self-exposure, pack it all away, and hand her over, reminding her, as he did, to be 'true'. But he, already, was 'false' – the suitcase had betrayed him. A third recourse is to extenuate it. Cressida in Howard Davies's Crimean *Troilus* (1985) went to the Greeks in her nightgown. Troilus tried fumblingly to cover her nakedness with his military greatcoat, a gesture meant to mark her both 'of Troy and Troilus', but when it fell away and exposed her to the hungry eyes of the Greek high command (an impropriety as great, given this production's vocabulary of costume, as setting Florence Nightingale naked in the officers' mess at Sebastapol) what Cressida experienced was gang rape. Her subsequent betrayal of Troilus was pragmatic. Her treatment had made her a whore; better, then, to accept Diomedes as 'guardian' and be visited in 'particular' than used 'in general' by the 'general' camp.

All of these versions accepted Barton's premise, that Ulysses' reading of 'false' Cressida is 'true' – that she is legibly the whore he writes her, 'set . . . down' for 'every ticklish reader' as 'sluttish spoils of opportunity' and 'daughter of the game' (4.5.61–63). Davies may have put a contemporary spin on things by locating Cressida as a victim to rationalize her harlot's progress, but like the others, he recruited design to his project to make Cressida explicit: Cressida was as she was designed. And the design ironed out her contradictions.

But is Ulysses, the play's chief machiavel and spin doctor, who also manipulates Achilles' public image to such devastating effect, to be trusted as the authority on Cressida? Who is Cressida? What is she, given that she provokes not just contrary valuations ('pearl'; 'spoils') in Troilus and Ulysses, but in herself, a conflicted sense of her self as two Cressidas. She has, she says, 'a kind of self resides with [Troilus]', but another 'unkind self, that itself will leave / To be another's fool' (3.2.146–148), an ambiguity of selfhood ironically mirrored in Hector's attempt in 4.5 to separate Ajax into his Greek and Trojan selves. Elsewhere in Shakespeare the collection of conventions we call 'character' proposes something we recognize theatrically as an essential self. It may develop, transform, go into hiding behind a disguise, betray or be betrayed. But it's (mostly) coherent, (mostly) continuous. In Cressida, though, the self is aware of a lived doubleness – or duplicity (an innocent looking semantic shift that registers the treacherous gap between seeming synonyms). As Troilus ends his voyeurism on Cressida with Diomedes in 5.2 flatly observing, 'This is, and is not, Cressid', another voyeur on the sidelines snorts, 'Will a swagger himself out on's own eyes?' (5.2.135). Thersites sees Cressida as one thing only. But perhaps Troilus is right. Perhaps the challenge Shakespeare constructs for this play is to put before us a Cressida, who, like the fair (but dark) lady of the sonnets is, in Eve Sedgwick's memorable term, 'oxymoron militant', a genuine contradiction.[14] Is it possible to play this self-division in the theatre? How do you 'design double'?

Ubiquitous, Absent, Iconic Helen

To address these questions, I need to shift my sights to Helen, Shakespeare's design coup for this play and a role he quite consciously constructs as Cressida's distorted twin. It is Helen – as seen in three performances – who cuts Shakespeare's subsequent designers free from caution and cliché to find a repertoire of daring visual language that projects the imagery Shakespeare scripts, but they don't 'wright', for Cressida. Designers understand Helen both as icon and iconoclast.

Helen is what this play is about. 'Ravish'd Helen', the Prologue tells us, 'that's the quarrel'. Her name tropes war – and love, for Helen is 'the mortal Venus, . . . love's visible soul' (3.1.31–32). She's everyone's 'matter'; hers, the definitive discursive body whose representation is continuously, opportunistically refashioned. When Troilus's political business urges it, Helen is 'a theme of honour and renown', an 'inestimable' 'prize' worthily 'stol'n' by 'crown'd kings' turned 'merchants'. But when he's not in the 'urging' vein, Helen is hideous – the 'daily paint' that lays the cosmetic blush on her 'fair' cheek is blood (1.2.91). Others figure Helen as 'mad idolatry', 'will . . . infectiously . . . affected' (Hector); 'woe' (Cassandra); 'a flat tamed piece' (Diomedes); 'a deadly theme' (Menelaus). Thersites makes her 'a placket', that is, the slit in a woman's petticoat that gives access to her privates. The whore-war for Helen is, in his rancid colloquialism, a 'war for a placket'.

Helen is also a set-up. She's framed as Cressida's *alter ego*. To begin with, it merely seems odd that they happen to keep turning up in the same conversations together. Later, it looks less like accident than policy. They're constantly compared, troped with the same metaphors ('pearl'; 'merchant'), crossed in identities, and, most bizarrely, fantasized as rivals. Helen, Pandarus tells Cressida, loves Troilus 'better than Paris'; Cressida, he tells Helen, 'is horribly in love with a thing you have' (3.1.95). At significant moments Helen's narrative inserts itself into Cressida's. Both

Patroclus and Ulysses remember Helen as they take, or spurn, Cressida's kiss in 4.5, and Cressida finally fetches up at Helen's old address, for her 'traitor' father Calchas 'keep[s] / At Menelaus' tent'; Diomedes and Troilus find her there. It's as though Helen constitutes the primary narrative that keeps surfacing through the palimpsest of individual women's histories – grounding, contaminating and over-determining them.

Helen and Cressida never meet. But then, women never do in *Troilus and Cressida* – Shakespeare makes a point of it.[15] Nor do they talk to each other. In the 3,500 or so lines of this play, women exchange exactly one line. When Cressida makes her first entrance in 1.2 inquiring, 'Who were those went by?', she's just missed Helen. But missing Helen turns out to be the play's in-joke, for Helen, Troy's 'quarrel', love's 'soul', the entire matter of the play, is entirely absent. Except for one, single scene, 3.1, placed smack in the centre of things, the play's axis.

In 3.1 Pandarus goes to Paris to deliver a message, its burden to instruct Paris to make his excuse if Troilus is missed at dinner. There's tedious chit-chat with a servant that repeatedly doubles Helen with Cressida, and then, finally, forty lines into the scene, Paris enters with what, by now, anticipation has roused us for, 'the face that launched a thousand ships / And burnt the topless towers of Ilium'.[16] Helen! What do we get? Disconcertingly, longueur. Unbelievably protracted puns on 'fair' and 'broke' that delay the message. The alibi in any case is so inept that Troilus's 'cover' is transparent: 'I spy', says Paris. There's some odd stage business as Pandarus seems to be fending Helen off. She wants a song; hard-pressed, he delivers, but only to deflect further interrogation: 'You spy? What do you spy? – Come give me an instrument.' The love song is really about sex, the 'generation of vipers'. Afterwards, they trade news, as if comparing Filofaxes: 'who's afield today?'; 'I would fain have armed today, but my Nell would not have it so.' Pandarus exits. Ten lines later, so do Paris and Helen: he wants her to use 'these your white enchanting fingers' to 'unarm our Hector'. 'Sweet,' says Paris, 'above thought I love thee.' The scene ends as desultorily as it began. We see no more of Helen.

Even in its nudging and winking this scene feels vacuous and vapid, merely going through the motions of 'tickling' (a favourite word in this play) its participants, a weary tease, though, as if the ritual of arousal is enervated, pointless – and unpointed. What does Helen mean when she says 'this love will undo us all'? Is this a staggering insight or banality? And what about Paris's 'I love thee'?

My response – Is that all? – is, I take it, precisely the reaction Shakespeare wants. His strategy is to withhold Helen, to ratchet up her mystique by circulating her reputation while preserving her body as an elusive mystery, incognito. When he finally does bring her on, the icon made flesh, anticipation is instantly wrecked in spectacular anti-climax, for the 'thing itself' inevitably fails to match expectation's idealization. As Shakespeare-the-designer understands it, there is nothing for Helen to do in this play. She must simply *be*. And her image – we only need to see it once – remains on our retina for the rest of the play, simultaneously delivering and deconstructing Helen as icon.

Three of Shakespeare's subsequent designers have spectacularly achieved this double Helen, putting in view both the 'pearl' and the contaminated 'carrion'. Anthony Ward designed a world for Sam Mendes' 1990 *Troilus and Cressida* littered with the junk of every conflict in history since Troy. Costumes made characters walking palimpsests. Agamemnon, in a slack, moth-eaten cardigan worn over an antique Roman breastplate, had to rifle through the debris of screwed-up briefing papers and scummy coffee mugs on the generals' map table to find his nameplate to shake under Aeneas's nose when the Trojan asked incredulously, 'Is this the great Agamemnon's tent?' Achilles, dangerous, hooded-eyed, his hair greased to outshine his leather trousers, his muscles on display under his black string vest, sat propped in the entrance to his tent, munching popcorn. Ulysses looked like Ulysses S. Grant;

Plate 13 Helen of Troy as gold-wrapped parcel. Sally Dexter in Sam Mendes' 1990 *Troilus and Cressida*.

Source: Joe Cocks photograph. Courtesy of The Shakespeare Centre Library, The Shakespeare Birthplace Trust, Stratford-upon-Avon.

118

Ajax, like the thing that lurks in the sado-masochist's basement in *Pulp Fiction*.

In 3.1, Pandarus, in white flannels and a striped Henley blazer that made one wonder how, after seven years' siege in Troy, he managed to keep up his 'Hooray-Henry' appearance, played straight man, for once, to an even camper servant whose lines on the 'mortal Venus' ushered in four bearers, carrying on to the darkened stage a palanquin. On it, a figure seated like a Buddha was wound round and round in a cloth-of-gold shroud. Paris presided over a choreography that was half ritual, half striptease and felt as if it must be his daily worship at this profane shrine to 'love's visible soul', for as he held the end of the gold cloth he walked in languid circles, and layer by layer unwrapped the parcel to Pandarus's goggle eyes. Underneath was Helen in red chiffon, as steamily voluptuous as Jane Russell, as dangerously desirable as her weight in dark chocolate. But the spectators' disappointment was audible. Was this the face that launched the thousand ships? It wasn't that she wasn't beautiful – simply that she wasn't enough. And that was the point. The design image contained its own interrogation. Was any woman worth this war? No. Was 'Helen', then, merely a legitimating fiction for the violence men intended

Plate 14 Helen of Troy (unwrapped) and Paris. Sally Dexter and John Warnaby in Sam Mendes' 1990 *Troilus and Cressida*.
Source: Joe Cocks photograph. Courtesy of The Shakespeare Centre Library, The Shakespeare Birthplace Trust, Stratford-upon-Avon.

to commit? Yes. Helen-the-woman was made over as totem, packaged by the politicians' PR men like some Golden Calf designed by Cadburys. As Sally Dexter played her, Helen was ripe, full-blown; her slow groping of Pandarus was, like lava flowing, a natural force. Her sudden insight that 'this love will undo us all' was as prophetic as any of Cassandra's visions, and as tragic, since, like hers, it was ignored.

In 1998, Tom Piper (in Michael Boyd's production) took the ritual-ization of Helen – and the troping of the erotic with the sacred that Ward's design had suggested – much further. In Piper's world, worship of the 'mortal Venus' was the national religion, Helen the divine to whom men knelt and the icon they used to front their political cause. And both icon and cause were debased.

Piper set *Troilus and Cressida* in a spare, whitewashed room, just across the Irish border into the IRA badlands, or perhaps in the Balkans. The Trojans had Irish accents; the room looked as if it had survived Sarajevo. The walls were bullet scarred, blackened with shelling. The stained glass fanlight was blown out over the altar in the corner (all that was left of any furniture), where a life-sized statue of the Blessed Virgin stood presiding over and inciting sectarian slaughter, a permanent spec-tator on human atrocity, her palms turned serenely outwards, distributing balm. Mostly, everyone ignored her, though clearly this was the 'doll' they were 'doin' it for'. But when Pandarus, a lank-haired Dublin clubman, alcoholic-gaunt, came looking for Paris in 3.1 he found black-shawled women kneeling in front of the Virgin, keening. There was something odd about the devotion, though. The priest, a Rumpelstiltskin transvestite in a surplice and skull cap who, like some-thing out of Breughel, punned leering profanities under the statue's holy gaze, clearly disconcerted Pandarus – he turned to go. But when he moved, the statue's head swivelled. Paris emerged from under her skirts in a backward somersault, wiping his pleasure off his grinning lips as he landed, sprawled, at Pandarus's astonished feet. The 'Virgin' descended from her plinth as her votresses cackled. Here was Helen.

The body swap was more than a *trompe l'oeil*. The gag worked in two directions, retrospectively to re-inform the notion of the Virgin who sanctifies slaughter as holy cause, but also pre-emptively, to substitute Helen (played by Sara Stewart) for Virgin and then to rewrite worship as blasphemy. Here was the stuff of farce: outrageous, impudent, carniva-lesque, but also offensive, iconoclastic. In representing a 'war for a placket' as a religious conflict, the image extended its reference beyond the play's local disputes to register all war as a version of lechery and war's 'sacrifice' as sacrilege.

Thirty years earlier, in 1968, the iconic – and iconoclastic – bodies

John Barton's production was interested in were male. While theatre censorship was still in force in England, the pressure theatre practitioners had been bringing to bear for years was finally reaching the crisis that would finish off the censor, but not until September. Barton's *Troilus* opened in August. Meanwhile, Ken Tynan's all-British *Oh! Calcutta!*, an erotic revue compiled of transvestite striptease, sex-fantasy tableaux ('a nun being raped by her confessor'), documentary (the history of underwear) and *outré* sketches (by John Lennon, David Mercer and Joe Orton) opened in New York. Lesbianism, simulated sex, 'all kinds of fetishes and sexual ambiguities' were in. But male homosexuality, was out. Tynan specifically excluded it as perhaps a taboo too far.[17]

If so, Barton, back in provincial England, and under the Lord Chamberlain's nose, used Shakespeare to put homosexuality squarely in view on the RSC stage. His designer, Timothy O'Brien, was inspired by

Plate 15 Achilles in drag as Helen of Troy. Alan Howard in John Barton's 1968
    Troilus and Cressida.
Source: Gordon Goode photograph. Courtesy of The Shakespeare Centre Library, The Shakespeare Birthplace Trust, Stratford-upon-Avon.

121

Attic vase painting to create 'friezes of bare-torsoed warriors in tiny kilts and huge, bird-like helmets'. Achilles was 'overtly homosexual', a 'high-camp posturer in tight gold braids', Hector, just as overtly, hetero – but his combat with Ajax was charged with homoeroticism, the warriors, like wrestlers, stripped to 'minuscule breech-clouts, buttocks and biceps straining'. Looking like 'metallic crested cock-birds' Barton's Trojans and Greeks met in a 'perverse iron mating dance', their combat a form of homosexual seduction desired by both sides.[18]

Women, though, were marginalized. Helen, modelled on late-1960s icons (Diana Dors, Jean Shrimpton – two brands of sex object instantly known to consumers), lounged on a litter in 3.1, her platinum blonde hair cascading down her back, a consciously clichéd representation. Later, though, Barton invented a return for Helen designed spectacularly to blow cliché apart . Hector's sportive combat with Ajax (4.5) was over and Greeks and Trojans were pursuing sport indeed, half-drunk from Agamemnon's conviviality, crowding towards Achilles's tent for the serious 'sport' to ensue. A flurry of movement in the direction of Troy turned attention to entering servants, carrying the litter everyone recognized. Menelaus sprang forward to claim his wife, the reclining figure whose blonde hair could be seen under her veil. But when the veils parted, it wasn't Helen but Achilles in drag in a lookalike Helen wig, enticingly opening his woman's wrap, displaying himself naked and inviting Hector to mount him. Later, as the midnight party scene reached its orgiastic climax, Achilles' 'Helen', wanting sex, beckoned Thersites ('a jigging carcass of syphilitic sores with a phallic red tongue lolling from a snoutish mask over his groin') – a shockingly diseased and distorted vision that burst apart both the apotheosis of Helen as icon and the idea of desire mapped on to her mortal body.[19]

All of these designs on Helen collaborated with Shakespeare's political narrative in *Troilus and Cressida*: they understood at a deep structural level how violence appropriates the erotic in this play, how blood is the warrior's keenest aphrodisiac. Male politics in *Troilus and Cressida* needs the woman, needs her, mystified, to legitimate its practices; needs her, objectified, to serve its objectives. In short, it needs Helen's discursive body as pretext. So it produces her as object, but in such a way that her performative body 'reduces' to mere mortality, demystified. Indeed, these designers were canny in showing how the 'real' Helen recedes, blocked by her images (the golden parcel, the benign statue) so that finally in Barton, as in Euripides and Herodotus, Helen isn't even on the scene. When Barton returned to this play for a third time, in 1976, Paris kept Helen on a golden leash; the Trojans, in council, represented her as a golden mask. But the Greeks possessed Helen, too: theirs, a life-sized

Plate 16 'Love, love, nothing but love!' for Helen, Paris, and Pandarus. Katia
     Caballero, Ray Fearon and Clive Francis in Ian Judge's 1996 *Troilus
     and Cressida*.
Source: Malcolm Davies photograph. Courtesy of The Shakespeare Centre Library, The
Shakespeare Birthplace Trust, Stratford-upon-Avon.

doll that travelled through the action, picked up and discarded and
finally adopted by Diomedes, the bitterest of her detractors. He flung her
over his shoulder and carried her to Calchas's tent where, propped
against a pillar, she watched his seduction of Cressida.[20]

For Cressida, though, Helen's appearance in 3.1 serves a different purpose: as curtain raiser and pre-text to her first meeting with Troilus.
There in the orchard in 3.2 he, like Paris, will make some such declara-
tion as 'Sweet, above thought I love thee.' Helen, I suggest, is the 'book
of sport' that teaches us to read what's 'set down' for Cressida in the next
scene.

Cressida's Glove

Shakespeare's designs for Helen – however they are fleshed out – manage
our interpretation of the role. Whatever else it is doing, Helen's performance tells a story that exceeds the playtext, teaches a 'politics of design'
and offers strategic information that equips me to return to the question
that frames the 'problem' of this 'problem' play – who is Cressida? In the

costume change in 4.4 Shakespeare tells us: she is something entirely, radically new, the woman who behaves like a man, who betrays like a man.

Certainly, Cressida confesses to a divided self in 3.2, but duplicity
(lived doubleness, internal division: we recognize in her the post-modern
self) is a condition of Cressida's role that Shakespeare maps onto her
from the beginning. Sex is politicized in this play, and she is made chief
spokesman [*sic*] – more ventriloquist than apologist – for the culture's
hypocritical double standards. Cressida is where this play begins, evoked
in the opening scene, the opening line, and variously valued as exotic
merchandise or household comestible. 'Her bed is India,' says Troilus;
'He that will have a cake . . . ,' says Pandarus.

When she enters in 1.2, she seems curiously de-centred, looking 'off',
wondering, 'Who were those went by?' Watchful, her speech is a series of
one-liners, all questions: 'whither . . . ?', 'What . . . ?', 'how . . . ?' But
when Pandarus enters with his interminable gossip she shows herself
knowingly provocative, a practised hypocrite (which, in Greek, is a
player) who stage-manages the scene Pandarus thinks he's directing by
matching wit blow for blow with him. Pandarus uses a fencing metaphor
to confess himself both routed and perplexed by her. 'You are such a
woman, a man knows not at what ward you lie' (l. 264). Is she for-ward?
To-ward? Back-ward? Or perhaps inscrutably in-ward?

We get an insight into the inward Cressida (as stunning as Prince Hal's
volte-face 'I know you all' speech in *1 Henry IV*) when, Pandarus gone, she
instantly transforms herself, shifting from the backchatting colloquial prose
they've been using into rhyming couplets. She discloses a strategy which,
like Prince Hal's, is based on 'knowing' politics – here, sexual politics:

> Words, vows, gifts, tears, and love's full sacrifice
> He offers in another's enterprise;
> But more in Troilus thousand-fold I see
> Than in the glass of Pandar's praise may be;
> Yet hold I off. Women are angels, wooing:
> Things won are done; joy's soul lies in the doing.
> That she belov'd knows naught that knows not this:
> Men prize the thing ungain'd more than it is.
> That she was never yet that ever knew
> Love got so sweet as when desire did sue.
> Therefore this maxim out of love I teach:
> 'Achievement is command; ungain'd beseech.'
> Then though my heart's content firm love doth bear,
> Nothing of that shall from mine eyes appear.
>
> (ll. 286–300)

Two voices seem to be speaking out of this soliloquy, produced by the contradiction between its form and content. The move into iambic pentameter gears up the speech by tautening and formalizing it, affectively pitching it at a higher level of discursive meaning than the chat that preceded it. But the chink and fall of the couplets is reductive; meaning is packaged as apothegm, the dead/deadening letter of inherited culture that cuts off interrogation of 'what everybody knows'. Where has Cressida learned this 'instruction'? Has it migrated from *Hamlet* – 'Fear it, Ophelia'? Here, though, the woman is recruited to voice what she isn't placed to resist, ventriloquizing patriarchal discourse which has been cast, evidently for easy internalizing, in the mnemonics of the nursery rhyme. The speech is neurotic, pragmatic, anti-romantic – yet its form is a sonnet. It's performed as a soliloquy, the theatre address that (supposedly) voices an 'authentic' self, but here it discloses strategic schizophrenia. Love's idealizing iconography, framing 'women' as 'angels wooing', is set against the cynical iconoclasm of 'things won are done'. By this agenda, to win at love, a woman must play false, act double. She must separate instinct from cultural performance, 'is' from 'shows', to divide what her heart holds from what her eyes show. The Cressida who leaves 1.2 has articulated the sexual politics of the divided self, become 'oxymoron militant'.

But if 1.2 casts her as watchful, it also represents her as watching, gazing at the male bodies of Troy's heroes, coming from the field, passing towards Ilium. Such 'passing' emerges as Shakespeare's prime theatrical motif in *Troilus and Cressida*. The Trojans 'pass' in 1.2, the Greeks, in 3.3, drilled by canny Ulysses; Hector passes from Greek to Greek in 4.5 as, earlier in that scene, Cressida passed down the same ranks. Helen passes from Menelaus to Paris, Thersites from Ajax to Achilles. Hostages pass each other in the dawn as unwittingly as Cressida is passed among male voyeurs in 5.2. All of these passings muster bodies across spectators' lines of vision in a choreography of evaluation that presents them for identification, interpretation, comparison, comment – icons provoking iconoclasm. The theatrical point seems to be to register that everyone has a double self. Hector the capitulator, Achilles the oath breaker, Diomedes the soiler, Troilus the savage, all have 'a kind of self' that, like Cressida's, 'resides', fixed, scrupulous and true, but has grafted to it, 'an unkind self, that itself will leave / To be another's fool' (3.2.146–147). If Helen is Cressida's distorted twin, just as certainly, Hector is another (most conspicuously in 4.5 when, expecting him, the Greeks get her instead; then, as she exits, he enters right behind). In *Troilus and Cressida*, such duplicity is the way things are.

And it's the designer who constructs stage pictures that deconstruct these icons. This, I take it, is the point of the strangely symbolist episode in 5.6 when Shakespeare brings on stage the material representation of War, a body in sumptuous armour that Hector hunts to death only to find inside a horror, an already putrefied corpse. The sumptuous armour dismantles everything Hector has invested in chivalry, unsays all his heroic saying and disarms him to Achilles' hero-satirizing slaughter. Shakespeare writes the death of Hector without a trace of sentimentality.

What 5.6 does for the war story, 4.4 does for the love story, dismantling fidelity in the costume change that unsays the saying of Cressida's anguished exit line from 4.2, 'I will not go from Troy.' Twelve lines later, she's back, and her entrance – like Macbeth's in murdered Duncan's 'borrowed robes' or Lear's in 'idle weeds' on Dover beach – writes a world changed. Cressida will 'go from Troy', and the stage picture says it all. Significantly, the glove she gives here with her vow will be recalled, satirically, in the following scene when Hector, swearing 'by Mars his gauntlet', mocks Menelaus: 'Your quondam wife swears still by Venus' glove' (4.5.178). Once again, a stray allusion twins 'false' Helen's career with Cressida's.

Does the costume change 'make Cressid's name the very crown of falsehood'? She does betray Troilus – but that's later. Here, I think something subtler – and harsher – registers, the gap the lovers themselves have acknowledged between desire and act, promise and performance. 'The will is infinite' says Troilus, and 'desire is boundless', but 'the act [is] a slave to limit'. So all those similes of 'big compare' the lovers traded in 3.2 come down in 4.4 to a pair of gloves. Shakespeare writes Cressida's costume change unsentimentally but also impartially, declining to 'make' Cressida anything except a woman with her gloves on dressed for travelling, a woman whose love story could go either way. That's what makes 5.2 so breathtaking a transgression. In 5.2 Cressida acts like Achilles: she betrays Troilus and fidelity as he betrays Hector and heroism. The play doesn't apologize for either of them.

Subsequent designers of this play, however, have overtly simplified things in far from impartial designs that load Cressida's costume change with significance and so over-determine her later scenes. In 1968, in a re-ordering that has become standard, John Barton cut 4.3 and ran 4.2 straight into 4.4. There was no costume change or exchange of tokens, and no doubt about Cressida's aptitude as sexual probationer. This Lolita-like Cressida spilling out of Timothy O'Brien's pseudo-Grecian dress was 'on the point of seducing her uncle before Troilus' came along, and moved on to Diomedes 'with equal facility.'[21] In the Greek camp, she 'gave herself away to the wise Ulysses by the increasing pleasure' with which she responded to the generals' kissing.[22]

Plate 17 Cressida in Troy. Francesca Annis and Mike Gwilym in John Barton's
1976 *Troilus and Cressida*.
Source: Reg Wilson photograph. Courtesy of The Shakespeare Centre Library, The
Shakespeare Birthplace Trust, Stratford-upon-Avon.

127

Plate 18 Cressida 'changed'. Francesca Annis with Achilles (Rosin Ellis) and
Patroclus (Paul Moriarty) in John Barton's 1976 *Troilus and Cressida*.
Source: Reg Wilson photograph. Courtesy of The Shakespeare Centre Library, The
Shakespeare Birthplace Trust, Stratford-upon-Avon.

In 1976 Chris Dyer's design was saner and cooler, but again Barton marginalized women while putting male bodies on display. Achilles and Patroclus strolled through the Greek camp holding hands; Troilus wore more between ankle and knee than between crotch and waist, while Francesca Annis's Cressida was hidden under a full-length jeballah. Again, Barton cut 4.3, erasing Shakespeare's costume change, but this time there was an exchange of tokens. Cressida accepted the heraldic sleeve Troilus had been wearing around his arm before running offstage to collect from the props table the glove she returned and gave him. Stylistically, the glove was 'off' – a *non sequitur* working like a bit of 'fancy dress' in an antique Troy where clearly no one wore gloves. If the token was made undecipherable, Cressida's costume change – placed between 4.4 and 4.5, her arrival in the Greek camp – was entirely legible; she'd apparently changed clothes somewhere *en route*. A Hostage Outfitter's, perhaps, in no-man's-land? She entered wrapped up, but when Diomedes 'symbolically disrobed her' before the generals, he revealed a Cressida metamorphosed into Greek courtesan.[23] The costume made her an exact replica of the Minoan snake goddess (*c.* 1600 BC) – a type of Eve – and offered a level of authenticity nowhere else on view in this production. Here under wraps, said the design, was the *real* Cressida. The laced-up bodice, cinched at the waist, curving into her groin and cupping her breasts with gauze that left her nipples revealed, delivered Cressida, wrote Wardle, as the 'assured sexual specialist whom Ulysses instantly recognizes'. She delighted in the kissing game, which began with Agamemnon chivalrously kissing her hand, proceeded through Achilles outpacing Menelaus to wrap her in his arms, and ended with Ulysses disgustedly shoving her away. An 'emotional gourmet', this Cressida demonstrated 'from the start' that she knew 'herself well enough to realize that she [was] not to be trusted'. Later, with Diomedes, there was 'no suggestion that she [succumbed] reluctantly. As before, she [held] off to make sure of the prize.'[24]

Cressida's wrap – a design motif Dyer borrowed from raver Achilles in 1968 and latterly instituted as a character marker – keeps turning up, on Carol Royle, next, in 1981. As Royle walked through the lines down-stage across no-man's-land, steel grilles clanged into place behind her, a maze that literalized her alienation from home, her new vulnerability as prize – or her new vocation. For when Diomedes unwrapped her for the Greeks and 'she emerge[d] in figure-hugging silk', she was, wrote Billington, 'in the proper sense, existential', as though Cressida were 'defining her character anew'.[25] In 1985 and in 1990 Cressida arrived among the Greeks wrapped in Troilus's greatcoat; in 1996, like a parcel in lengths of silk that came off self-consciously, seductively, helped by

Diomedes, as Victoria Hamilton played her diffident warming to wantonness in front of Troy's siege-scarred walls. Unwrapped, she stood before the generals in a sex-enhancing gold dress cut to point the way to her privates.

In none of these versions did the lovers exchange the sleeve, the glove, and the meanings those tokens trope; instead, ribbons, scarves or armbands played stand-ins. Liz da Costa's Crimean costumes in 1985 were placed to accomplish the signifying work Shakespeare scripts, for in this period design the minute attention to spats, braces, boots and hats evoked a world which would have made total sense of Cressida in 4.4 – if she'd been dressed for Victorian travel, in hat and gloves. Instead, Davies's production violated its own rules of stylistic engagement to opt for heightened sensation and anachronism: Cressida in her nightgown meant, in 4.5, 'anything goes'. All versions made Cressida, arriving in the Greek camp, available to the generals in provocative ways that she was represented – to greater or lesser extent – as self-authoring. Even more telling, da Costa (1985) and Clancy (1996) introduced an additional costume change for Cressida in the night scene with Diomedes (5.2). Juliet Stevenson's Cressida entered looking like a blowsy Carmen, hair down and bunched to dangle over one ear, peasant blouse lowered off her shoulders. Hamilton's, in red gold-shot taffeta – literally, the scarlet woman – dropped yet another wrap as she entered, eyes transfixed on Diomedes who uncovered himself naked to the waist, grappled her, and drove his hungry hand into her crotch. Both costumes were straitjackets for Cressida, imposed, not grown into, that hijacked the scene, closing off all narrative directions but one and leaving no doubt how the assignation with Diomedes would end. The costumes screamed 'whore'. Where had they come from? Certainly nothing in Stevenson's performance had suggested that her Cressida kept anything like that gipsy get-up in her wardrobe. Had she stopped by the same Hostage Outfitter's who kitted out Francesca Annis in 1976?

These productions took Ulysses' word on Cressida. Indeed, in 1996, *Cressida* took his word on Cressida. Fascinated by the carnal, Hamilton's gaze lingered on Diomedes in 4.4 when he first addressed her, and later, she turned to look back at him as Troilus led her away. In 4.5, she was delighted with the kissing 'game' and her own power to deal Menelaus the rebuff that made him the men's laughing stock. Meeting each encounter with pleasure she was clearly unaware that she was performing the steps to an ancient choreography, triple-turning herself from Agamemnon to Achilles to Patroclus – to a whore. Abruptly, though, pleasure stopped when Ulysses trained his silken sarcasm on to her. He held unbroken eye contact as he made her his butt in the 'daughter of the game' speech, shared with his appreciative, leering colleagues ranged behind him who, hearing Hector's flourish sound his arrival from Ilium, bawled in unison, 'The Trojan's trumpet'. Cressida, turning to go, heard them cry 'strumpet'. She froze. Then her head snapped around, to fix her shocked gaze on smug Ulysses, and her face crumpled. Somehow able to read last night's sex with Troilus on her body, he knew she was tainted. In this reading, it was Ulysses who made Cressida a whore.

Stevenson played this scene to a very different conclusion. Her Cressida slapped Agamemnon and wiped the first kiss off with the back of her hand, but her disgust only served as sexual taunt. A split second of suspended animation erupted into the competitive male frenzy of a gang rape, the kisses shoving her from 'encounterer' to 'encounterer'. Cressida left the scene contaminated, her nightgown manhandled, a victim of male violence whose only recourse – it seemed – was Diomedes' protection. But not quite. For Stevenson found in Shakespeare's lines a Cressida who neither solicited the generals nor surrendered to them. Instead she managed utterly to rout them, rebuffing Menelaus with wit that tented his wounded virility to the quick, and putting Ulysses – for the only time in this play – on the losing side of discourse. 'May I, sweet lady, beg a kiss of you?' asked Ulysses. Stevenson's Cressida barked out her answer, 'Why, beg then' and snapped her fingers, gesturing imperiously towards the ground.

Ulysses stood rigid, near meltdown. But once Cressida had gone, he took his revenge behind her back by trashing her as 'daughter of the game', an outburst heard as hysterical over-compensation by Nestor and Agamemnon who swapped significant glances. What Stevenson demonstrated is that Shakespeare's Cressida is no victim, rather, a canny player who scores heavily in the gendered power games of 4.5 and exits having forced Ulysses to expose his own neurosis, not her status. And that means that she enters to Diomedes in 5.2 genuinely un-determined; her betrayal of Troilus is, then, a real choice, so what happens in 5.2 is tragedy, not farce. Ultimately, though, Stevenson couldn't play out what she'd discovered in Shakespeare's text, for given da Costa's deterministic design, a Cressida who still had choices to make in 5.2 was unsustainable. Her 'fancy dress' had already made the choices for her.

In writing Cressida 'authentic Greek courtesan', 'scarlet woman', 'gipsy jilt', 'whore', instead of, as Shakespeare designs her, a woman with her gloves on, each of these productions implicated itelf in the very practices the play sets up for satire – simply reproducing the 'natural' misogyny the narrative circulates for derision and discredit. They could see well enough what was going on in the other half of the play, that the war narrative is Shakespeare's satire on chivalry, for they clarified that by design. Plainly, though, they weren't reading Shakespeare's sexual satire in *Troilus and Cressida*.

Is Shakespeare's 'text' so difficult? Let me unravel what those productions didn't interrogate, the tangled logic of patriarchal discourse this play puts on trial, by granting their premise – Cressida is a whore – then asking them simply, 'When did she fall?' Was it when she stopped 'hold[ing] . . . off' and went to bed with Troilus? Does sex make a woman a whore? It does in *King Lear* where she who is known only as the 'whoreson['s]' mother gets that title because she has a 'son [Edmund] for her cradle ere she has a husband for her bed' (1.1.12). Sex is inevitably generative in Shakespeare. Recall Helena, triumphantly pregnant after Bertram's 'one-night stand' in *All's Well*, or Isabella, militant for chastity in *Measure*, arguing the straight move from the single act of unlawful sex to unlawful progeny. See, too, her 'sisters', Julietta and Kate Keepdown, the one, a 'fornicatress', the other, a 'punk', both of them mothers. In patriarchal discourse, she who bears the illicit child, not he who fathers it, is criminalized. The child is the evidence against her, not him. Then, since only married sex prevents the making of whoresons, it follows that all women who commit unmarried sex must be whores. And their crime, written (as it must be) on their body, is conspicuously legible.

Observe that in *Troilus and Cressida* while nobody, not Pandarus, Troilus or Cressida, talks of marriage, they do talk of the other ('if my lord get a boy of you . . . ,' leers Pandarus). But this must mean that in taking Cressida to an unmarried bed Troilus, the play's Petrarchan idealist, adventurer to India for perfect pearls, emblem of virginity and swearer of 'truest' vows that 'truth can speak truest', is a maker of whores. He's following the career of his big brother Paris, one who, 'like a lecher, out of whorish loins' is 'pleas'd to breed out [his] inheritors' (4.1.64–65). Who does this double standard indict: Cressida, Troilus, or a patriarchal set-up that instantiates these sexual politics? If Troilus is responsible for making Cressida a whore, is he not, then, also responsible for making her incapable of being true, since whores, by definition, are 'false'? One could, of course, gloss Troilus's hysteria, 'False, false, false', against Antony's hypocritical railing at Cleopatra, 'I found you as a morsel cold upon / Dead Caesar's trencher' (3.13.121–122). But if Ulysses can read sex on Cressida and call her whore, does this not implicate him as literate in the language 'her foot' supposedly 'speaks'? Is he another Gloucester in *Lear*, a namer of whores because a maker of whores? Or is she legible to Ulysses because her appetite for the carnal, whetted by her first 'dish of fool', grows ravenous and gives her away as she samples the generals? In this reading, Troilus's mistake was to throw

132

himself, raw meat, to a carnivore. And what of Diomedes, he who impre-
cates against 'puling cuckold[s]' and dishonour-palating 'lecher[s]', who
sees that whores make men monsters, if not that men make women
whores. If Cressida is a whore, what is he, her 'encounterer'?

The satiric truth is that men in this play need the whore like they need
the goddess. Helen and Cressida anchor the third term, hold down the
notional place of the 'beloved' in the permutating series of erotic triangles Shakespeare's narrative sets up: Cressida, Troilus, Pandarus;
Cressida, Calchas, Antenor; Cressida, Troilus, Diomedes; Cressida,
Patroclus, Thersites; Helen, Menelaus, Paris; Helen, Pandarus,
Alexander; Helen, Hector, Troilus. None of these are equilateral. They're
skewed because they are everywhere predicated on a kind of queasy
voyeurism, displacement or surrogacy – the pander at the door, at the
elbow – that frames them as deviant. But this local 'queering' of relationships works to expose cultural asymmetries, in terms Eve Sedgwick
has taught us to read, that foreground an essential incongruity. In these
triangles, women figure in the erotic equation, *but don't count*. For what
these triangles are actually tracing is a 'calculus of power' that is struc-
tured between men, that traffics in women as 'exchangeable, perhaps
symbolic, property' whose 'primary purpose' is to 'cement the bonds of
men with men'. The woman is the '"conduit of a relationship" in which
the true *partner* is a man'.[26] In the Sonnets, as Sedgwick observes, this
exchange between men is celebrated. Male to male exchange sets its
'heterosexualizing campaign' in a 'context of heterosexual socialization'
where desire functions to 'consolidate partnership with authoritative
males in and through the bodies of females'.[27] In *Troilus and Cressida*,
though, the homosocial is trashed, the 'conduit' polluted, and the
exchange contaminated, debased and infected. Men are not homophobic
in this play. They don't fear men; it's worse than that. They despise
them, mock them, satirize them, humiliate them, hold them as abjects in
contempt. That is, they treat them like women. The male desire this play
traffics in deracinates male bonding. In their separate erotic triangles,
Helen and Cressida still figure as the *tertium quid* that, like the surveyor's apparatus, works to fix other positions. But where they stand,
how they are represented, positions the audience to inspect the patriarchal edifice – like Troy, a monolith (but already shifting on its 'basis',
doomed); like the Greek camp, hollow factions holed up in hollow tents,
as though to trope empty ideology. From the point of view of design, it
is critical to Shakespeare's discursive project in *Troilus and Cressida* that
Cressida be put in view as a woman who does not absorb the gaze but
rather reflects it back; that we see her, not sensational in herself, but neu-
tral, a woman in gloves. What Shakespeare's satire requires us to attend

to are the male practices that construct Cressida. The men, not the costume, make her the whore.

Alternative Positions

There is, I am arguing, a subversive Cressida-play inside *Troilus and Cressida*. If directors and designers haven't quite found it yet it may be because, in the post-war theatre, the play has been captured for other cultural work – men's work. And if contemporary accounts are to be believed, the capture was purely accidental. When John Barton submitted his production budget for his 1968 *Troilus* the men in the finance office of the perennially strapped-for-cash RSC came back to him with worries – wasn't all the armour his designer wanted for the warriors 'going to come a bit expensive'? Barton agreed he could cut costs by putting his warriors in skirts, the 'tiny kilts' or 'baby-doll shorts and jockstraps' reviewers saw on opening night that were, after all, 'traditional' – which Barton, a classicist as well as a director, knew perfectly well.[28] In the war scenes, Barton thought his boys could save even more production money by stripping nearly naked – to breech cloths – coincidentally making the whole design concept authentic by summoning up images

Plate 19 Warriors stripped for combat. John Barton's 1968 *Troilus and Cressida*.
Source: Gordon Goode photograph. Courtesy of The Shakespeare Centre Library, The Shakespeare Birthplace Trust, Stratford-upon-Avon.

from Attic pottery of muscled wrestlers in clinches and lithe runners in perpetual hot-foot pursuit around the surfaces of wine jars. Thus associated, naked male flesh would be read (without censors' objections) through the classics.

This account may come close to the truth. Money did matter, and 'tradition', strategically wheeled in, could satisfactorily authenticate the lavish undress urged by the budget. But I suspect Barton had more up his sleeve than a deficit. In 1968 the hot topic was sex, and Barton was perfectly placed to debate it. For the theatre is one of the public spaces where cultures practise sex, where they perform representations of what they recognize as a standard repertoire, but also where they rehearse alternative positions. I'm thinking here of Louis Montrose's 'anti-structures', his notion that performance promotes cultural innovation by putting into play 'marginal experiences that do not simply invert structural norms but rather temporarily liberate "human capacities of cognition, affect, volition, creativity" from their usual constraints' into a space where they can contemplate change.[29] If Barton didn't imagine Cressida's radical possibilities as 'anti-structure', he did see *Troilus and Cressida* as a text for speculating on the anti-structural possibilities of other 'marginal experiences'. On his stage, near-naked male bodies would embrace in voluptuous combat that registered war as copulation between male partners. In short, Barton would invent *Troilus and Cressida* – protected by 'Shakespeare', guarantor of High Culture – as theatre's core text for representing homoerotic desire and homosexual subculture long in advance of any cultural theorization of these issues in academic, gay or straight analysis.

Famously, Philip Larkin put a date on these things in Britain: 'Sexual intercourse began / In nineteen sixty-three.'[30] Six years earlier, Arthur Miller's *A View from the Bridge* was refused a public performance licence in London by a Lord Chamberlain who objected to its Act 2 'homosexual' kiss. Four years later, Joe Orton, cultural anarchist and Jack Cade of black camp, urged himself in his diary as he revised *What the Butler Saw*, 'Sex is the only way to infuriate [the over-30s Establishment]. Much more fucking and they'll be screaming hysterics in next to no time.'[31] From the opposite end of the political spectrum, Law Lord Patrick Devlin agreed with Orton: since sexuality, he claimed, possessed an inherently subversive power, sex was a subversive activity which the law had a duty to suppress.[32] The following season, Tynan's anti-suppressant *Oh! Calcutta!* opened in New York, and Barton's *Troilus and Cressida*, in Stratford. Review headlines greeted it with *double entendres*: 'A Queer Twist to Shakespeare'; 'Meanwhile, back at the Trojan camp . . .'; 'Achilles's fatal flaw'.[33] Harold Hobson in *The Sunday Times* thought it contained scenes 'as daring as I expect to see even after the censorship is abolished', and Ronald Bryden in *The Observer* commented parenthetically that '(in actual area of revealed human skin, London's avant garde cellars [the private subscription theatres where the Lord Chamberlain's writ of censorship didn't extend] lag acres behind the Avon)'.[34]

Of course, Barton's interpretation could have justified itself to its critics as simply picking up what's thick on the ground in Shakespeare's text, its (sexualized) interrogation of male power positions which casts the husband Menelaus as a 'puling cuckold' and the lover Paris, under Helen's power, as 'womanish' (what early modern usage meant by 'effeminate'). His little brother looks to be going along the same route:

> Call here my varlet, I'll unarm again.
> Why should I war without the walls of Troy,
> That find such cruel battle here within? (1.1.1–3)

After the Prologue, these are the opening lines of the play, and its keynote. Masculinity is hysterically stressed out in *Troilus and Cressida*, and men are no better than limp-wristed 'luvvies'. 'Dainty' Achilles 'Lies . . . / Upon a lazy bed' while Patroclus, 'like a strutting player', 'pageants' the generals in scurrilous jokes, mocking the 'still and mental parts' of war as girls' stuff – 'bed-work, mapp'ry, closet-war' (1.3). Is this what so infuriates Ulysses, that Achilles is making a girl out of him? It looks like love of Patroclus is keeping Achilles in bed; in fact, it's a woman, 'one of Priam's daughters'. So, like Paris and Troilus, Achilles is 'girled' by love. Effeminacy, not homosexuality, is Ulysses' taunt in 3.3 (though on Barton's stage, these two would be conflated). When Achilles' masculinity collapses in 5.1 the 'boy' Patroclus is roused to desperate virility, arming himself as Achilles in the armour everyone recognizes. But to this performance, he's only a travesty player-quean whose 'conceit / Lies in his hamstring'. Patroclus falls before Hector, the 'boy-queller', like a girl.

What Barton did in 1968, when 'homosexuality' was still the only term reviewers knew for describing what they saw on stage, was to use this densely problematic male text to speculate on alternative masculinities, to 'practise sex' under cover of an 'Establishment' text located via design in an ancient Greek past (where, it could be supposed, they certainly did things like that, and did them differently).[35] In this 'tribal Mediterranean world where wealth consists in bracelets, herds and lives taken', it was natural (wasn't it?) for 'bare-torsoed warriors' to strip to G-strings to meet in combat performed as a 'mating display perverted from its natural use towards each other, and death'.[36] Natural (wasn't it?) for

Hector's meeting with Achilles to present a 'kind of travesty marriage', and for that orgiastic rite between 'high-camp posturer' and seductive hard-man to reach orgasmic climax with the couple locked together, Achilles' legs wrapped around Hector's waist.

Of course, every level of this representation contained distortion. Alan Howard's 'extraordinary Achilles: a prancing, bespangled queen with dyed blonde hair and shaved legs' was recognized by reviewers as an 'absurdly sensational piece of exaggeration' for, they pointed out, neither Homer's nor Shakespeare's Achilles was homosexual but rather 'decently bisexual, like Plato's Alcibiades and a million other virile young Greeks.'[37] Barton quite wittingly queered what, as an academic, he certainly knew about erotic culture in the classical world where the virility of the homosexual orientation of male desire was self-evident. But unwittingly, he also queered what wouldn't be known about early modern erotic culture until Alan Bray's *Homosexuality in Renaissance England* discovered it a decade later, that practices called 'homosexual' for the first time in the 1890s were scattered among various possibilities in the 1590s, none of them synonymous with Victorian 'homosexuality'.[38] So Howard's Achilles didn't belong to Homer's Sparta or to Shakespeare's London, but he didn't belong to Swinging Sixties Chelsea either. He was actually a high camp anachronism left over from the 1940s, reminiscent of 'flaming' Quentin Crisp patrolling Portsmouth for 'something in uniform', whose get-up in drag as Helen tied transvestism to homosexuality and homosexuality to 'whoops-my-dear' effeminacy – a Gordian knot of pop-culture stereotyping that Marjorie Garber is still trying to disentangle thirty years later.[39]

Still, such distortions – witting or unwitting – were insignificant compared to Barton's audacious achievement. His 'Greek camp' put on mainstream view a representation of a subculture whose post-war urban presence was increasingly visible and articulate,[40] and he associated that subculture not just with effeminacy in Achilles but with virility in Hector, Ajax, Aeneas, Antenor, all of them displaying bodies that celebrated masculinity in built physiques. For while Barton had waived his costume budget, he'd 'insisted' that 'the soldiers' physiques . . . would have to look convincing', so he sent his actors to the gym for weight training, 'a body-building course,' said the *Daily Mail* under the headline 'Tough for Trojans', designed 'to fill out their uniforms'.[41] (Did the *Mail* know those 'uniforms' were G-strings?) If audiences had ever seen anything like these spectacularly built bodies where muscle mass troped male potency and everything – almost – showed, it would have been in the movies, in peplum films. Richard Dyer counts some forty-five of these films in London between 1957 and 1965. Peplum films were practically the only place where male nudity, that is, white male nudity or even semi-nudity, was on view in popular fiction until the 1980s. Low-budget, mostly Italian-made, these adventure flicks inspired by classic texts from Homer to the Old Testament featured heroes called Hercules, Ulysses, Spartacus – sometimes side by side – who came on screen in posing pouches and skimpy skirts – the 'pepla' – to face every adversity from roaring lions to massed armies wearing little more than muscle definition.[42] Putting his Greeks and Trojans in pepla Barton recruited to his project imagery that was both elite and popular, classical and contemporary, glamorous and B-grade, hetero and homo, since peplum he-men were desired by both sexes. This was imagery that equipped theatre reviewers of *Troilus and Cressida* to read the 'voluptuous' exchange when Hector squared up for combat with Ajax as both erotic and virile, homo and hetero. Homosexuality worked in this production like one of Montrose's 'anti-structures', representing itself not (or not only) as lassie-laddism between poofters, a residual cultural idea, but, framed in the discursive terms of an emergent cultural idea, as male power. In succeeding years, it would be this second image of gay culture, as empowered, confident and defiantly unheterosexual, that would move out of theatre's cultural rehearsal rooms and onto Britain's streets and full public awareness.

In the event, however, Barton's direction turns out to have been very costly for *Troilus and Cressida*. His first write-off was Cressida, for as one reviewer after another observed, in Barton's '"boys-will-be-boys-my-dears" environment', Cressida 'hardly gets a look in'.[43] His second write-off was the play itself. In 1968, Barton's ideas were outrageous, anti-Establishment, agitational – they declared this play up for grabs and continuous rethinking. In 1976 they returned – the 'standard' reading of the play. And then this 'standard' subsequently settled into the 'authorized' *Troilus and Cressida* that directors have been reproducing ever since. Where the theatre imitates itself, not life, however, it grows decadent, reactionary. So, in 1976, when, again, Achilles was 'a camp queen', Irving Wardle found Barton's self-quotation dulling: 'We never sense the deadly killer inside the preening superstar, and for all his displays of giggling hysteria he never gets the chance to go the whole hog with Hector in his tent.'[44] By 1981, the theatre's failure to keep pace with street politics and gay culture in the 'real' world cost it credibility. Paris's 'orgy with a group of mincing acolytes' and Achilles's 'rouged nipples' and 'salacious dance, fingers clicking and bracelets jangling' weren't offensive because they shocked 'straight' morality but because they mindlessly quoted clichés that grotesquely travestied gay relationships.[45] As Robert Cushman observed, the RSC's 'reactionary equation of homosexuality

Plate 20 Hector meets Achilles with Troilus behind – Greek 'camp'. Louis Hilyer, Philip Quast and Joseph Fiennes in Ian Judge's 1996 *Troilus and Cressida*.
Source: Malcolm Davies photograph. Courtesy of The Shakespeare Centre Library, The Shakespeare Birthplace Trust, Stratford-upon-Avon.

with decadence once thrilled the critics [but] it destroyed the company's credibility with everyone else for nearly a decade. It's hardly worth reviving now.'[46] Yet it continued to be revived. In 1996, Ian Judge recycled the same worn sensations, but now the gap between cultural discourse and theatre cliché was obvious to everybody. So Judge's homosexualized narratives read like self-parody in a production that was universally slated: 'Bare buttocks galore'; 'A triumph for the wrong camp'; 'like Frankie Howerd in a camp sit-com called Up Phrygia'; 'sexuality is everywhere and nowhere, spreading a tired theatrical gloss on passion and eroticism'.[47] Within the space of thirty years, Barton's subversive undress

139

dwindled into Judge's decorative 'fancy dress', where it provided no leverage for dislodging the performance stereotypes it circulated but merely indulged 'feelgood camp'.

But where does this leave Cressida? Mostly, without 'a look in', for Barton set in motion a cultural hijack of this text at the RSC that has appropriated it for coy flirtation with sexual decadence and a safely dangerous fantasy of homosexuality which, carried out for homosocial purposes, has produced increasingly narcissistic, thoroughly Othered, self-reflections ever since. The play, locked by productions in a closed circle of congratulation that misses Shakespeare's satire entirely, turns out to be about men and their partnerships, not radical, but retro. It reproduces the structures of male exchange that Sedgwick observed in the Sonnets and a disenchanted women's movement observes in culture at large. Back in Barton's 1968, the Wilson government instituted legal reforms of birth control, divorce and abortion (along with homosexuality and theatre censorship), but the emergent ideology still retained 'time-honoured' residual assumptions about dominance and subordination. Female sexuality might be recognized in a way it had not been before, but it was still constructed from the point of view of the male.[48] Forty years on, Cressida is still a casualty of 1960s-style conservative politics. When Juliet Stevenson's 'changed' Cressida is produced as gipsy slut, or Victoria Hamilton's, as scarlet woman, we are seeing costume masking political appropriation.

* * *

Smart actors learn how Shakespeare's design works and how to collaborate with him to author themselves. Simon Russell Beale, in 1990, brilliantly consulted what he called the 'institutionalized machismo' of Shakespeare's text to discover for Thersites an alternative position, as both insider and outsider, that enabled him to critique the range of masculinities the play has on offer, from Ajax's absurd self-obsession with his own magnificence to Achilles' dangerous, self-annulling egotism and Patroclus's debilitating neutrality. Russell Beale figured Thersites's dissidence in his costume, which he compiled out of cultural signifiers that operated as self-parody. His filthy pinstriped trousers held up by an Eton tie had clearly lived a previous life in the City, while his flasher's mac with its CND and Gay Lib badges (a bizarre reinvention of Cressida's wrap) had just as clearly been a regular in Soho. Topping out this get-up, though, the leather skull cap tied incongruously like a baby bonnet under his chin made him look like a WWI fighter pilot or a seventeenth-century alchemist. This Thersites intellectually disdained the stupidity of war. It was hard to tell whether he wore his surgical gloves to cover some hideous disease or to protect himself from contamination by forced fraternizing with dolts whose suicidal idiocy might be infectious. The bile he spat was more than metaphor. It dripped like a condiment into Ajax's silver-service dinner which the muscle-bound dope proceeded to scoff. 'He reminds you,' said Paul Taylor, 'of an anthropomorphized storybook animal – Toad, say, dressed up as the washerwoman.'[49] When Russell Beale's Thersites had had enough of Ajax's numbskulled cuffing and packed up to change sides, protruding from the stuff stuffed inside his plastic carrier bag was his jester's bauble, a curious antique from a sweeter, vanished age. At the end, when he was left after Cressida's last exit, he picked up the scarf she'd dropped and, curious, sniffed it. This Thersites, then, was a pastiche of English culture that summoned male power images to dismantle them.

Actors who are less inquiring or less powerfully placed to challenge their director's design concept will be victimized by costume. In the RSC's 1998 touring production of *Troilus and Cressida*, for example, Patroclus was cross-cast. Elaine Pyke played him transvestite as a boyish figure reminiscent of Julie Andrews's *Victor/Victoria*, in 1920s trousers, waistcoat and cropped hair. 'Not altogether fortunate casting,' wrote Paul Taylor, 'since it makes Achilles look as though he's knocking off the Winslow Boy.'[50] More damagingly, the costume, not erasing the actor's gender but inviting the audience to read the female body beneath, played disturbingly, and worse, misogynistically, with this sexualized ambiguity, most explicitly in 4.5. Shakespeare's hostage exchange has Patroclus taking two kisses from Cressida; this production lingered over those kisses, charging them with a disturbing eroticism that exploited the sensation of same-sex coupling. Then, as a finale to the hand-over, Patroclus took Cressida in his – or was it her? – arms and began to dance, slowly and sensuously, a tango that troped sex. Reviewers read this as male rape; young women spectators, as the director's lesbian fantasy, which deliberately recruited the cross-dressed woman to the business of shaming and polluting Cressida.[51] In the 'fancy dress' this production devised, Pyke's Patroclus was finally as much a hostage to representation as Cressida was to fortune – a further demonstration of design's power, as Michael Ratcliffe observed, to 'flatter or disturb the dreams of spectators'. Where costume is concerned, the theatre's interests are always vested.

5

REMEMBERING EMILIA

Gossiping hussies, revolting housewives

The status of the evidence required to reconstruct performances depends on the success of two necessarily problematic procedures – spectating and tattling . . . Often the best hedge against amnesia is gossip.

Joseph Roach, *Cities of the Dead*, 1996

Hedging Amnesia

The remembering I want to do begins with a performance memory from *Othello*, an image of two women, close together, talking. (In its way, the image is arresting because so unexpected. Nothing has prepared for it. Before now, men have been intimate, men have put their heads together and gossiped while women have kept aloof from each other, the one wary; the other, oblivious.) Now, one woman sits, undressed to her bodice, almost a child, ready for bed. Her head 'hang[s] all at one side', her chin pressing on to her bare shoulder, sagging dispiritedly. The other has helped her 'unpin', letting down her plaits, removing petticoat and corset, layer after layer of Victorian white lawn and linen, kind clothes for the heat of Cyprus. Now she stands behind her, erect, hands deft, brushing her hair. Their bodies seem suspended in the surrounding darkness, illuminated only by the oil lamp on the dressing table. One tells a story that the moaning wind in the background makes haunting, ghostly: 'My mother had a maid call'd Barbary . . .' Then she starts to sing, pummelling her fist against her heart, almost in mockery of the song's lament: 'Willow, willow, willow.'

They share gossip: 'This Lodovico is a proper man'; 'I know a lady in Venice would have walk'd barefoot to Palestine for a touch of his nether lip.' And with the gossip, they share other contraband, illicit information:

142

Plate 21 'This Lodovico is a proper man.' Emilia (Zoe Wanamaker) unpins
      Desdemona (Imogen Stubbs) and gossips in Trevor Nunn's 1989
      Othello.
Source: Joe Cocks photograph. Courtesy of The Shakespeare Centre Library, The
Shakespeare Birthplace Trust, Stratford-upon-Avon.

> O, these men, these men!
> Dost thou in conscience think, – tell me, Emilia, – . . .

Their intimacy produces secrets: the contents of the one locked drawer the enraged husband shook and tugged but could not open when, so short a time ago, he ransacked the room for evidence of adultery. Now, as one woman looks furtively away, the other, big-eyed with anticipated danger, finds a key. The drawer yields its cache – a child-sized box of chocolates. The women, like schoolgirls, their nervousness burst with a peal of laughter, hunch up side by side conspiratorially to share the sweets and their final reflections which the chocolates will do nothing to sweeten: 'I do not think there is any such woman.'

The older woman, the one with the deep voice, gravelly from years of hauling itself over shag tobacco and up the stem of the little pipe she habitually smokes (or perhaps from other abuse) responds: 'Yes, a dozen.' Then she sits, hands folded in her lap, gazing steadily out into the far distance, into the black hole that is her marriage, and adds more:

> But I do think it is their husbands' faults
> If wives do fall . . .

Later, their heads will lie close together one last time as again they share perplexity in secret knowledge:

> What did thy song bode, lady?
> Hark, canst thou hear me? . . . Willow, willow, willow.

Remembering Emilia

This quiet scene of women's intimacy, conversation, gossip, is one I am remembering from Zoe Wanamaker's extraordinary performance of Emilia opposite Imogen Stubbs in Trevor Nunn's chamber play *Othello* at the RSC's Other Place in 1989 (then on film for television a year later). It reminds me of the moment late in *Hamlet* when, Osric just gone, Horatio and the prince converse. 'If it be now,' Hamlet reflects ''tis not to come. If it be not to come, it will be now. If it be not now, yet it will come . . . Let be.' His repose, his willingness to 'Let be', seems to speak beyond immediate anxieties, to release him from the traumatic imperative that has mandated his life in the play – the male obligation to revenge. In 'Let be,' Hamlet achieves the knowledge he needs to live – then exits to the duel. So in *Othello* Emilia finds in the unique privacy of this women's scene, which privileges women's talk, women's bodies, women's thoughtful work upon the cultural imperatives that organize their lives, reflections that, while they do not release women from patriarchal confines, at least claim some space for manoeuvre, some terms of survival and settlement within them. 'Then let men know . . . ,' says Emilia, finding the knowledge Desdemona needs to live. But even as she speaks, she is preparing Desdemona for the bed she has laid with her wedding/winding sheets, the bed both of them will occupy, not long hence, as corpses.

I want to re-read *Othello* through Wanamaker's performance, a performance that opened up Emilia's story to detailed scrutiny, putting in view what it invited spectators to read as the suppressed narrative of Shakespeare's play, a narrative whose subject is suppression. Wanamaker understood *Othello* as a failed gossip text, the secrets women share unable to save their lives, and Emilia as profoundly tragic: she located her tragedy in the staggering discoveries that Emilia, a naively collusive patriarchal abject, made about male power. The prize, and price, of her hard learning was nothing less than her voice, a voice that welled up in her throat involuntarily, almost as if strangled, but once released, spoke 'liberal as the air'. It defied silencing to assert the clamorous truth that rewrites Desdemona's ending by redeeming her contaminated death from slander. Paying for speaking, Emilia dies, but not before, in Wanamaker's performance, she rewrote abjection as female heroism, reconfiguring the entire map of the play's meaning to let spectators see a 'secret' *Othello* inside the play they thought they knew.[1] *Othello* is a narrative of strangeness, of 'erring barbarians', cannibals and anthropophagi, the 'unhoused' of Othello's so resonant expression – a race narrative that puts Othello at its centre. But Wanamaker's Emilia showed it to be as powerfully, as problematically a narrative of the familiar, the 'housed', grounded in a domestic narrative of true and truant housekeeping. Men in this play look outwards (from windows, citadels, battlements), and they fraternize over a world map whose patriarchal territories they make it their business to police – 'Rhodes . . . Cyprus . . . other grounds, / Christian and heathen' (1.1.29–30). Women are located in interior spaces, confined in the father's house, admonished to 'speak indoors', their management directed to 'house affairs'. All the women of this play are 'housewives'. As if to express the futility of their culture's project to restrict them, however, the very tropes that confine women 'indoors' in *Othello* simultaneously undo confinement, offer women 'outdoors', as 'public commoner[s]' (4.2.75), transgressives. So Bianca, the 'housewife', is, oxymoronically, also a 'customer', transacting business in a marketplace where, 'selling her desires', she 'Buys herself bread and clothes' (4.1.94–95). Desdemona is the 'hussy', truant to her 'house affairs' who, evidently itching for excitement across her father's threshold, idles over the outlandish traveller's tale. Emilia is told to 'speak indoors' because, conspicuously, she is speaking 'out'. These transactions between outward and inward neatly, if unwittingly, collude with Iago's project of ocular manipulation, his scheme to 'puddle' men's seeing by turning the masterful outward gaze obsessively inward, on to unmappable female interiors. When men 'discover' that they can know domestic space only as unknowable, housekeeping fails in *Othello*, women leave home. Ultimately, this play is Shakespeare's divorce narrative, a narrative that begins with Desdemona, but ends with Emilia.

The narratives of strangeness and the familiar are co-dependants in *Othello*, written on to bodies that make them legible in performance. Most obviously, the racialized narrative, enacted through Othello's body, speaks through the obsessive, demonized discourse of darkness to mobilize (white) cultural fantasies that associate blackness with savagery and sexuality. The play's domestic narrative – the one that interests me here – is both more and less spectacular. Before it, too, learns obsessiveness, this narrative speaks through the entirely colloquial, even banal discourse of misogynistic gender stereotyping, mobilizing (male) cultural fantasies that work to regulate women's bodies by regulating their speech. Gender, as Maureen Quilligan observes, is 'one social role ideologically grounded in the physical body', and the terms in which early modern gender stereotyping expressed itself (terms that recent feminist scholarship has made utterly familiar) explicitly connect the policing of women's bodies to the policing of their language, seeing women's bodies as most dangerously 'in-bodied' when they are in speech.[2] By such logic, acts of speech (that find, in *Othello*, metonyms in body parts – tongue, lips, mouth, hand) figure carnal activity, so that silence tropes continence and the liberal tongue, the incontinent body of the whore.

In both narratives Iago is the originator of discourse, then its wrecker; the first inventor of misogyny and racism; later, the pornographer, literally, writing women 'whore', the denigrator writing the black man black and blackening all with his tainting. Both narratives – with perverse significance, as I will argue – circulate as 'woman's talk', as gossip. For gossip, it turns out, is what this play talks. It's *Othello's* most idiosyncratic discursive habit, the rhetorical strategy the play employs for speaking itself performatively. It is, of course, a practice identified both with gender and with bodies, for gossip belongs to 'her indoors'. There were, as I will show, excellent historical reasons why this was so; why, located in domestic interiors as 'women's talk', gossip was suspected, dangerous; and why, grounded in the gendered body, its traffic should be so ambiguous. Gossip was licensed 'naturally' to women, yet made those who traded in it licentious; it was what women were – and what they mustn't be. In *Othello*, though, and this is one of the play's perversions, gossip isn't what women do. It's men's talk. Early on, Iago cannily strips (good) women of speech by mobilizing a warped syllogism (silence equals chastity; all women talk; all women are whores), whose logic registers female virtue only in absence, the absence of expression. Women can never contest Iago's major premise (silence equals chastity) without demonstrating his minor one – so proving his conclusion, while, perversely, they can only challenge his minor premise by rendering themselves expression-less. The 'good' housewife Emilia is dumb. But what Iago strips from women, he appropriates to himself, playing the (discredited) 'woman's part', the gossip's part, in *Othello* and to Othello, as scene after scene puts in view scenarios of 'monstrous' relation: Othello, Cassio, Roderigo, Montano, Lodovico stand centre stage, Iago hanging upon them like the 'bauble' strumpet Cassio claims he can't shake off, tumid lips thrusting into their ready ears, his latest tattle a parody of erotic penetration.

In 4.3, though, Emilia reverses Iago's perverse mastery, repossessing 'women's talk' and finding the voice that defeats him. Her capitulation into speech, of course, is a capitulation into the very stereotype her silence so far has evaded. It is one of this play's most testing ironies that its narratives work, finally, to trouble all that they propose by preserving mischievous contradiction and validating the very stereotypes they simultaneously dismantle, the 'false truths' they set up for trashing. As one narrative 'proves' the lie that black Othello is the savage barbarian, so the other 'proves' the lie that 'super-subtle' Emilia is, indeed, the 'whore of Venice'. For Emilia finally does betray her husband, and in the very terms he imagined, capitulating from model housewife – the silent 'her indoors' – to 'extravagant . . . stranger', 'unhoused' by her decision to 'be in speaking, liberal as the air'.

As Zoe Wanamaker's Emilia sat eating Desdemona's chocolates in 4.3 she was answering the cultural construction of women Iago had premised from the opening scene of the play. In 5.2, she would have more to say. Where did Wanamaker find this part? To start, I want to think about Emilia in Shakespeare's playtext.

Finding the Part

In *A Midsummer Night's Dream* Peter Quince is passing out parts to *Pyramus and Thisbe* when Bottom interrupts him. 'What is Pyramus?' he demands. 'A lover or a tyrant?' (1.2.17). Like *Pyramus*, *Othello* is a play that assigns parts with obsessive (if controversial) discursive particularity. What is Michael Cassio? 'A great arithmetician', one who no more 'the devision of a battle knows' than 'a spinster' (1.1.19, 23–24). Roderigo? 'A snipe', Iago's 'sport and profit' (1.3.383–384). Bianca? 'A housewife that by selling her desires / Buys herself bread and clothes' (4.1.94). Othello is 'the thicklips', the 'old black ram', the 'extravagant and wheeling stranger / Of here and everywhere' (1.1.66, 88, 136–137); Desdemona, the 'maiden never bold', she who 'shunn'd / The wealthy curled darlings of our nation' to run instead – 'O treason of the blood' – 'To the gross clasps of a lascivious Moor' (1.3.94; 1.2.68; 1.1.169, 126). And Iago? His part is the ultimate evacuation of self that, enigmatically, leaves him pure part, in a position to appropriate all other parts: 'I am not what I am' (1.1.65). Only Emilia misses out. 'What's her history?' 'A blank' (*Twelfth Night*, 2.4.108–109).

No one much bothers about Emilia's part. Cinthio, Shakespeare's source, gives his ensign a (nameless) wife – a fellow Venetian – whose company 'Disdemona' seeks out on Cyprus, but she's a bit player, not instrumental, even though she's the story's sole survivor and putative 'author'. Editors brush past her. M.R. Ridley lists Shakespeare's changes to Cinthio without noticing that he radically rewrites the ending not just to anchor it on Emilia but to construct it entirely around her tragic self-revelation and disclosure. E.A.J. Honigmann suggests that 'Emilia repays some attention' – then has nothing more to say about her.[3] In the theatre, Emilia doesn't merit priority casting; on film, directors – Orson Welles, 1952, Oliver Parker, 1995 – habitually cut the part so drastically that what is left is a caricature. Faye Compton in 1952 played what remained of her as a sturdy games mistress; Joyce Redman (in Stuart Burge's 1965 film with Olivier as Othello), as a *commedia* soubrette.

It doesn't, of course, look, to begin with, as if Shakespeare is going to make much of Emilia either. She's plucked out of the air, a procedural afterthought to the muggy business in the Senate: 'Prithee, let thy wife attend on her,' Othello orders Iago, providing for Desdemona to follow him to Cyprus (1.3.295). Is the ensign's wife, like the ensign, under Othello's peremptory command; like him, on call to rouse from sleep in the middle of the night to pack her bags for travel to the ends of the civilized world? Does she even know this young bride she's commanded to attend? Where would they, why would they ever meet, she, a subaltern's wife, Desdemona, a senator's privileged, cloistered daughter? ('How got she out?' asks Brabantio, staggeringly, of Desdemona's elopement.) In Trevor Nunn's claustrophobic, class-conscious mid-Victorian setting where social gradation registered in the precise arrangement of brass tunic buttons on the men's cavalry uniforms, it was perfectly clear that their paths had never crossed. Desdemona was a stranger, not just different in class from Emilia, different in species. Emilia watched her from a cautious distance, the impulsive girl whose giddy love, written on her incandescent face, demonstrated that she had nothing in common with her. One category of difference between them registered superficially in understated details of costume: the chatelaine at Emilia's waist, the rolled-up sleeves, the plain brooch at her high collar. But what really distinguished them was presented through their bodies, in how the Self performed what it thought about the Self. Desdemona, utterly unself-conscious, oblivious to her body, possessed patrician easiness, was used to servants dressing her. Wanamaker's Emilia was always on guard, on duty, alert to protocol and boundaries, watchful, reserved.

When Emilia eventually enters the play, on the quayside at Cyprus in 2.1, she is hardly less de-anonymized: unnamed, silent at first, she utters only two half lines in the scene. But her 'cover' suddenly vanishes when Cassio's presumptuous 'bold . . . courtesy' turns all attention upon her, taking her as its excessively engrossing object. Even as he kisses her, however, he ignores her to address her husband:

> Let is not gall your patience, good Iago,
> That I extend my manners; 'tis my breeding
> That gives me this bold show of courtesy.
> (2.1.97–99)

Retorting, Iago reverses Cassio's idealizing 'courtesy', makes Emilia instead the dumb butt of his misogynistic joke:

> Sir, would she give you so much of her lips
> As of her tongue she has bestow'd on me,
> You'ld have enough.
> (2.1.100–102)

Here, in a demotic nutshell, is the trope whose *double entendres* sexualize speech and make speech sexually compromising, the trope that determines to manage women's bodies by managing the cultural space of women's discourse.

Can Emilia, who later reveals she's under the jealous surveillance of a husband whose imagination's 'seamy side' is always on the look-out to abuse her, welcome Cassio's 'courtesy'? Can she rebuff it, the flattering attention of Iago's senior officer? Such social questions are relevant to performance, for though silent, Emilia performs through her reticence, and yet, whichever way she plays the scene, she'll be wrong-footed; that's how Shakespeare has constructed it. Wanamaker's Emilia, huddled from the storm on the luggage she'd hauled unaided into the scene, registered an anxious glance at Iago (Ian McKellen), who 'tsk-tsked' fussily when Cassio closed in to kiss her. Still, as much as these questions are relevant to performance, they are irrelevant to consequences, for as the pained blankness that settled upon Wanamaker's face as she submitted to them further registered, Cassio's kisses aren't about courtesy to women. They're aimed at Iago, a perverse homosocial exchange 'between men' that masks homophobic rivalry, their intention to goad gall. In that Cassio's disclaimer, working over Emilia's body, works also to activate the phallic imaginary into fantasies where women will function 'merely' as dupes and pawns of male rivalry, this moment presages things to come.

Iago's cheap banter mocking 'lippy' Emilia is, of course, demonstrably wrong. Emilia hasn't uttered a word, a silence Desdemona marks in speaking up for her – 'Alas! she has no speech.' How does Emilia's silence work here? If she speaks, she confirms Iago's slander. If she doesn't, she either colludes with it, confounds it, or perhaps buys Iago's approval with the only coin that purchases it. Silent, she shrugs off Iago's typecasting as 'loose' woman, but that, it seems, merely gives him an excuse to load her with other parts, parts, he insists, that belong to women in common, parts that make them common. So, singled out for 'courtesy', Emilia becomes exemplary of the 'common', punningly pronounced in Iago's next line:

> Come on, come on, you are pictures out o'doors
> Bells in your parlours; wild cats in your kitchens;
> Saints in your injuries; devils being offended;
> Players in your housewifery;

'And,' he concludes, 'housewives' – that is, 'hussifs', 'hussies' – 'in your beds' (2.1.109–112).

As her husband clowned for the troops, weaving among them while they roared with barrack-room laughter, punctuating each of his gags with an obscene gesture of tongue, arm and fist, Wanamaker's Emilia gazed indulgently, her weary smile bending her stiff upper lip, wearing Iago's contempt as if it were a joke. Desdemona protested a second time, 'Fie upon thee, slanderer!' (l. 113). But even as Desdemona defended her, it was clear that Emilia's loyalty lay with Iago. When Desdemona came to sit beside her, Emilia arched her body impercepti- bly out of touch. Desdemona scanned the distance for Othello's sail and wept; Emilia gazed away impassively – and whistled through her teeth.

This scene on the quayside, which so puzzled earlier editors (Ridley could explain Iago's 'cheap backchat' only as Shakespeare's miscalculated 'sop to the groundlings'[4]) is, in fact, brilliantly calculated and placed. It stands liminally, on the threshold of Cyprus, to provide the preliminary information upon which the rest of the play depends, to map what Pierre Bourdieu would call 'the universe of what is taken for granted' here.[5] It is an initiation into discourse – a verbal analogue to the baptismal sea storm the Venetians have just passed through – that sets out the legiti- mating fictions, the cultural protocols that frame the sexual politics Iago manipulates to such devastating effect. In a play that destroys women, this quayside exchange licenses their destruction. 'I know our country disposition well,' Iago will claim. What he 'knows' is what women are – 'pictures', 'wild cats', 'devils' 'housewives'. He knows, that is, Emilia's 'part', a demonized part she cannot deny because protesting instantiates it, a part he will fit to Desdemona, too, and with obsequious care, dis- close to Othello across Act 3. Crafted from misogynistic, even pornographic 'old paradoxes', the cultural 'truth' that constructs the 'woman's part' is, in truth, a sad old joke, fit only, says Desdemona, 'to make fools laugh i'th alehouse'. It's prattle – but it's prattle that, pre- senting as 'truth', gives fools 'the cause' to kill the wives their prattle makes whores.

It is crucial that this exchange be transacted over Emilia's head. As the original slandered wife of this play she is Desdemona's proxy here. Her predicament, compressed into those six lines traded between Cassio and Iago, maps the space between idealization and pornography that Desdemona will later occupy. Moreover, by constituting her prestige as a wife in her silence, Iago effectively gags Emilia, a devastating move in a theatre like Shakespeare's, hungry for words, where subjectivity links to speech. Every part Iago constructs for her – gossip, scold, mad woman, drab, all of them women who tell tales – predicates transgressive speech, but in Emilia, produces submissiveness, conformity, the model house- wife. At least until the end.

As these ideas (that come into play first in Venice, in the street beneath Brabantio's window, and later, in the Senate, in Othello's remembering) fix upon Emilia, we begin to see the performance work the play has cut out for her. Her 'blank' is the secret history that the play will write, and that she will radically revise in *Othello*'s final moments.

Here on the quayside, though, the whole history of women is, as Iago thinks, already known. A male-authored narrative circulated among men, it takes its place among the other male narratives that constitute *Othello*.

Travellers' Tales and Domestic Interiors

Almost nothing happens in *Othello*. Cassio gets drunk, a brawl breaks out, Desdemona drops her handkerchief, Emilia hands it to her husband. For the rest, the play is constructed out of narratives: tales, stories, reports, news, gossip, prattle.[6] It begins mid-conversation – 'Tush, never tell me' – with Roderigo repelling news he finds incredible and doesn't want to hear; it ends with Lodovico condemning himself to 'relate' a story he doesn't want to tell, one he knows 'would not be believ'd in Venice' though its tellers 'should swear' they 'saw 't'. Framed between Roderigo's 'Tush' and Lodovico's 'relate', *Othello* is compiled of one fantastic story after another. First, there's the story of the elopement, which Brabantio, like Roderigo, finds unbelievable and so explains in terms of other stories:

> is there not charms,
> By which the property of youth and maidhood
> May be abus'd? Have you not read, Roderigo . . . ?
> (1.2.171–174)

Then, the story of Othello's life, which is also the story of the wooing – a seduction story which works, in the Senate, a second seduction, this time on the Duke:

> Her father lov'd me, oft invited me,
> Still question'd me . . .
> I ran it through . . . I spake of . . . all my travel's history;
> . . . of antres vast, and deserts idle . . .
> And of the Cannibals, that each other eat;
> The Anthropophagi, and men whose heads
> Do grow beneath their shoulders.
> (1.3.128–144)

The story of the handkerchief:

> that handkerchief
> Did an Egyptian to my mother give,

She was a charmer . . . there's magic in the web of it;
A sibyl . . .
In her prophetic fury sew'd the work;
The worms were hallow'd that did breed the silk,
And it was dyed in mummy, which the skilful
Conserve of maidens' hearts.

(3.4.54–73)

Finally, the story of the life retold, a narrative that makes Othello both agent and victim, slayer and slain, storyteller and story told, its 'hero' a double man – Moor and barbarian:

in your letters . . . Set you down this,
And say besides, that in Aleppo once,
Where a malignant and a turban'd Turk
Beat a Venetian and traduc'd the state,
I took by the throat the circumcised dog,
And smote him thus.

(5.2.341, 350–355)

Observe: *Othello*'s stories spontaneously expand, re-author themselves in the subsequent telling; that's how story behaves here. Ignorant of Desdemona's 'gross revolt', Roderigo somehow owns more details than he's been told, elaborates the tale as he retells it:

At this odd-even and dull watch o'the night,
Transported . . . with a knave of common hire, a gondolier,
To the gross clasps of a lascivious Moor.

(1.1.124–126)

The stories the play tells are 'extravagant', 'wheeling'; they're brought from Aleppo and Egypt, and from further afield, from the 'unhoused' wilderness of Libya's deserts, from the place of barbarity, from the cannibals. But here's an irony: they're told, as it were, 'indoors'. The incredible tale is situated in the domestic interior, its 'extravagant' strangeness inserted into household space dense with household stuff – puppies, spinsters, figs, skillets, tinder boxes, beds, handkerchiefs. In *Othello*, the house is both a location and a discursive space. Brabantio stands '*at a window*' (Q. S.D.), his house solidly under his feet, to hear a wild tale 'proclaim[ed] . . . in the street': 'Look to your house'; 'Are all doors lock'd?'; 'you are robb'd'; 'an old black ram / Is tupping your white ewe' (1.1.69, 80, 85–86, 88–89). Desdemona, Brabantio's close-kept 'jewel', keeps her father's house, manages its domestic affairs, until her father's 'oft invited' house guest disturbs her business by bringing extravagance over the threshold. Listening, wrapt, to Othello's tales of 'battles, sieges, fortunes . . . disastrous chances . . . accidents . . . hair-breadth scapes'; to tales of anthropophagi (how unlike the 'wealthy curled darlings of our nation' who loiter limply at Brabantio's doors), Desdemona plays truant to huswifery. Even when she's summoned home from strangeness by 'the house-affairs' that 'draw her thence', she persists in breaking house, turning cannibal, devouring the tale that tropes the man:

> And ever as she could with haste dispatch,
> She'ld come again, and with a greedy ear
> Devour up my discourse.
>
> (1.3.148–150)

What does 'the house' count for in this play? The opening act is set against a series of houses: Brabantio's in scene 1; a public 'house', as Othello calls it (1.48), the Sagittary, in scene 2; inside the state house, the Senate, in scene 3. 'The house', as this spread of reference suggests, tropes patriarchy, property (among it, daughters), family, name, lineage, public stature, political power. But 'the house' also figures the 'housed', like Desdemona, against the 'unhoused', Othello of the vagrant 'tented field'(more different, even, than black and white). It tropes insiders, and the superior cultural knowledge, or narrative, they own, assumptions that are implicit in Brabantio's withering, 'This is Venice, / My house is not a grange' (1.1.105–106) and in the kind of insider knowledge Iago mobilizes against the 'stranger' Moor, who never seems more nearly Venetian than when he cracks an in-house joke: 'Let housewives make a skillet of my helm . . .' (1.3.272).

What is the status of *Othello*'s narratives? Are they true? Do spectators, does the play, credit the fantastic traveller's tale, the anthropophagi, the 'men whose heads / Do grow beneath their shoulders'? What about that sibyl – 200 years on the job – and those 'hallow'd' silk worms? Was the handkerchief really dyed in virgin blood distilled from maidens' hearts?[7] Or is this poppycock, framed to make Venetian insiders snort with derision, like sneering Iago, trashing Othello's 'history' as nothing but 'bragging', 'fantastical lies' (2.1.222). Is *that* the truth?

What the play reveals is that it doesn't matter. Whatever their status, the tales *work*. Spectators even see Othello's 'fantastical' narrative perform seduction upon the duke who, ravished, thinks 'this tale would win my daughter too' (1.3.171). Information about the irrelevance of truth to a story's effectiveness is crucial, because, of course, the most fantastic tale this play intends to circulate is not the one about the outlandish cannibal or even the sibylline handkerchief. It's the utterly fantastic story Iago passes off for 'true' about 'her indoors', a narrative that claims to know Desdemona is false because it claims to 'know our country disposition well' and so knows the narratives that constitute its 'true' histories. In short, it's a narrative that trafficks between the phallic imaginary and cultural construction, looped through the circuit of Iago's confident insider 'knowledge'. Everyone knows what women are like – just as everyone knows what cannibals are like. In Venice, their history is adultery. So 'It cannot be that Desdemona should long continue her love unto the Moor . . . . When she is sated with his body, she will find the error of her choice; she must have change, she must' (1.3.342–343, 351–353). Must she? It doesn't matter. Like Othello's story of the handkerchief, Iago's narrative will work – it 'will do, as if for surety' (1.3.388).

Gossip, Groom-ing, Monstrous Birth

To see the epic traveller's tale domesticated, told indoors where it is produced as truth but simultaneously mocked as 'prattle', is to see *Othello* practising a kind of miscegenation, a mixing not of race but of discursive categories. For domestic space, space indoors, is properly the privileged space of women and women's talk, a space Iago contaminates as he perversely insinuates himself into it, usurping its discourse to appropriate *Othello* as his gossip text. There he both engenders the tales his 'invention' 'labours' to 'deliver', and stands chief gossip to the 'monstrous birth' that he delivers as the malignant child of his fantasy.[8]

What is at stake here, as Iago's plot drives deeper and deeper into interiors, finally to target the marriage bed, is nothing less than the wreck of intimacy. So I want briefly to map the space Iago spoils, the domestic sphere of housewifery and gossip as it was theorized in language Shakespeare's audience would have known from common precept, from Elizabethan sermons and Jacobean conduct books. In them, the good wife was the housewife, her space indoors. 'Not a streetwife, one that gaddeth up and down,' said the Puritan Robert Cleaver in 1614, following St Paul, but one who stays at home and 'avoids gossiping further than the law of good neighbourhood doth require'.[9] Henry Smith, in a 1591 marriage sermon, explicated this taxonomy with tedious emphasis:

> We call the wife *housewife*, that is housewife, not a street wife like Thamar [Gen. 38:14], nor a field wife like Dinah [Gen.

34:1], but a housewife, to show that a good wife keeps her
house: and therefore Paul biddeth . . . women that they be
chaste and keeping at home: . . . as though home were chastity's
keeper. And therefore Solomon depainting the whore setteth
her at the door [Prov. 7:12], now sitting upon her stalls, now
walking about the streets.[10]

The tortoise was the beast women should model themselves on. Even the
careful Newcastle merchant Ambrose Barnes advised his daughters to
adopt it as the 'emblem of a woman who should be a keeper at home',
for 'the tortoise seldom peeps out of its shell'.[11]

Yet, as Cleaver observes, a good wife must not be reclusive: she has
responsibilities to 'good neighbourhood'. 'The woman that gaddeth
from house to house to prate confoundeth herself, her husband, and her
family.' But 'a woman is to go abroad' in errands of 'employment and
provision in household affairs', to 'come to holy meetings', and 'to visit
such as stand in need'.[12] What constituted 'need'? Significantly, the necessary work of attending childbirth – supervising labour, standing witness
to birth – which strictly excluded men; then visiting the new mother
across the thirty days of her lying-in, her time 'in the straw' (as John
Chamberlain colloquially put it), a 'privilege . . . which 'longs / To
women of all fashion' (*The Winter's Tale*, 3.2.101–102).[13] Admonished
by the rubrics of the 1559 *Book of Common Prayer* (issued at Elizabeth's
accession and again, with minimal revision, in 1604, at James's) not to
defer 'the baptism of infants any longer than the Sunday, or other holy
day, next after the child be born', it was the godmother's duty to present
the infant for baptism while the mother kept *accouchée*.[14]

Answering for the infant in baptism, godparents of either sex stood
'godsib' – that is, 'sibling', 'god related', to the child. Latterly (in the
hundred years between Chaucer's *Tales* and Fabyan's *Chronicles*)
'godsib' corrupted to 'gossip' and went on, waywardly, to move from
identifying a person to, interchangeably, troping a speech practice – as
in Viola's, ' . . . make the babbling gossip of the air / Cry out "Olivia!"'
(*Twelfth Night*, 1.5.242–243). By the time Shakespeare was thinking
about it, the sacramental function of gossip was already absorbed and
dispersed into the social – practised, for example, in Cleaver's unlegis-
lated 'law of good neighbourhood' that made 'gossiping' the charitable,
and wholly approved, business of bringing conversation to the house-
bound mother. 'Gossip' was certainly women's work and, potentially,
carnivalized work, at least as portrayed in Thomas Middleton's outrageously obscene *A Chaste Maid in Cheapside*. There the complaisant
cuckold Allwit's kept wife lies-in like the Countess of Salisbury – *her*

childbed hangings of white satin embroidered with gold and pearl notoriously cost £14,000 (according to John Chamberlain's hot gossip in
January 1613[15]). Crowding Mrs Allwit's notorious bed, a pack of raddled 'gossips' defines the 'holy' breed – backbiting between mouthfuls
of sweetmeats, their spilt secrets and other indiscretions (some left as
puddles under their stools as they stagger home) multiplying with the
rounds they drink.[16]

Located in the private, feminized space of birth and the ritual space of
baptism, early modern gossiping brought together ideas of the sacred
and the profane, of the mystified and the raucously demystified, of paternity confirmed – and potentially abused.[17] Just as the gossip's feast
performed, in David Cressy's phrase, a 'profane pastiche of the christening ceremony' in the wetting of the baby's head, so likewise it
commonly privileged sexual banter, and worse, licentious activity,
promiscuous exchange that mocked as always futile paternity's claim
exclusively to know and name its own children.[18] As the Porter exclaims
of the crowds thronging the christening feast in *Henry VIII*, 'Have we
some strange Indian with the great tool come to court, the women so
beseige us? Bless me, what a fry of fornication is at the door! On my
Christian conscience, this one christening will beget a thousand'
(5.3.51–53). The social gossip was an intimate, a sharer of close secrets:
she talked indoors. But she was also a 'commoner', a 'gadder'. For to
visit the woman lying-in, the gossip was forced to walk abroad, to leave
the household that guaranteed her own reputation. The gossip, then,
paradoxically refashions Cleaver's housewife into a figure of ambivalence.

Historians like Bernard Capp, putting actual social practice against
contemporary patriarchal theorizations like Cleaver's, read gossiping as
a form of early modern networking, a way for 'ordinary women' in seventeenth century England to 'create their own social networks and their
own social space', 'a semi-separate domain outside the family structure
and beyond male control', a 'subculture' where they could operate 'a *de
facto* authority', particularly over sexual conduct. As Capp observes,
'Reputation – especially sexual reputation – was central to every woman's
social position', and 'Gossip was a speedy, free and powerful sanction.'[19]
Theorizing the important cultural work gossip performs, Patricia Meyer
Spacks maps not just gossip's content but its form, method, situation,
even its politics, in language, like Capp's, that reads usefully against
Othello. Spacks understands this most public form of private talk as a
female form, a 'function of intimacy', whose 'participants use talk about
others to reflect upon themselves, to express wonder and uncertainty and
locate certainties' and to 'enlarge their knowledge of one another'.
Gossip 'provides a resource for the subordinated', 'a crucial means of

self-expression, a crucial form of solidarity'.[20] Implicitly voyeuristic, it imagines what goes on behind closed doors, traffics in forbidden knowledge, exploits an erotics of power and exerts imaginative control: it appropriates, claiming others' experience by translating it into 'story'. So, for Spacks, gossip 'subliminally recalls ancient belief in the magic of language'; 'telling stories,' she writes, 'takes possession of other lives', an illusion of mastery that constitutes a form of wish-fulfilment even as it seeks to control competition. Just as gossip 'is a catalyst of social process', it is also, of course, a highly theatricalized discourse. It sets up a dialogue between knowledge and ignorance, initiated and uninitiated; it plays with power as much between the gossipers as between gossip and authority; it works, I would argue, as Shakespeare's playhouse did, transgressively, to raise questions 'about boundaries, authority, distance, the nature of knowledge', and to demand 'answers quite at odds with what we assume as our culture's dominant values'.[21]

Before Iago, the gossip figure Shakespeare's culture knew in representation was a female figure, her apparatus and sphere the over-determined territory of the feminine carnivalesque: Noah's frampold wife, second mother to mankind, armed with her distaff and flanked by 'gossips' she unceremoniously dumps when the flood waters wash over her feet in the Mystery play that still survived in performance in Shakespeare's youth; Chaucer's much-married gap-toothed Rabelaisian Wife of Bath; Lady Centaur, the monstrous college president and professor of abortions in Jonson's school-for-scandal *Epicoene*; Titania's gravid Indian votaress; the witches in *Macbeth*, collectors of arcane relics from the midwifery they practise ('finger of birth strangled babe'). Outrageous, gross, over-exaggerated, these gossips inhabit bodies that constantly exceed the texts they occupy in scenes that celebrate dangerous female intimacy and alliance even as, by suggesting insubordination, they demystify male authority.

In *Othello*, Shakespeare regenders this model. Iago, playing the woman's part he denies Emilia, is Othello's self-made gossip, gossip to the project as gossip is the project. He first conceives his plot in obstetric terms by imagining Othello and Desdemona in the act of copulation, 'making the beast with two backs' and parenting monstrous progeny ('coursers for cousins, and gennets for germans'), then figures himself as mischief's midwife patiently attending those 'many events in the womb of time, which will be delivered' (1.1.115, 112; 1.3.369–370). Later, joking on the quayside, he has more of this imagery to hand, metonymizing the projection of his monstrous 'conception' as a pregnancy and troping fertile male invention with bizarre male birth: 'My Muse labours, / And thus she is deliver'd' (2.1.127–128). The metaphors that fester under the surface of Iago's text erupt again, disgustingly, only lines later, when he imagines men's fingers transformed to 'clyster-pipes' (l. 176), high-tech instruments of primitive gynecology used by physicians like Shakespeare's son-in-law, John Hall, to intervene in stalled deliveries.[22] Just as Iago figures Desdemona the demon godmother, able to 'win the Moor . . . to renounce his baptism' (2.3.334), so he fantasizes himself, autochthonically, his plot's mother, midwife, godmother, all: 'I ha't, it is engender'd; Hell and night / Must bring this monstrous birth to the world's light' (1.3.401–402).

Practising first on Roderigo, the Moor's proxy, then on Othello, Iago assumes a gossip's intimacy, always at hand, taking possession of their lives by telling stories, prattling, offering information that he presents as simultaneously 'common' – 'what we men know' – and reserved, that simultaneously mystifies and grossly demystifies women. So, to the dupe Roderigo, he makes 'virtue' 'a fig', 'love', 'merely a lust of the blood', 'courtesy', 'lechery' and Desdemona, Cassio's *rara avis* who 'paragons description, and wild fame', a 'super-subtle Venetian' whose 'frail vow' must collapse when, 'sated with his body', she finds 'the error of her choice'. 'She must have change, she must' (2.1.62, 1.3.357, 351–352). Roderigo knows ''tis not possible' and 'cannot believe that in her'. He cannot, that is, believe the very imputation of corruptibility on which his hopes of 'enjoying' Desdemona depend. Yet he persists in being duped. How like Othello, duped by the intimacy of the only experienced married man in the play, the one who 'know[s] our country disposition well' and knows:

> In Venice they do let God see the pranks
> They dare not show their husbands: their best conscience
> Is not to leave undone, but keep unknown.
>
> (3.3.205–208)

All this insider knowledge Iago offers in an economy of male-bondedness and solidarity that mimics the gossip's feast, an economy of exchange ('put money in your purse'; 'she must have change') that masks his own presumption to cultural superiority and works, almost magically, to re-order alienation in *Othello*. For if the play's performative narrative positions the black man as the spectacular Other, what Iago's gossip narrative achieves, by turning Desdemona into 'story', is to identify another, stranger Other. Doing so, Iago cynically recruits the alien Othello into the self-promoting ranks of the native, the 'us' who 'know our country disposition well', even as he projects on to the female Other the 'true' fiction of dishonesty – gossip – that controls the narrative and drives it towards the murder that will validate not just male knowledge and male power but male honour as well. Desdemona *did* 'deceive her father, marrying you'; she *did* 'give out such a seeming':

> Not to affect many proposed matches,
> Of her own clime, complexion, and degree,
> Whereto we see in all things nature tends;
> Fie, we may smell in such a will most rank,
> Foul disproportion; thoughts unnatural.
>
> (3.3.210, 213, 233–237)

The deception of the father predicates the deception of the husband. The 'we' recruited to this knowingness knows what must happen next: 'she must die, else she'll betray more men' (5.1.6).

The gossip's intrusion that men fear will usurp their own domestic space, ousting them from their own hearths – like Allwit held at bay by his wife's boozing cronies – is realized, grotesquely, when, in yet another inversion, Iago finally achieves the divorce of man and wife he said Brabantio would seek in 1.2: 'he will divorce you.' In 3.3, Iago kneels with Othello. He echoes the compulsive, eroticized language newly discharged from Othello's mouth to swear the death of love and intensifies its thrust to orgasmic climax, exchanging the vow that blasphemously mocks marriage in perverted 'service':

> Iago doth give up
> The excellency of his wit, hand, heart
> To wrong'd Othello's service.

'Now art thou my lieutenant,' Othello responds, and Iago, in pleasured triumph, cries, 'I am your own for ever' (ll. 472–474, 485–486). It seems that the handkerchief concealed upon him works exactly as Othello's story of its magic says it will, making Iago 'amiable'. With Desdemona declared dead, Othello and Iago plight new troths, pledge hands and hearts. The travesty marriage performed – in a second elopement? – the groom and monster bride rise, their unnatural coupling shortly to produce a terrible premature birth. It will be brought to light tangled in Othello's wedding sheets by the Moor who will 'groan' in the throes of his 'strong conception', his 'labour' delivering Desdemona dead.

Playing Emilia/Reading Performance

Iago is ubiquitous in *Othello*. Preternaturally busy, a tireless jack-in-office, he's always around, organizing the beginnings of scenes, tidying up their endings, manoeuvring, manipulating, and absent only from 2.2 – the ten-line announcement of the nuptial celebrations – and from 4.3 – the scene that makes his absence felt, the 'willow' scene. Ian McKellen's precise, buttoned-up Iago was the company's 'old woman', a domestic fusspot in uniform, smoothing imagined wrinkles out of camp beds, straightening order papers, tugging his tunic; 'cooking' the punch for the wedding carouses, then swilling the basin and smartly tidying it away after Cassio was sick in it; deftly bandaging Roderigo's thrashed head and combing his hair with his fingers; holding Desdemona, after Othello's fury, in his arms and rocking her like a child; twining his fingers into Othello's as he swore to be his 'own for ever'. Everything about him was clipped – the moustache, the consonants. His intimacy, however, (he touched everyone constantly, except Emilia) was clinical, remote; his tactility, the mortician's touch. In soliloquy, his face hardened into a death mask.

Emilia's presence in *Othello* plays very differently. By the middle of the play, she's appeared in only three of nine scenes and spoken some dozen lines, all but two to Cassio. She speaks not a word to Desdemona until 3.3, the scene in which she hands the handkerchief over to Iago.

Zoe Wanamaker told the story of Emilia's distance, watchfulness. She made spectators see Emilia, not Iago, as the play's principal observer, both bound to, and alienated from, its domestic narrative – one whose service to Desdemona would be 'trimm'd in forms, and visages of duty', in 'shows', not in 'duteous and knee-crooking . . . bondage', an 'officer' who would follow Iago's advice and keep her heart attending on herself (1.1.50, 45–46, 51). On the quayside, she couldn't make sense of Othello and Desdemona's love: of the way, when he came ashore, it stopped his breath in his throat and him in his tracks, of the way it launched her into space, as into orbit, caught in Othello's arms. The lovers' kiss was incomprehensible. She watched, horribly fascinated, wary. Then it became clear why. Never taking his grossly gaping eyes off the couple, Iago moved around the tight playing space to Emilia, wrenched her head towards his mouth, brutally ground his face into hers, then casually pushed her aside. The lovers' kiss acted like an aphrodisiac on this voyeur whose gestures, as if played in a tilted mirror, were a perverse imitation, his copy-cat kiss, masturbation. Emilia stood momentarily rooted, her face registering incomprehension: this was a woman Iago never touched, a woman confused when he did, a wife damaged by the casual, promiscuous abuse he'd just demonstrated.

Again in 3.3 the two marriages were cruelly juxtaposed. The heat of the morning was already intense, the cicadas rasping, the shutters around the sand parade ground tight shut against the sun's battery when

Emilia – her high-collared white shirt starched stiff – brought Desdemona's fan to her where she sat, at ease, with Cassio, promising to work his reinstatement. Every gesture of Emilia's was taut, economical, even repressed; Desdemona's hands, eyes, head, body moved with childish impulsiveness, unselfconscious abandon. Her speech, impetuously, implied childish secrets, huge conspiracies, as when, immediately after Cassio's abrupt exit she confided to Othello, 'I have been talking with a suitor here . . . .' (3.3.43). Tellingly, Emilia silently repaired Desdemona's mistakes. The glass of lemonade she handed Othello like a libation to a god brought tears to his eyes; Emilia spooned in the sugar Desdemona hadn't known to add. Then she sat in a white canvas camp chair rolling her own cool glass back and forth across her cheeks as she watched Desdemona adoringly bully Othello – 'To-morrow . . . ? to-morrow night, or Tuesday morn . . . ?' (3.3.59, 61) – and again embrace him, again disappear into his arms, kissing him with such profound love that Emilia had to look away. She turned her gaze up towards Iago, standing ramrod straight, staring like a basilisk, like Milton's Satan gazing on Paradise. The kiss lingered. Iago glanced sideways, found Emilia's eyes. The emptiness between them was a wasteland.

Why does Emilia hand over the handkerchief? Wanamaker told that story clearly. She was kept offstage at 3.3.283 when Desdemona re-entered alone, swinging a gold watch from a chain, comically imperious, summoning Othello from work. When he spoke miserably of 'a pain upon my forehead, here', she took her handkerchief from where she kept it, against her heart, childishly sure of her remedy: 'Let me but bind your head . . . .' The handkerchief was ridiculously small; Othello batted it away, struggled to his feet, exited leaning into Desdemona, who suddenly stopped, remembered something, turned. The handkerchief! She crossed back to the table – and retrieved the watch. The theatre lights went down for the interval. The handkerchief lay where it fell in the parade ground sand – tantalizing, innocent, a piece of litter, a time bomb.

The second half opened with an orderly crossing the parade, spotting the handkerchief, retrieving it, draping it over the back of a chair, exiting. Emilia entered and sat, for the first time allowing her body to relax. She lit her tiny tobacco pipe, drawing the smoke down deeply into her lungs and slowly exhaling, catching sight of the handkerchief. She rose to fetch it from the chair, ran it speculatively across her hand, and began, 'I am glad I have found this napkin' (l. 294). Her soliloquy in the theatre panned across the audience (on film, she speaks directly to the camera). For the first time, then, Emilia occupied a performative space of access to her spectators like the space Iago owned from the outset. This intimacy felt illicit, as though some optical economy had swivelled round and spectators who'd watched Emilia through a telescope saw her pinned to a microscope slide. Such looking was unbearable, for Emilia's soliloquy, as Wanamaker delivered it, anatomized a terrifying void. Reporting, bemusedly, that Desdemona 'reserve[d]' the handkerchief 'evermore about her, / To kiss, and talk to', her voice suddenly cracked, the fissure breaking open like a bereavement, a conflicted reaction that spoke of longing, loss – and contempt, for Desdemona's infantilism was pathetic. And yet, a passion that, Promethean-like, could animate even a handkerchief: how Wanamaker's Emilia yearned for such warmth in the nuclear winter of her marriage to her 'wayward husband' whose inclinations were as imperative as they were incomprehensible. What would Iago do with the handkerchief? 'Heaven knows, not I,' Emilia said simply. But it was the next, despairing line that contained the whole narrative of her abjection: 'I nothing know, but for his fantasy'. This was a woman who, like Ophelia after the nunnery scene in *Hamlet*, could think, could know nothing. She had ceded intelligence in order to survive in a world where her reality was entirely the mad construct of male imagination, Iago's 'fantasy'. Did Shakespeare leave Emilia's history 'a blank' precisely to signal that she has no history outside of Iago's pathological invention?

This Emilia's defeated willingness to 'nothing know' marked her collusion with that fantasy. What was at stake, though, was painfully clear when Iago entered to challenge her, 'How now, what do you here alone?'. His eyes moved like a hooded cobra's, swiftly patrolling the empty parade ground. 'Alone' bore the weight of accusation, told of a life for Emilia under constant surveillance, for 'alone' sarcastically implied the opposite – illicit assignation – the darting eyes seeking suspects. Emilia's response – 'Do not you chide!' – was a cry of anguish that discovered her to be as effectively monitored, infantilized by paternalism's punitive strictures as Desdemona, conversing with a handkerchief, was by its benevolence. To appease this angry father was to offer 'I have a thing for you' (l. 305). In this performance, then, handing over the handkerchief was Emilia's pathetic attempt to buy a moment's approval from a sadistic husband who needed to humiliate and punish her.

Magically, though, it appeared that the handkerchief was going to work to make this 'loathly' wife 'amiable'. 'What will you give me . . . ?' she asked, in a voice calculated to reverse the power relationship between them, to set up as barter the exchange she knew Iago desired. Pulling the handkerchief slowly from her side-pocket placket sexualized that exchange. As Iago spoke 'A good wench, give it me,' he held out a hand, inviting Emilia to approach. She stood behind him, her arms

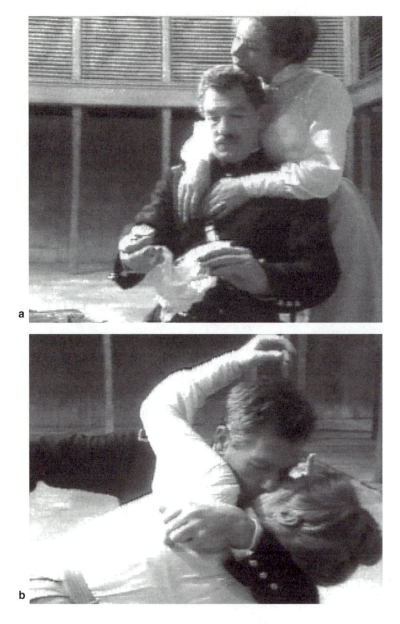

Plate 22 (a) Emilia hands over Desdemona's handkerchief to Iago. (b) Emilia
paid for the handkerchief. Zoe Wanamaker and Ian McKellen in Trevor
Nunn's *Othello*, BBC, 1990.
Source: BBC/RSC.

164

circling his neck, her lips grazing his hair, as he spreadeagled the hand-kerchief on the table. His gesture felt obscene. But she'd mistaken Iago's desire for the handkerchief as desire for her, a miscalculation he mocked by answering her 'What will you do with it . . . ?' by brutally pulling her on to his lap, grinding his fist into her crotch and his mouth on to hers until she gagged. Was this his demonstration of what he 'will do with it'? By the time he released her he'd already palmed her pipe and had it in his mouth, lit, an oral substitute that clearly pleased his groping lips. 'Go, leave me,' discarded her. But she stood, rooted, as on the quayside, by this show of 'love' that felt like rape. It was as though she was struggling towards comprehension, towards knowing. But then to 'nothing know' prevailed: Emilia did as she was told.

Under the glare of the next day's mid-morning sun Emilia sat with her head down at her work in 3.4 as Desdemona restlessly searched the parade ground, wondering 'Where should I lose that handkerchief, Emilia?' The response, 'I know not, madam,' was formal, even curt. In the symbolic economy that both defined and discriminated these two women, Emilia and Desdemona would never be closer in representa-tion – nor farther apart – than in this moment, set up as a conscious pairing of them as exemplary housewives, models of good and bad housekeeping. Emilia was dutiful, methodical, poring over her ledger, deaf to distraction from rhetorical questions as she entered bills and totted up columns; Desdemona, the slatternly 'hussy', was rummaging in a litter bin for what she had carelessly mislaid. She didn't hear the edge in Emilia's voice when she asked of Othello, 'Is he not jealous?', nor did she see her head raised, suddenly alert, when Othello entered and began his story. Abruptly, Emilia closed her book, hugging it to her as she retreated from Othello's menacing telling, inches from Desdemona's terrified eyes, of the Egyptian, the sibyl, the worms, the magic. The theatre made this scene a composition in double focus, siting Othello's narrative of strangeness and Desdemona's struggling reaction in the foreground where the exchange made one kind of sense, against Emilia in the background, frozen upon his words, where her horrified watchfulness mapped responses that reinterpreted Othello's telling to make another kind of sense of it. Certainly, she was hearing the story of the handkerchief – her face registered her rising panic. Could she, now, tell the truth? Could the handkerchief be returned? Was it too late, the magic already irretrievably lost in the handling? Simultaneously, however, Emilia was *watching* a story – one she knew familiarly, a story of domestic abuse. Confusingly to her, the narrative wasn't where she'd left it, but rather displaced, shifted from one house-hold on to another, so that Othello was playing Iago's part and, uncannily, Desdemona her abject self. In this abuse narrative, male power, male appetite, possessed, authored and mastered women's lives by mastering the narratives that wrote their histories. The lost handkerchief figured Desdemona's lost plot. When Othello roared for it, his voice slamming like a fist into Desdemona's shaken, uncomprehending face, Emilia seemed to be recognizing Desdemona for the first time. She knew that violence. It made Desdemona suddenly, horribly familiar: their stories, as it turned out, belonged to a shared narrative that connected them to the whole history of 'what women are'. But whereas earlier, on the quayside, Iago's version of that history sensationalized women as active, dangerous, transgressive, Emilia knew women were merely instrumental to men's hungry fantasizing, fodder – a neat trope, did she but know it – for the self-consuming jealousy gnawing at men's innards. The play's true cannibals were its household anthropophagi – husbands:

'Tis not a year or two shows us a man:
They are all but stomachs, and we all but food;
They eat us hungerly, and when they are full,
They belch us.

(3.4.100–104)

This insight marks the pivot point of Emilia's play. However tentatively, she here begins to articulate a countertext to Iago's totalizing discourse, troping the domestic (food, stomachs) with the fantastic (men cannibalizing women) to produce an image whose components are utterly mundane but whose operation is grotesque, bizarre. Reminiscent of that original speech that brought strangeness into collision with familiarity (Othello's fantastic 'history' contextualized to Desdemona's housewifery) Emilia's speech here also unwittingly glosses Iago's project as he pursues it in scenes counterpointing hers across Acts 3 and 4.

For while Emilia and Desdemona continued, ignorantly, to occupy a space of unremarkable domesticity (the housekeeping accounts in 3.4 troped that space), where headaches and handkerchiefs were consequential but not loaded with monstrous significance, Iago, narrating his version of the traveller's tale, was conducting Othello deeper and deeper into a heart of darkness, a *terra incognita* of female sexuality where household stuff turned monstrous. Moreover, he was seducing the Moor into crediting his 'fantastical lies' by telling them in household language, locating them as home truths – knowledge gained as one went about the daily business of suffering toothaches, telling dreams, watching a man wipe his beard, learning 'our country disposition well'. The more fantastical, the more credible, for each observation brought home to Othello (the discursive intimacy of Iago's gossip works at a literal level) some new information that served to transform the house Desdemona kept into an alien place, stranger even than those 'antres vast and deserts idle' of Othello's wanderings, a place of barbarity. Here, the murderous savagery Iago was working Othello up to would find a 'natural' home.

In the undisputed prehistory of this play, Othello violated Brabantio's house, robbing it of its 'jewel', Desdemona, 'abus'd, stol'n . . . and corrupted' (1.3.60). Not insignificantly in this scheme of things she, her father's object, is as mystified in Brabantio's account as the handkerchief is in Othello's. The traffic in witchcraft woven through both narratives binds them associatively. Confessing Brabantio's charge, Othello reduces it – not 'stealing', exactly, mere 'taking away': 'That I have ta'en away this old man's daughter, / It is most true: true, I have married her' (1.3.78–79). Daffing aside those 'spells and medicines, bought of mountebanks', mind-altering drugs that Brabantio imagines 'wrought upon her', forcing 'nature so preposterously to err', Othello claims his only 'mighty magic' was his 'tale' (1.3.61, 106, 92, 162). But for all his rationalizing, Othello cannot undo the affect of his violation upon Brabantio, nor the way Brabantio represents it, nor the way his abuse of Brabantio's house automatically displaces on to Desdemona; she, figured 'abused . . . corrupted', is, afterwards, by definition, corrupt. 'O thou deceivest me / Past thought!', says Brabantio to his absent daughter (1.1.165–166); and 'Look to her, Moor . . . . / She has deceiv'd her father . . .' (1.3.292–293). This is true. Desdemona has deceived her father. Her deception is, then, the ineradicable datum written into the opening of the play; the one truth Iago, in all his economical dealings in that commodity, can draw on baldly: 'She did deceive her father, marrying you' (3.3.210).

And that deception, 'naturally', as Iago insinuates, diagnoses a disposition to deceive again. Inevitably, as the Aeschylean logic of this play has it, Othello's violation of Brabantio's house – like Macbeth's 'Bloody instructions which, being taught, return / To plague th'inventor' (1.7.9–10) – will return to violate his own; Desdemona, in the return, will be made the instrument of that violation, not the 'abus'd' but the abuser.

These ideas are revisited in 4.2, showing the metaphors that have driven this play, so much of it about male possession reconfigured as demonic possession, pursued to an appalling performative conclusion that monstrously inverts them. In the first interior scene since the Senate, Othello goes indoors. He's seeking information – gossip? – in the women's room, needing to interrogate women's stories, women's speech, women's privacy. Astonishingly, that is, he conducts the scene that's never staged in plays that turn on misinformation. He goes to the reliable source; he asks the questions that tell the truth, that make the handkerchief irrelevant. But then he trashes it all. Why? Because by speaking, Emilia confirms what Othello, Iago-ed, now knows, 'our country disposition'. That is, she confirms the misogynist scheme that marks the speaking woman as the incontinent whore. Acting upon his 'knowledge', Othello reframes his own house as a place of pollution: Emilia is a bawd; the house, a brothel; its discourse, cunning. And in this domestic economy, Desdemona functions as Othello's new model housewife, 'her indoors', a secret 'closet' of perversion: 'a subtle whore, / A closet, lock and key, of villanous secrets' (4.2.21–22).

Wanamaker's Emilia stood in the centre of Desdemona's pathetically sparse furniture, indomitable, dignified, fearless, handing over her chatelaine, the keys to the house, when Othello, fingers snapping, demanded them as he rummaged through Desdemona's coffer. He flipped the pages of her missal for secreted letters, pawed her jewel box and found nothing, but could not penetrate the final mystery, the one locked drawer. Emilia looked coldly upon this frenzy. Her report of Desdemona was definitive:

> if she be not honest, chaste, and true,
> There's no man happy, the purest of her sex
> Is foul as slander.
> (4.2.17–19)

When Othello fulminated, 'Some of your function, mistress, / . . . Your mystery, your mystery' (4.2.27, 30), Emilia knew exactly where his metaphors were taking him. Summoned to him, Desdemona did not. As though hearing a foreign language, she understood 'a fury' in his words, 'But not the words' (ll. 32–33). As his mind lurched more violently into the gross distortions of pornographic fantasy, though, Emilia was forced to yield her ground: 'Dispatch!' (l. 30) roared her dismissal from the scene. But the Emilia who 'shut the door' and left 'procreants alone' was not the abject of 3.3; this Emilia was militant. And when she was summoned back, Othello completing his grotesque parody of careful housekeeping by throwing the brothel-keeper's fee at her feet – 'there's money for your pains; / I pray you turn the key, and keep our counsel' (ll. 92, 94–96) – Wanamaker's Emilia moved to Desdemona, who was collapsed, stunned 'half asleep', and, for the first time in this production, *touched* her, smoothing her tangled hair away from her tear-bloated face.

Desdemona's response to Othello's battering was a whispered

instruction, a *non sequitur* as Emilia heard it, dense with premonition: 'Prithee, to-night / Lay on my bed our wedding sheets; remember, / And call thy husband hither' (ll. 105–107). Emilia's response was an outburst, and as the discovered voice that struggled up into her throat reached full cry, she came close to knowing the truth:

> some eternal villain,
> Some busy and insinuating rogue,
> Some cogging, cozening slave . . .
> The Moor's abus'd by some outrageous knave,
> Some base notorious knave, some scurvy fellow . . . .
> (4.2.132–133, 141–142)

Iago had to cut this off, to gag Emilia. 'Speak within doors,' he barked; 'You are a fool, go to.' But for the first time, McKellen's Iago was rattled. He'd seen – and heard – something he couldn't control.

Ironically, though, at that moment of first physical contact from Emilia, Desdemona, numbed, oblivious to it, unwittingly marked the distance still between them. She'd summoned Iago. She'd needed male counsel, male affirmation: 'Am I that name, Iago?' (l. 119). She wanted advice: 'What shall I do to win my lord again?' (l. 151). Emilia's wants were simpler: 'A halter' to hang a rogue. Desdemona, damaged (the blow in 4.1 had sent her sprawling; the battering in 4.2 left her curled in a heap on the floor), was still conformist: 'his unkindness may defeat my life, / But never taint my love' (ll. 162–163). Emilia, damaged, was darkly dissident: ''Tis not a year or two shows us a man.'

These women, then, when they came together in 4.3, the willow scene, were not natural allies, certainly not sisters bonded in common cause. Their business was practical ('Prithee unpin me'), and their talk first avoided each other, offering other women's narratives as proxies for their own: Desdemona's 'My mother had a maid called Barbary'; Emilia's 'I know a lady . . . would have walk'd barefoot to Palestine'. As they talked, history – women's stories, different from those told by men – flooded into the scene, connecting these two women to generations of mothers and maids and wives and abandoned loves whose lived lives, not male culture's secondhand constructions, told 'what women are'. Iago worked fiendishly in this production to mystify women; McKellen was always mopping sweat off his brow. Here, as it turned out, men were the inscrutable mysteries – 'O, these men, these men!' – who 'prov'd mad', who betrayed and 'did forsake' women. Women were suicidally constant. The scene drifted across registers, through *non sequiturs*, offering women's private speech as an alternative discourse, conversation differently tuned, differently organized to what had gone before. Memory interrupted speculation and speculation lapsed into instruction. The tense quality of the near-monosyllabic pentameters ('He hath commanded me to go to bed') unwound into demotic, prosaic chat ('I would not do such a thing for a joint-ring; or for measures of lawn . . . ud's pity'). Dialogue moved, seemingly by lateral thinking, into song-as-parallel-text, story glossing story. The melody, marked by Desdemona beating time against her heart, was a soundtrack of sorrow that harked back ironically to that earlier song from another world, Iago's rowdy 'cannikins', the repetitive 'Willow, willow, willow' somehow remembering other repetitions, 'think . . . think . . . think'; 'honest . . . honest . . . honest', and detoxifying them.

As they talked, isolated in the halo of lamplight, Emilia and Desdemona achieved intimacy, shedding defences as Desdemona shed layers of clothes, getting down, performatively and discursively, to naked truth. 'Dost thou . . . think . . . Emilia . . . ?' In a word, Desdemona and Emilia were gossiping, that is, playing into the very fantasized, demonized stereotype the play had, throughout, distanced from women, while men, discursive transvestites, appropriated its practices and dangerous contamination. Iago was the gossip, Roderigo, Cassio, Othello his girly dupes. Putting feminized discourse into men's mouths had made it monstrous; now that got 'corrected'. Gossip came home to its 'right' place.

The effect for spectators was like a whiplash. Women's continence, the sensationalized object of men's anxiety whose real subject was the men themselves, a trope for their paranoid uncertainty about their own sexuality, had so far in *Othello* been positioned beyond reproach, so that men's fears looked ridiculous, their credulousness, stupid. Now women were placed to undo all that, located performatively in the discursive space of suspicion, the gossip space. So while the stories they were telling told of women's fidelity, loss, rejection, betrayal, abjection, of so much weeping that women's 'tears . . . soften'd the stones', formally, the stories simultaneously told the tellers as gossips. And as gossips, Emilia and Desdemona were not just compromised but dangerous: their gossip revealed that they knew things they shouldn't. Paradoxically, then, spectators had to read this beautifully delicate scene of women's intimacy as a text paralleled by a countertext scanned through the confirmatory apparatus of Iago's pornographic fantasy. Observed through the lens of that warped text, Desdemona, undressing, revealed not just a vulnerable female body but a sensual one; Emilia, telling of the Venetian who would have walked barefoot to Palestine for a kiss, disclosed the very female appetites Othello despaired of ever controlling – 'That we can call these delicate creatures ours / And not their appetites!'

(3.3.273–274). At the same time, however, her hypothetical 'would have' evidently marked his anguish as self-inflicted paranoia; Emilia's Venetian 'gossip' never actually made the journey her desire disposed her to. And yet, however ingenuous the narrative content of the scene, its performative situation framed it as incriminating – the women were gossiping. Ergo, they had to be transgressing. Thus, when Stubbs's Desdemona, guilt written on her face, found the key to her private drawer and moved to unlock it, spectators knew what was coming. The drawer would reveal what they didn't want to see, the secret that would discover the women to be the very hussies their fathers and 'honest' friends proclaimed them. So when that drawer produced nothing more dangerous than chocolates and suspense sagged into audible sighs of relief, spectators perhaps reflected that, like Othello, against all the evidence of sense, they had been momentarily Iago-ed; so imperative is the misogynistic presumption of women's deceit. Nunn's production had found a way of representing the radical self-contradiction written into the scene both at the level of actors' performances and spectators' responses.

The poignancy of the scene registered in the painfully tentative moves Emilia and Desdemona made towards and away from each other, parallel to but wholly unlike the obscene, aggressive homoerotic bonding of Othello and Iago in 3.3. Wanamaker's Emilia stared stonily away as Desdemona, the battered wife, still declared that her love 'approve[d]' Othello's 'stubbornness, his checks and frowns' (l. 20). She performed her servant business efficiently, unpinning Desdemona, answering crisply her sudden terror of a noise she couldn't name, 'It is the wind' (l. 53), and turning to go when dismissed, 'Now get thee gone; good night' (l. 57). But as she turned, Desdemona suddenly clutched her around the waist, clinging like a child. Disconcerted, Emilia unpeeled her grasp. But Desdemona's anguish stopped her in her tracks. 'O, these men, these men!' opened an artery into Desdemona's heart. Emilia turned back, sat down, contemplated the question Desdemona put to her with such fervent incredulity, 'Wouldst thou do such a deed, for all the world?' (l. 63). The comic outrageousness of Emilia's answer, using 'male' logic and rhetorical casuistry to re-present relativistically Desdemona's mystified and absolute 'wrong' as no mystery at all, but merely 'a wrong i' the world' that could be 'quickly . . . right' if you had 'the world for your labour' (ll. 79–80), made the women laugh out loud in contemplation of such a carnivalized utopia. The laughter dissolved the strangeness between them. This moment made Stubbs's Desdemona decide to unlock the drawer, to share her secret with Emilia, quid pro quo, as she knelt at her side, her head almost in Wanamaker's lap.

But the contraband Emilia handed back in exchange was bitter stuff.

171

Plate 23 'O, these men, these men!' Imogen Stubbs and Zoe Wanamaker in Trevor Nunn's 1989 *Othello*.
Source: Joe Cocks photograph. Courtesy of The Shakespeare Centre Library, The Shakespeare Birthplace Trust, Stratford-upon-Avon.

Women betray their husbands, 'no question'. 'But,' she went on, prob-
ing pain, 'I do think it is their husbands' faults / If wives do fall.' This
was no liberationist manifesto but a catechizing that discovered male 'err-
or', that saw all men as 'extravagant and wheeling strangers' who 'slack
their duties, / And pour our treasures into foreign laps', who 'break out
in peevish jealousies', 'strike us', 'scant our former having in despite'. A
dozen secret histories seemed to be buried in the subtext of this totalizing narrative. Where, by the way, had all those 'treasures' gone that Iago
had extorted from Roderigo, 'jewels' sufficient to have 'corrupted a
votarist' (4.2.189)? Certainly, not on to Emilia. Desdemona had already
worked out for herself that men were mere mortals: 'We must think /
Men are not gods' (3.4.144–145). Still, reluctant sceptic that she was,
she was not prepared to credit Emilia's outright heresy here, which was
all the more threatening because the analogy she drew between 'them'
and 'us' was unassailable: 'Let husbands know, / Their wives have sense
like them.' Nor could Desdemona defend Emilia's charge: 'What is it
that they do, / When they change us for others?' As her logic was fault-
less, her conclusion was inescapable:

> Is it sport?
> I think it is: and doth affection breed it?
> I think it doth. Is't frailty that thus errs?
> It is so too. And have not we affections?
> Desires for sport? and frailty, as men have?
> Then let them use us well: else let them know,
> The ills we do, their ills instruct us so.
>   (4.3.97–103)

Indisputably, says Emilia, men hold the power; what she required was
that they use it responsibly. Because women are not without power: 'we
have some grace, / Yet have we some revenge' (ll. 92–93).

For Stubbs's Desdemona this was too much information. She fixed the
lid back on to the chocolate box, dismissing Emilia with a final 'Good
night'. But with an impulse just as sudden as Desdemona's earlier, Emilia
reached forward to clutch Desdemona, holding her as though she were
precious, rocking her. Suddenly she straightened and started away, but
stopped as she overheard Desdemona, kneeling at her prie-dieu, once
again consulting patriarchal authority: 'God me such usage send, / Not
to pick bad from bad, but by bad mend!'

So Emilia's 'gossip' was discredited as 'bad'. A shadow of wry pain
crossed her sorrowful face. When she exited, she and Desdemona were as
far apart as ever.

This awful failure of words between the women was the critical subtext that underwrote their final scene together, 5.2. On the bed laid by Emilia with her wedding sheets, Desdemona fought like a tiger for life, crying out 'O Lord, Lord, Lord!' as she thrashed and gulped air until Othello, pushing his huge bulk down upon her, pressed the breath out of her. Rolling away, he lay beside her, panting from the struggle, then, hearing her, dead, speak again those same words he'd smothered, ('My lord, my lord!'), he started up, appalled ('What voice is this? Not dead? not quite dead?'). He pressed the pillow on to her face again, again bore down – and again heard the voice – 'What ho, my lord, my lord!', followed by insistent knocking that forced his attention from the bed to the noise at the door, making him realize the voice was Emilia's.

For Emilia's voice uncannily picked up where Desdemona's was stopped, and as this scene went on, gathering momentum, more and more urgent, Wanamaker's Emilia was seen to have internalized Desdemona's voice, to be ventriloquizing that voice and finally finding the full pitch of her own. Everything in this scene depends upon speech and silence, narratively in terms of the story that will be told or suppressed, performatively in terms of the tropes that saturate it, making speaking the urgent dynamic, the physical work that must get done here. Wanamaker's Emilia at the door wanted to speak with Othello; Othello knew she would 'sure speak to my wife'; the sound of Desdemona's death rattle made Emilia push past Othello – 'What cry is that? . . . it is my lady's voice.' Pulling Desdemona upright, shaking her, Emilia urged, 'O lady, speak again . . . speak!' But Desdemona's utterance was inaudible. Emilia, ear to her mouth, turned her strangled sounds into words, speaking her last line for her: 'A guiltless death I die.' 'O, who has done this deed?' cried Emilia in her own voice. Again, Emilia interpreted Desdemona's ghastly pangs, took on Desdemona's voice, speaking up for her what was inaudible in Desdemona, 'Nobody, I myself.' Emilia lay Desdemona back against the pillows, gently, as though the body might break, then sat silent, frozen. 'You heard say . . . ,' said Othello. 'She said so, I must needs report . . . ' answered Emilia dully.

That is, Desdemona's dying words, translated instantly into report, authorized the latest of latest narratives, set it circulating out amongst the cannibals and anthropophagi, the Egyptian seers and prophetic sibyls – a 'natural' history of women's betrayal. And that's where the story would end if it weren't for Othello's next move, Iago-like, to discredit what 'she said' as truth, with a substitute narrative even more outlandish than the tale Emilia 'must needs report' – a narrative which ironically works to unravel the whole story. 'She's . . . a liar . . . ' he roared at Emilia, and as the two of them circled the death bed, exchanging violent 'iteration' –

'thy husband . . . '; 'my husband . . . ?' – over the corpse, Emilia roared her own report – 'He lies!'. 'Speak,' she urged Iago when the crowd her bellowing had summoned stood around the bed where Desdemona lay in full view. Iago told the appalling truth, all of it in a clipped couplet: 'I told him what I thought, and told no more / Than what he found himself was apt and true.' When she persisted, 'You told . . . ', he barked in her face 'go to, charm your tongue.'

For a split second, Wanamaker's Emilia froze, stopped in her tracks by a fascinated concentration on Iago's voice, as if hearing him for the first time. What was at stake here was more than the revelation of the truth that would destroy her husband, the mastery of the narrative that would end the story in Desdemona's innocence, not defamation. The ownership of speech was at stake. Would Emilia obey? How much easier to obey; to let the 'lie' stand; to 'nothing know, but for his fantasy'. Desdemona had stopped Emilia talking in 4.3. Iago wanted her gagged now. But Emilia resisted. She was 'bound to speak' so that this narrative wouldn't go Iago's way. 'What, are you mad?' His contempt was palpable. Then, 'I charge you get you home.' Their exchanged looks exposed their entire marital history, 'home' as a lock-up garage housing charmed tongues and madness. Even now, though, habits of abjection died hard. Emilia asked permission of the patriarchy: 'Good gentlemen, let me have leave to speak'; apologized ''Tis proper I obey him', but then declared 'not now'. The divorce crisis that had haunted this play from the beginning finally arrived with the true and loyal housewife staging her 'gross revolt' in monosyllabic observation, 'Perchance, Iago, I will ne'er go home.'

Yet even now, as Othello told his version of events, his officers moved to huddle around him where he sat at the foot of the bed, male solidarity positioned to see things from Othello's eyes as he urged his evidence of marital infidelity – a handkerchief. Emilia looked wild. Again, Iago warned: 'Hold your peace.' But Emilia was now deeply dangerous, would tear down the patriarchy with her bare hands, would 'be in speaking, liberal as the air, / Let heaven, and men' – her fierce iteration spat the word – 'and devils . . . / All, all cry shame against me, yet I'll speak.' 'Villainous whore!' cried the 'honest' husband, even now seeking consensus from the men around him, and validation from the old dependable stereotype that could be relied upon to unmask Emilia, the 'erring' wife, for what her speaking made her – the 'cunning whore of Venice', 'filth' who 'liest!' And staggeringly, that exhausted equation between speech and incontinence looked like it might prevail. They nearly believed him, as Emilia cried out desperately, 'I do not, I do not.' A rumble like the thunder he was summoning rose out of Othello's throat. Iago lunged across the bed, pulling Emilia backwards into him, her eyes widening as she felt the blade slide between her ribs. Then, as the men's and women's narratives again diverged, Gratiano charged after Iago while Emilia, asking, 'Lay me by my mistress' side', returned to gossiping with Desdemona. Her language of intimacy, spoken against Desdemona's cheek, restored women's real histories to the narrative, locating Desdemona's and Emilia's, the latest 'history', among them. 'What did thy song bode, lady?': her reference was secret, incomprehensible to any of the men looking on. Dying, Wanamaker's Emilia fumbled to pull the wedding sheets smooth around dead Desdemona as she softly sang 'Willow, willow, willow'. Here was a space, like Glenn Close's Gertrude found on the side of the grave raining petals with her requiem down on Ophelia's dead face in Zeffirelli's *Hamlet*, that belonged only to women, that opened an aperture on to an alternative narrative that might have been. And as Wanamaker's Emilia reached for Desdemona, stretching across the sheets to fold the dead hand in hers, their bodies touched in speaking: 'Hark, canst thou hear me?'

* * *

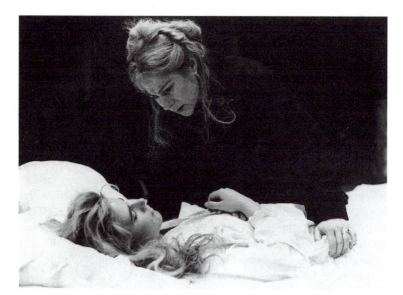

Plate 24 'What did thy song bode, lady?' Zoe Wanamaker and Imogen Stubbs in Trevor Nunn's 1990 *Othello*.
Source: BBC/RSC.

At the end, Emilia hedges amnesia. Refusing to forget, she remembers in the scene present a past scene of women's gossip – 'What did thy song bode, lady?' – and, in remembering, turns memory into performance. She sings Desdemona's song. That is, she re-enacts Desdemona's death in the song Desdemona sang to remember another woman's death, offering her voice as a substitute for Desdemona's, putting that voice back into play even as the music in her throat chokes in a death rattle: 'Willow, willow, willow.' Emilia performs on Desdemona the work theatre performs on culture, work that is always the work of remembering. But remembering with a difference: for Desdemona's death as Emilia enacts it is not the same death Desdemona herself performed. Theatre's recapitulations give scope for improvisation, innovation. The 'ludic space' – Roland Barthes' term – is reconfigured.[23] The bed where Desdemona lies, the bed that obsesses male fantasy in *Othello*, finally produces the 'ocular proof' craved by the narrative, implicating Desdemona in a love triangle. But it's Emilia, not Michael Cassio, who makes up the numbers loading the tragic bed. Telling again, Emilia tells different. Was Desdemona a 'strumpet', 'turn'd to folly'? A 'liar gone to burning hell'? Emilia answers with 'true' tattle that changes Desdemona's ending – 'Moor, she was chaste, she lov'd thee, cruel Moor' – and tattle that changes her own ending, for Emilia dies not Iago-dumbed but 'speaking as I think'.

Remembering Wanamaker's Emilia I, too, am hedging amnesia with gossip, re-performing performance in a different mode, translating spectating into tattle. My aim is to contribute something to what Joseph Roach calls 'genealogies of performance', after Jonathan Arac's 'critical genealogies' – excavating 'the past that is necessary to account for how we got here and the past that is useful for conceiving alternatives to our present condition'. Performing the ending, Wanamaker's Emilia invents that which requires me never to forget. Performing Wanamaker performing Emilia, I want her performance remembered, for as her Emilia, at the end, accounted 'for how we got here', so she likewise embodied 'alternatives to our present condition'. Remembering performance for me is not just history but prophecy. Accurately recalling the past, we can make shrewd guesses about what's to come. I notice that the question Emilia puts at the end is an open one: 'What did thy song bode, lady?' In that openness I hear an invitation to future performers, spectators and tattlers to engage in performance, and with performance; to play the play and to gossip about it; to sing – and to 'bode'.

NOTES

PREFACE

1 Clifford Geertz, 'Thick Description: Toward an Interpretive Theory of Culture', in *The Interpretation of Cultures*, New York, Basic Books, 1973, pp. 3–32.

2 Barbara Hodgdon, 'Replicating Richard: Body Doubles, Body Politics', *Theatre Journal* 50 (1998), p. 208.

3 Joseph Roach, *Cities of the Dead: Circum-Atlantic Performance*, New York, Columbia University Press, 1996, p. 30.

4 Stephen Orgel, 'Nobody's Perfect, Or, Why Did the English Stage Take Boys for Women?', *South Atlantic Quarterly* 88.1 (Winter 1989), pp. 7–30. Orgel's article effectively raised the temperature under the rather less provocative question – 'How many people crossdressed in Renaissance England?' – opening Jean Howard's seminal article (and first salvo in the ideological debate it set off), 'Crossdressing, the Theatre, and Gender Struggle in Early Modern England', *Shakespeare Quarterly* 39 (Fall 1988), pp. 418–440. To call the crossdressed players 'boys' is not just provocative but misleading. It is clear from Philip Henslowe's playhouse accounts that women's roles were played by adult male actors. See, for example, entries on f. 37 and f. 43v of his *Diary* itemizing payments 'to geue the tayller to by tynssell' for 'bornes [William Bird, alias Borne] womones gowne', probably to fit him, as subsequent entries suggest, for the title role in *Alice Pierce* (R.A. Foakes and R.T. Rickert, *Henslowe's Diary*, Cambridge, Cambridge University Press, 1968, pp. 72, 85). The ingrained habit, in the face of documentary evidence to the contrary, of 'boying' the players partly rests on a misreading of Cleopatra's assertion that she would rather die than 'see / Some squeaking Cleopatra boy my greatness / I'th' posture of a whore'. Her comment isn't metatheatrical and certainly doesn't dissolve the illusion of her performance, for Cleopatra isn't a boy player drawing attention to the boy's body beneath the role. She's a man. And what she's saying is, 'Compared to the real me [that is, Shakespeare's 'me'], any re-presentation of me [on a Roman, or a rival London stage] will be diminishing – mere child's play.'

5 Jonathan Dollimore, Steve Brown and Susan Zimmerman, quoted in David Cressy's circumspect and wide-ranging revisionist survey of the politics of crossdressing in *Travesties and Transgressions in Tudor and Stuart England*, Oxford, Oxford University Press, 2000, pp. 92–115.

6 Asking, 'How aware is the audience of the 'boy' and how does that affect response?' Dawson answers, 'The simple answer and certainly that supported by what eyewitness accounts exist is that the audience by convention simply ignored the gender of the actor, reading him as her.' See 'Performance and Participation: Desdemona, Foucault, and the Actor's Body' in James C. Bulman (ed.), *Shakespeare, Theory, and Performance*, London, Routledge, 1996, p. 40. Confirming that response in the modern theatre, Peter Holland comments on the Cheek by Jowl *As You Like It* that in this crossdressed, all-male production, 'Gender became a construct of performance, and sexuality was placed within the control of character, not actor.' See *English Shakespeares: Shakespeare on the English Stage in the 1990s*, Cambridge, Cambridge University Press, 1997, p. 91.

7 See Chapter 2.

8 Philippa Berry, *Shakespeare's Feminine Endings: Disfiguring Death in the Tragedies*, London, Routledge, 1999, p. 166.

9 Dawson, 'Performance and Participation', p. 37.

1 BODY PARTS – OR PARTS FOR BODIES

1 Citations follow the Arden *King Lear*, Kenneth Muir (ed.), London, Routledge, 1991. In an account of *The True Chronicle History of King Leir*, pp. xxiv–xxxiv (extracts appear in an appendix), Muir observes that 'in all the sources known to have been used by Shakespeare, with the one exception of the old play, Cordelia commits suicide', p. xxxi. That is strictly true, except that the suicide occurs five years later, after a counter-revolution that installs her nephews as rulers. The chronicles and epic poems notwithstanding, in the 'old' play she lives at the end.

2 Ludmilla Jordanova, 'Happy Marriages and Dangerous Liaisons: Artists and Anatomy' in Deanna Petherbridge (ed.), *The Quick and the Dead*, Manchester, Cornerhouse Publications, 1997, p. 100.

3 Keir Elam, '"In what chapter of his bosom?": Reading Shakespeare's Bodies' in Terence Hawkes (ed.), *Alternative Shakespeares 2*, London, Routledge, 1996, p. 145.

4 Anthony B. Dawson, 'Performance and Participation: Desdemona, Foucault, and the Actor's Body' in James C. Bulman (ed.), *Shakespeare, Theory, and Performance*, London, Routledge, 1996, p. 31.

5 Elam, '"In what chapter of his bosom?"', p. 144. See also Mary Douglas, *Natural Symbols: Explorations in Cosmology*, New York, Pantheon, 1970; Michel Foucault, *Discipline and Punish: The Birth of the Prison*, trans. Alan Sheridan, Harmondsworth, Penguin, 1977; Mikhail Bakhtin, *Rabelais and His World*, trans. Helene Iswolsky, Bloomington, Indiana University Press, 1984; Thomas Laqueur, *Making Sex: Body and Gender from the Greeks to Freud*, Cambridge, Massachusetts, Harvard University Press, 1990; Jonathan Goldberg, *Sodometries: Renaissance Texts, Modern Sexualities*, Stanford, Stanford University Press, 1992; Peter Stallybrass, 'Patriarchal Territories: The Body Enclosed' in Margaret Ferguson *et al.* (eds), *Rewriting the Renaissance: The Discourses of Sexual Difference in Early Modern Europe*, Chicago, University of Chicago Press, 1986; Laura Levine, *Men in Women's Clothing: Anti-theatricality and Effeminization 1579–1642*, Cambridge, Cambridge University Press, 1986; Gale Kern

Paster, *The Body Embarrassed: Drama and the Disciplines of Shame in Early Modern England*, Ithaca, Cornell University Press, 1993; Jonathan Sawday, *The Body Emblazoned: Dissection and the Human Body in Renaissance Culture*, London, Routledge, 1995.

6 Dawson, 'Performance and Participation', p. 31.

7 Dawson, 'Performance and Participation', p. 41.

8 Dawson, 'Performance and Participation', pp. 41, 44.

9 Janet Adelman, *Suffocating Mothers: Fantasies of Maternal Origin in Shakespeare's Plays*, Hamlet *to* The Tempest, London, Routledge, 1992, p. 127.

10 Elisabeth Bronfen, *Over Her Dead Body: Death, Femininity and the Aesthetic*, Manchester, Manchester University Press, 1992, pp. 65, 208.

11 The word was contemporary to Shakespeare's theatre. Philip Henslowe entered in his Diary (f. 117v) a payment to 'John thare the 23 of octob*er* 1602 to paye vnto the paynter of the properties for the playe of the iij brothers'; these may have included 'a tabell & a coffen' elsewhere itemized. See R.A. Foakes and R.T. Rickert (eds), *Henslowe's Diary*, Cambridge, Cambridge University Press, 1968, p. 218.

12 See Peter Stallybrass, 'Transvestism and the "Body Beneath": Speculating on the Boy Actor' in Susan Zimmerman (ed.), *Erotic Politics: Desire on the Renaissance Stage*, London, Routledge, 1992, pp. 64–83. Stallybrass and I arrive at a similar notion of 'vexed looking', but whereas he fixes his gaze narrowly upon the boy player undressing, I widen the focus to encompass all demands upon the audience to 'Look there!'

13 For a much fuller mapping than I can present here of the early modern discovery of the 'undiscover'd country' of death see Michael Neill, *Issues of Death: Mortality and Identity in English Renaissance Tragedy*, Oxford, Clarendon Press, 1998, an indispensible *A–Z* of this 'natural' landscape constructed by mankind's imagination. See also Marjorie Garber's *Coming of Age in Shakespeare*, London, Routledge, 1981, rpt. 1997, pp. 213–241.

14 Foakes and Rickert, *Diary*, pp. 277–278.

15 Foakes and Rickert, *Diary*, p. 279.

16 Norman E. McClure (ed.), *The Letters of John Chamberlain Vol. I*, Philadelphia, American Philosophical Society, 1939, pp. 194–195.

17 Foakes and Rickert, *Diary*, p. 297.

18 Peter M. Sacks, *The English Elegy: Studies in the Genre from Spenser to Yeats*, London, Johns Hopkins University Press, 1985, pp. 1–2.

19 Roland Mushat Frye, *The Renaissance Hamlet: Issues and Responses in 1600*, Princeton, Princeton University Press, 1984, pp. 205, 206. I quote Frye's book extensively in this section for the wealth of visual material it compiles, particularly from English sources. His commentary has been superseded by Michael Neill's masterly study, *Issues of Death*, which gives a very full account of *Hamlet* but, while interested in tropes of the apocalypse, makes only passing reference to *King Lear*. See in particular Neill's section on 'Tragedy and the Funereal Arts', where his interest is on narrative closure and discursive bodies.

20 Quoted in Frye, *The Renaissance Hamlet*, p. 212.

21 Frye, *The Renaissance Hamlet*, p. 210.

22 Frye, *The Renaissance Hamlet*, p. 212. The painting, Frye continues, 'was among the earliest bequests to Dulwich College' – established and endowed

by Edward Alleyn – and 'may have come as part of the 1626 gift from Alleyn's private collection, which had hung in his own home.'

23 Frye, *The Renaissance Hamlet*, p. 232. Shakespeare might have been familiar with the *transi* in Southwark Cathedral: dating from the fifteenth century, it displays the emaciated corpse of an Augustinian canon of the Priory of St Mary Overie. His rib cage protrudes, his face is a skull. The shroud has slipped off the back of his tonsured head – rather bizarrely, his hair is beautifully coifed – and falls modestly around his pelvis, held in place by one bony hand.

24 Frye, *The Renaissance Hamlet*, p. 232.

25 Quoted by Julian Litten, *The English Way of Death: The Common Funeral Since 1450*, London, Robert Hale, 1991, p. 66. This drawing, afterwards, was Donne's daily contemplation and served, *post mortem*, as the cartoon for his monument in St Paul's.

26 *Calendar of State Papers Venetian IX* (1592–1603), edited by Horatio Brown, London, HM Stationery Office, 1897, p. 338.

27 Ashmole ms. 830, f. 18. Printed in Mrs Maxwell Scott, *The Tragedy of Fotheringay*, London, Sands & Co, 1925; first published 1895, p. 260.

28 *Calendar of State Papers Venetian X* (1603–1607), edited by Horatio Brown, London, HM Stationery Office, 1900, p. 3. Letter dated 12 April 1603.

29 Tanner ms. 78, f. 129, printed in Maxwell Scott, *The Tragedy of Fotheringay*, p. 251.

30 Stonyhurst ms. Ang. A. iii. 77. I am indebted for the transcript of this manuscript to Catherine Loomis who contextualizes and analyses the document in 'Elizabeth Southwell's Manuscript Account of the Death of Queen Elizabeth [with text]' in *English Literary Renaissance* 26:1, 1996, pp. 482–509. Attending the queen at her death were Ann Russell, Lady Warwick (daughter of the second Earl of Bedford, who had waited upon Elizabeth since her accession); Philadelphia Carey, Lady Scrope (first cousin to the queen and younger sister to Kate Carey, Countess of Nottingham [d. 1602], Elizabeth's closest and best loved companion); and Elizabeth Howard, Lady Southwell (author of the Stonyhurst ms. and daughter to Kate Carey and Charles Howard, Earl of Nottingham). Julian Litten, in *The English Way of Death*, p. 42, is hardly correct in discrediting the story by discrediting 'Mistress Southwell' as 'a minor courtier' and 'a Roman Catholic'. See, too, John Chamberlain's long letter to Dudley Carleton on 30 March 1603: 'no doubt but you shall heare her Majesties sicknes and manner of death diversly related: for even here the papists do tell strange stories, as utterly voyde of truth, as of all civill honestie or humanitie. I had a goode means [Chamberlain's friend, William Gilbert, was the Queen's physician] to understand how the world went, and finde her disease to be nothing but a setled and unremovable melancholie.' For all Chamberlain knew, 'the body was not opened but wrapt up in seareclothes and other preservatives', McClure, *Letters*, pp. 188, 190. But he was writing a full month before the queen was interred.

31 McClure, *Letters*, pp. 188, 190.

32 Sidney Lee, *Stratford on Avon*, London, Seeley & Co, 1885, p. 46. Doubts about the story's veracity – though not its circulation – abound. See Patricia Wainwright, *Trinity Tales*, The Parochial Church Council of Holy Trinity, Stratford-upon-Avon, 1983, pp. 28–29.

33 In the *Iconologia* Caesar Ripa's Truth was a naked woman looking at the sun. First published in Rome in 1593 without illustrations, Ripa's book of emblems was reissued in 1603 with illustrations. It was in this form, according to Rosemary Freeman in *English Emblem Books*, London, Chatto, 1948, that 'it reached England and soon became a source-book for Jacobean personification', p. 79.

34 Both re-genderings are painfully apt, for Lear, while he makes his daughters monsters, makes himself the mother. See Carol Chillington Rutter, 'Eel Pie and Ugly Sisters in *King Lear*,' *Essays in Theatre* 13:2, 1995, pp. 135–158, and Adelman, *Suffocating Mothers*, p. 113.

35 *King Lear*, directed by Peter Brook (1971), Columbia Pictures, in association with the Royal Shakespeare Company; designed by Wahkevitch and Anggard; Lear: Paul Scofield; Goneril: Irene Worth; Regan: Susan Engel; Cordelia: Anne-Lise Gabold; Fool: Jack McGowran. Released: 22 July 1971. Distributed by RCA Columbia on video. See, too, Jack Jorgens, '*King Lear*: Peter Brook and Grigori Kozintsev' in *Shakespeare on Film*, Bloomington, Indiana University Press, 1977, pp. 235–251; Peter Holland, 'Two-Dimensional Shakespeare: *King Lear* on Film' and Kenneth S. Rothwell, 'Representing *King Lear* on Screen: From Metatheatre to "Meta-Cinema"' in Anthony Davies and Stanley Wells (eds), *Shakespeare and the Moving Image: The Plays on Film and Television*, Cambridge, Cambridge University Press, 1994, pp. 50–68 and 211–233; and Barbara Hodgdon, 'Two *King Lear*s: Uncovering the Filmtext,' *Literature and Film Quarterly* 11:3, 1983, pp. 143–151.

36 *King Lear*, directed by Adrian Noble; designed by Anthony Ward; Lear: Robert Stephens; Goneril: Janet Dale; Regan: Jenny Quayle; Cordelia: Abigail McKern; Fool: Ian Hughes. Opened 20 May 1993.

37 *King Lear*, directed by Nick Hytner; designed by David Fielding; Lear: John Wood; Goneril: Estelle Kohler; Regan: Sally Dexter; Cordelia: Alex Kingston; Fool: Linda Kerr Scott. Opened 11 July 1990.

38 Ted Hughes, *The Birthday Letters*, London, Faber and Faber, 1998.

2 SNATCHED BODIES

1 See Grigori Kozintsev, *Shakespeare: Time and Conscience*, translated by Joyce Vining, New York, Hill and Wang, 1966, which looks back on his theatre production of the play and contains his production diary of the film; Jack J. Jorgens, 'Image and Meaning in the Kozintsev *Hamlet*,' *Literature and Film Quarterly* 1:4,1973, pp. 307–315; Jay Halio, 'Three Filmed *Hamlet*s,' *Literature and Film Quarterly* 1:4, 1973, pp. 316–320; Edward Quinn, 'Zeffirelli's *Hamlet*,' *Shakespeare on Film Newsletter* 15:2,1991, pp. 1–12; Michael P. Jensen, 'Mel Gibson on Hamlet,' *Shakespeare on Film Newsletter* 15:2, 1991, pp. 1–6; H.R. Coursen, *Shakespearean Performance as Interpretation*, Newark, University of Delaware Press, 1992; and Felix Barker, *The Oliviers: A Biography*, London, Hamish Hamilton, 1953, which appears to be the text Olivier raided for his subsequent autobiographies.

2 All quotations of *Hamlet* follow the Arden *Hamlet*, Harold Jenkins (ed.), London, Routledge, 1993; quotations of all other Shakespeare plays follow *The Complete Works of Shakespeare*, David Bevington (ed.), 4th ed., New York, Harper Collins, 1992.

3 Q1 and F evidently derive from playhouse copy (notoriously, the Q1 stage directions read like a record of stage business: '*Leartes leapes into the graue*' and, two lines later, '*Hamlet leapes in after Leartes*'). It's unlikely that Ophelia's 'body' was a dummy. Props were costly to make and maintain in the Elizabethan theatre – an unnecessary expense when an actor was on hand to play dead. Philip Henslowe's inventories of properties held in stock by the Admiral's Men at the Rose in the 1598 – the only playhouse inventories of their kind – itemize a number of body parts but no corpses; see R. A. Foakes and R.T. Rickert, *Henslowe's Diary*, Cambridge, Cambridge University Press, 1968, pp. 316–325.

4 John Dover Wilson, quoted in Jenkins (ed.), *Hamlet*, 390n who observes that 'the stage affords many instances of the supposed dead rising from their [open] coffins'. The communal 'parish coffin', also called a 'shell', was used for funerals but not burials – it went back to the church from the grave to await its next occupant while the corpse, wrapped only in its shroud, settled into the ground. Aristocratic corpses were normally embalmed, wrapped in a shroud and cerecloth, then in lead, and coffined. Is Ophelia's corpse made 'common' by 'common' burial? For another reading of Ophelia's burial see Roland Mushat Frye, *The Renaissance Hamlet: Issues and Responses in 1600*, Princeton, Princeton University Press, 1984, pp. 243–253. For more on burial custom, particularly the practices of embalming and dressing the corpse for the grave, see Julian Litten's comprehensively illustrated *The English Way of Death: The Common Funeral Since 1450*, London, Robert Hale, 1991.

5 Barbara Hodgdon, 'Two *King Lear*s: Uncovering the Filmtext,' *Literature and Film Quarterly* 11:3, 1983, pp. 143–151.

6 Hodgdon, 'Two *King Lear*s', pp. 143, 144.

7 In conversation.

8 Laurence Olivier, 'An Essay in Hamlet', in Brenda Cross (ed.), *The Film Hamlet: A Record of its Production*, London, Saturn Press, 1948, pp. 9–15, esp. p. 12.

9 Both Vertinskaya and Simmons were eighteen years old when they played Ophelia. As Felix Barker tells it, when Olivier asked Simmons to take the part, she was (although a veteran of eleven films), 'At first . . . so amazed and overawed that she said she couldn't possibly do it. Olivier told her he was quite sure she could, and . . . explained the part to her' (Felix Barker, *The Oliviers: A Biography*, London, Hamish Hamilton, 1953, p. 258). Although she read her audition speech 'a little falteringly' Olivier discerned in her 'great natural talent' and felt her 'warmth and sensitivity' would 'make up for her lack of experience'. She was, in short, a child he could tutor. In *Shakespeare: Time and Conscience*, Kozintsev imagined Ophelia as 'a small, slender girl', p. 218; 'a sweet girl, half a child, whom they turn into a doll', p. 255, and although Bonham-Carter was twenty-four when she played Ophelia, Mel Gibson's Hamlet saw her as 'still a child . . . fourteen years old and just beginning to awaken sexually . . . . too young to be sexual, and besides, Hamlet would never use her in that way', Jensen, 'Mel Gibson on Hamlet', p. 1.

10 Olivier, *On Acting*, London, Weidenfeld and Nicolson, p. 198.

11 For a brilliant psychoanalytic reading of this filmtext, see Peter Donaldson's

Shakespearean Films/Shakespearean Directors, London, Unwin Hyman, 1990, pp. 31–67.

12 See Donaldson, *Shakespearean Films*, pp. 39–51; and Olivier, *On Acting*, p. 198.

13 Olivier had the wall decorations – hazel sprigs and lovers' knots – copied from frescoes at Notley Abbey, which he'd bought in 1944.

14 On this sequence, see Laurence Olivier, *Confessions of an Actor: An Autobiography*, New York, Simon and Schuster, 1982, p. 122; and Olivier, *On Acting*, p. 198.

15 Of the Millais painting, Showalter in 'Representing Ophelia' says, 'The artist rather than the subject dominates the scene. The division of space between Ophelia and the natural details Millais has so painstakingly pursued reduces her to one more visual object; and the painting has such a hard surface, strangely flattened perspective, and brilliant light that it seems cruelly indifferent to the woman's death', p. 85 – except, of course, that Ophelia in Millais's painting is not dead. For an account of his model, Elizabeth Siddall, that complicates the relationship between artist and subject and explores the idea of the 'muse', see Bronfen, *Over Her Dead Body: Death, Femininity, and the Aesthetic*, Manchester, Manchester University Press, 1992, pp. 168–178.

16 In his 1967 film *King Lear*, Kozintsev uses the same cut to a bird in flight to symbolize the soul. So does another Russian *Hamlet*, the BBC's *Animated Tales* version. Ophelia dematerializes at the end of an arched corridor as, sweetly mad, she leaves Elsinore, an ethereal waif in white, who reappears crossing a reed marsh. A splash is heard. A heron, startled by the noise, rises out of the reeds and flies into an eternal vanishing point.

17 The burial scenes in Olivier, Kozintsev and Zeffirelli all run between eight and nine minutes; Ophelia is on camera for twenty-four, thirty-two, and thirty-eight seconds respectively.

18 See Michael MacDonald, 'Ophelia's Maimed Rites,' *Shakespeare Quarterly* 38, 1986, pp. 308–317. 'Slapstick tragedy' is Arthur Lindley's coinage in 'The Unbeing of the Overreacher', *Modern Language Review* 84, 1989, pp. 1–17, esp. 1.

19 On the burial of suicides, see Jenkins (ed.), *Hamlet*, 376n and 388n, and Michael MacDonald and Terence Murphy, *Sleepless Souls: Suicide in Early Modern England*, Oxford, Clarendon Press, 1990, pp. 42–49. Desecrated burial was a folk custom tolerated by the Church but not formalized in canon law until 1662. See Frye, *The Renaissance* Hamlet; Clare Gittings, *Death, Burial and the Individual in Early Modern England*, Beckenham, Croom Helm, 1984; and J.V. Holleram, 'Maimed Funeral Rites in *Hamlet*,' *English Literary Renaissance* 19, 1989, pp. 65–93.

20 On the idea of the grave as mystified space, see MacDonald and Murphy, *Sleepless Souls*, pp. 45–46.

21 On profaning the moment, see Lynda E. Boose, 'The Father and the Bride in Shakespeare,' *PMLA* 97, 1982, pp. 325–347.

22 The Folio, too, contains a version of this stage direction, but I rely on Q1 here because of that quarto's proximity to early modern stage practice. See Steven Urkowitz, 'Good News about "Bad" Quartos' in Maurice Charney (ed.), *'Bad' Shakespeare: Revaluations of the Shakespeare Canon*, London, Associated University Presses, 1988, pp. 189–206; and Random Cloud,

'The Marriage of Good and Bad Quartos,' *Shakespeare Quarterly* 33, 1982, pp. 421–431. An elegy on Richard Burbage, perhaps by John Fletcher, confirms that Q1 records stage practice: 'Hee's gone & with him what a world are dead . . . / . . . young Hamlett . . . . / Oft haue I seene him leap into the graue . . .'; quoted in E.K. Chambers, *The Elizabethan Stage* 4 vols., Oxford, Clarendon Press, 1923, vol. 2, p. 309.

23 Like Jean Simmons, Winslet was entirely new to Shakespeare, though not to film. In *Jude*, she'd played Sue Bridehead, elaborating Sue's sexual anxiety and making her a figure of powerful affect, qualities Branagh may have wanted for Ophelia. In casting her, Branagh was certainly aiming at box-office receipts, but as one who aspires to Olivier in so much, he may also have seen himself playing Larry to Winslet's Jean.

24 For a discussion that dismantles the idea of the Shakespearean text as the fixed site of performance see W.B. Worthen, *Shakespeare and the Authority of Performance*, Cambridge, Cambridge University Press, 1997.

25 If there were a Victorian version of Hogarth's *Harlot's Progress*, Holman Hunt's *Conscience* would hang in the narrative sequence just before Millais's *Ophelia*. His fallen woman, her hair streaming down her back, rises from the lap of her lover who lounges at a piano, a scene, observes Andrew Motion, in *Wainewright the Poisoner*, London, Faber and Faber, 2000, that 'seventeenth-century Dutch paintings of women playing the spinet had made . . . a standard symbol of sexual availability', p. 77. Her eyes are fixed expectantly on what lies beyond the wide-open French windows (which the viewer sees reflected in the wall mirror behind her). Is it freedom she seeks in the world beyond her bourgeois prison-drawing room, or death? For a discussion of Holman Hunt, du Maurier, their representation of the woman's body, and a contextual reading of the Victorian myths of womanhood and vampirism that informs *Hamlet*, see Nina Auerbach, *Woman and the Demon*, Cambridge, Massachusetts, Harvard University Press, 1982. See, too, Bronfen, *Over Her Dead Body*, pp. 313–323. The visual quotation Winslet's Ophelia makes most insistently, particularly in the funeral scene, is of Elizabeth Siddall as portrayed by Rossetti and Millais.

26 The new line is 'My lord!'; the reassigned speech is the letter from Hamlet (2.2). The first interpolation adds a bizarre twist to the narrative, for it makes Ophelia, still ignorant of her father's death, the one who warns Hamlet that soldiers are after him.

27 'Gate' has been a euphemism in theatre since Aristophanes wrote *Lysistrata*.

28 The most infamous cemetery in England, Highgate has been the site of several bizarre funerals, among them Lucy Westenra's in *Dracula* and Elizabeth Siddall's in real life. Siddall, Dante Gabriel Rossetti's wife and model for *Beata Beatrix*, was Millais's Ophelia. When she died in February 1862 of an overdose of laudanum (perhaps a suicide) Rossetti expressed his grief and guilt by burying with her his only copy of his last poems. Some years later he changed his mind and ordered an exhumation of the body so the book could be retrieved. The story quoted from Bronfen in *Over Her Dead Body* uncannily recalls Shakespeare's Ophelia and weirdly predicts Winslet's: 'In [Rossetti's] absence, his friends gathered together at Highgate Cemetery on 4 October 1869, a bonfire was lit to dispel unpleasant smells and in the light of the flames the coffin was lifted once again out of the grave, opened and the little green book removed. Supposedly,

because the body was so well preserved, or because the spectators . . . were mesmerized by the effect, Siddall . . . is said to have appeared radiantly beautiful, a figure of fine pallor among an abundance of red golden hair', p. 177. The connection between Lucy Westenra, Ophelia and Winslet is equally teasing. In a diary entry made a week before her death Lucy writes, 'Well, here I am to-night, hoping for sleep, and lying like Ophelia in the play, with "virgin crants and maiden strewments"' – the garlic wreath Van Helsing makes her wear – 'Good-night everybody', Bram Stoker, *Dracula*, Harmondsworth, Penguin, 1984 (first published 1897), p. 161. Within days of her funeral, the un-dead Lucy is walking on Hampstead Heath, which borders Highgate Cemetery. Reporting strange incidents on the Heath, the *Westminster Gazette* tells of a number of children lured away at sunset by a 'bloofer lady', and continues: 'A correspondent writes us that to see some of the tiny tots pretending to be the "bloofer lady" is supremely funny . . . [and] naively says that even Ellen Terry could not be so winningly attractive as some of these grubby-faced little children pretend – and even imagine themselves – to be', p. 213. Ellen Terry was, of course, the Victorian theatre's most celebrated Ophelia.

29 I am grateful to Dr Timothy Healy for conducting a post-mortem examination of Ophelia.

30 See also Barbara Hodgdon, '*William Shakespeare's Romeo + Juliet*: Everything's Nice in America', *Shakespeare Survey* 52, Cambridge, Cambridge University Press, 1999, pp. 88–98.

3 SHADOWING CLEOPATRA

1 Most pre-1970s production photographs aren't really that. Angus McBean, for instance, who photographed Ashcroft in 1953, always held his own photocalls, set-up compositions under special lighting. For a discussion of production photography that proposes 'a materialist poetics of photographic evidence' see Barbara Hodgdon, '"Here Apparent": Photography, History, and the Theatrical Unconscious' in Edward Petcher (ed.), *Textual and Theatrical Shakespeare: Questions of Evidence*, Iowa City, University of Iowa Press, 1996, pp. 181–209.

2 For a brilliant reading of this production, see Hodgdon, 'Doing the Egyptian', in *The Shakespeare Trade*, pp. 74–109.

3 *The Play Pictorial* 9, 1906, p. 54.

4 See the range of representations reproduced in Lucy Hughes-Hallett, *Cleopatra: Histories, Dreams and Distortions*, London, Vintage, 1990, but notice that Alma Tadema's painting, Fig. 33, has been cropped, cutting off the black attendant who waits at Cleopatra's elbow. See, too, Mary Hamer, *Signs of Cleopatra: History, Politics, Representation*, London, Routledge, 1993.

5 Both film stills are reproduced in Hodgdon, *The Shakespeare Trade*, Figs. 24 and 26. And see Hamer, *Signs of Cleopatra*, pp. 104–134.

6 Hodgdon, *The Shakespeare Trade*, Fig. 31.

7 On black, mass cultural representations of Cleopatra see Francesca T. Royster, 'Cleopatra as Diva: African-American Women and Shakespearean Tactics', in Marianne Novy (ed.), *Transforming Shakespeare: Contemporary Women's Re-visions in Literature and Performance*, New York, St Martin's Press, 1999, pp. 103–125.

8 On the vexed question of how critics read Cleopatra's blackness see Janet
   Adelman, for one, in *The Common Liar: An Essay on Antony and Cleopatra*,
   Oxford, Oxford University Press, 1973, who found it 'slightly alarming'
   that criticism hadn't 'speculated more widely about the issue of Cleopatra's
   color, particularly since directors have to make these kinds of decisions for
   every production', p. 182. But why only 'slightly' alarming? When G.K.
   Hunter was writing about Othello's colour in *Dramatic Identities and
   Cultural Tradition*, Liverpool, Liverpool University Press, 1978, he started
   from the assumption that the Moor's colour mattered a great deal, and that
   it was his business as a critic 'to suggest what it was possible' for his blackness to have meant. By contrast, Cleopatra's self-reference perplexes
   Adelman. What does Cleopatra mean when she calls herself 'black'?
   For Adelman, her 'use of the word is by no means clear'. Hedging the question with avoidance as obvious as Adelman's, the black academic Eldred
   Jones in *Othello's Countrymen*, London, Oxford University Press, 1965,
   resorted to euphemisms to talk about Cleopatra's colour and how it might
   have indexed her legibility on stage – that is, on Shakespeare's stage, for
   Jones didn't even begin to imagine a black Cleopatra on any contemporary
   stage in England or America. Wole Soyinka, the black African poet, playwright and academic, likewise yielded to euphemism. Confessing in
   'Shakespeare and the Living Dramatist', *Shakespeare Survey* 36, 1983, pp.
   1–10, that he'd 'winced' through 'the entire night' of the RSC's most
   recent *Antony and Cleopatra*, he was finally able to account for Cleopatra's
   performance only as a deliberate send-up: 'Perhaps the RSC knew that it
   had a problem in persuading even an English audience to accept any interpretation of Cleopatra by an English actress.' Errol Hill's *Shakespeare in
   Sable: A History of Black Shakespearean Actors*, Amherst, University of
   Massachusetts Press, 1984, made explicit what Soyinka didn't say, that
   'textual references to her color . . . leave no doubt' that Shakespeare wrote
   Cleopatra black, but he could produce no theatre record in England or
   America of any black performance. See also Antony Barthelemy, *Black
   Face, Maligned Race: The Representation of Blacks in English Drama from
   Shakespeare to Southerne*, Baton Rouge, Louisiana State University Press,
   1987; Jack D'Amico, *The Moor in English Renaissance Drama*, Tampa,
   University of South Florida Press, 1991; Ania Loomba, *Gender, Race,
   Renaissance Drama*, Oxford, Oxford University Press, 1989; bell hooks,
   Black Looks: Race and Representation, Boston, South End Press, 1992, and
   Michael Neill, editor of the latest Oxford *Antony and Cleopatra*, Oxford
   University Press, 1994, who thinks that 'the issue of racial difference in
   Antony and Cleopatra' is 'relatively insignificant', p. 87.
9 Richard Dyer, *White*, London, Routledge, 1997, pp. 24, 13.
10 Soyinka, 'Shakespeare and the Living Dramatist', p. 3.
11 To some extent I collapse what a more detailed history would keep separate.
   The histories of race in England and America are defined by origins and
   therefore utterly distinct; America's conditioned by slavery, Britain's, by
   imperialism.
12 Dyer, *White*, pp. 23, 24, 31, 32.
13 Jan Nederveen Pieterse, *White on Black: Images of Africa and Blacks in
   Western Popular Culture*, New Haven, Yale University Press, 1992, p. 172.
14 Dyer, *White*, p. 28.

15 For an important account of the 'representational technologies' belonging
   to Egypt and Rome that 'produce structurally dissimilar subjects' but that
   ultimately sees Cleopatra as a sequence of performances, 'invested with all
   the property that goes with the playhouse', and that remains curiously
   unmaterialized performatively, see Linda Charnes, *Notorious Identity:
   Materializing the Subject in Shakespeare*, London, Harvard University Press,
   1993, pp. 103–153, esp. pp. 135, 128.
16 Michael Billington, *Peggy Ashcroft*, London, John Murray, 1988, p. 146.
17 Richard Huggett, *Binkie Beaumont: Eminence Grise of the West End Theatre
   1933–1972*, London, Hodder and Stoughton, 1989, p. 383.
18 Margaret Harris, for Motley, commented that the costumes were designed
   in deference to Evans' age. See Michael Mullin, *Design by Motley*, Newark,
   University of Delaware Press, 1996, p. 112.
19 Footage is preserved at the National Film and Television Archive, London.
   By contrast, across the same theatre season, only 340 performances of
   Shakespeare, all told, were given in London, including Michael Redgrave's
   Macbeth at the Aldwych, Donald Wolfit's *Hamlet*, *Othello* and *Lear* at the
   Savoy, and Alec Guinness's *Richard II* at the New Theatre.
20 Peter Higgs at the British Museum tells me that she has recently been
   reclassified, dated to the late Republican period, 40–30 BC, and therefore a
   contemporary of Cleopatra, but, without a royal diadem, unlikely to be a
   Hellenistic monarch. She is now thought to be Syrian.
21 Ivor Brown, *The Observer*, 3 May 1953; Peter Fleming, *The Spectator*, 8
   May 1953; Philip Hope-Wallace, *Time and Tide*, 8 May 1953. Famously,
   Langtry (frequently billed as the 'Jersey Lily'), played Cleopatra in 1890.
   Her real name was Charlotte le Breton. Ironically, then, English Lily was
   'Other'-wise Jersey French.
22 Harold Hobson, *The Sunday Times*, 3 May 1953.
23 *Birmingham Gazette*, 15 May 1953.
24 *Royal Leamington Spa Courier*, May 1953.
25 *Wolverhampton Express*, 29 April 1953.
26 Hope-Wallace's question has been asked, by one critic or another, of every
   Cleopatra ever since.
27 It was this sort of racist-imperialist thinking that would provoke the Suez
   Crisis three years later.
28 *Daily Mail*, 1 May 1953. See also Kathleen Tynan, *The Life of Kenneth
   Tynan*, London, Phoenix, 1995, p. 80.
29 The specific 'Frenchwoman' Tynan perhaps had in mind for Cleopatra was
   Sarah Bernhardt; but for an insight into the interpenetrating discourses of
   sex, race, and the foreign in Tynan's life, particularly as they were put in
   view in *Oh! Calcutta!*, see Kathleen Tynan, *The Life*.
30 Pieterse, *White on Black*, p. 186.
31 See, for example, Ivor Brown in *The Observer*, 3 May 1953; David Lewin in
   the *Daily Express*, 29 April 1953; the *London Evening News*, 29 April 1953.
32 Ashcroft and Robeson may have been lovers. Certainly, they exchanged love
   letters, Billington describing her as 'spiritually charmed and physically
   enthralled' to him and quoting her saying, 'I had never thought consciously
   about racism' until *Othello* 'put the significance of race straight in front of
   me and I made my choice where I stood', *Peggy Ashcroft*, p. 41. Infamously,
   reviewing Robeson's Othello, James Agate demonstrated precisely the

'manifestations of racism' Ashcroft was opposing. He wrote: 'his hands appeared to hang below his knees and his whole bearing, gait and diction were full of humility and apology, the inferiority complex in a word', quoted in Billington, *Peggy Ashcroft*, p. 41.

33 Kenneth Tynan, the *Daily Mail*, 1 May 1953.

34 *London Daily Herald*, 29 April 1953.

35 For re-reading this production and locating its blackness for me I am grateful to Roger Howells, who was there at the time, and later was stage manager at the RSC for thirty years.

36 Hodgdon, *The Shakespeare Trade*, p. 43.

37 The phrase, which seems to have originated with Nunn, was quoted in the souvenir programme and widely in press releases, but for an example of how the cycle, under different direction, might have been politicized, see Sally Beauman's *The Royal Shakespeare Company: A History of Ten Decades*, Oxford, Oxford University Press, 1982, p. 316. For Beauman, Nunn's Roman season charted an evolution from 'tribalism to authoritarianism, to colonialism, to decadence.'

38 *Coventry Evening Telegraph*, 'Stratford 72 Extra', 14 July 1972.

39 Terence Hawkes, *Meaning by Shakespeare*, London, Routledge, 1992, p. 43.

40 David Isaacs, *Coventry Evening Telegraph*, 3 August 1972. 'The worst kind of English liberalism' would be put in view four months later when the RSC staged in London the Arden-Darcy collaboration, *Island of the Mighty*. The project led to the biggest internal political crisis in the company's history as RSC 'liberals' tried to confront and discuss post-imperialist realities – but simply didn't know how. The script's subjects were Arthurian legend, Ireland and the Empire.

41 See for example Lynda E. Boose's '"The Getting of a Lawful Race": Racial Discourse in Early Modern England and the Unrepresentable Black Woman', p. 37, in Margo Hendricks and Patricia Parker (eds), *Women, 'Race', and Writing in the Early Modern Period*, London, Routledge, 1994, pp. 35–54. See, too, illustrations, reproduced in Richard Dyer's *White*, pp. 54, 55, from *Harper's Weekly* 9, December 1876, and *Punch*, 29 October 1881, that analogized not just Negro/Irish, black/white, south/north, primitive/civilized but also human/subhuman: both 'Paddy' and 'Sambo' in these cartoons are apes.

42 Peter Lewis, *Theatre Records* (Series A: vol. 83, 119), 16 August 1972; Felix Barker, *Evening News*, 16 August 1972; Don Chapman, the *Oxford Mail*, 16 August 1972.

43 The 'history' presented here as 'truth' is largely Plutarch, qualified by the observation that he would hardly have been impartial since, for family reasons, he hated Cleopatra.

44 Benedict Nightingale, the *New Statesman*, 25 August 1972; B.A. Young, the *Financial Times*, 16 August 1972; 'K.P.C.', the *Gloucester Citizen*, 16 August 1972; the *Stratford Herald*, 18 August 1972.

45 'Genuine' was placed as a rhetorical contrastive in Chapman's review to set up his facetious (racist) joke about 'the – one hopes *feigned* – piping eunuchs.'

46 Geoffrey Parsons, the *Morning Star*, 18 August 1972.

47 Kenneth Hurren, *The Spectator*, 19 September 1972.

48 *Guardian*, 16 August 1972.

49 In conversation, 18 October 1998. Benedict recounts that even at the read-through she was hypersensitive to rehearsal-room politics, for she 'had committed a terrible *faux pas* when [she] auditioned' for Charmian. She'd jumped speeches: 'My eye just went on to the next line – all of Charmian's scenes are with Cleopatra – and suddenly John stopped me! "That's Cleopatra's line," he said, quite sharply. "*You're* reading for Charmian!"' Some days into rehearsal, another, even more revealing incident occurred. Benedict had recently played an acclaimed *Medea* and had been given, at the end of the run, Medea's necklace as a token of her director's admiration – a stunning (and strangely totemic) scallop shell on a gold band, emblem of prophecy, sorcery, Medea's dark female power. Benedict now wore it constantly, as a sort of 'signature', until, in the middle of one day's rehearsal, Caird suddenly interrupted the scene and told her to remove it. 'That's when,' says Benedict, 'I knew I should be playing Cleopatra.' Instead, she wore the necklace as Zenocrate.

50 Malcolm Rutherford, the *Financial Times*, 7 November 1992; John Peter, *The Sunday Times*, 8 November 1992.

51 Paul Taylor, the *Independent*, 7 Novembr 1992.

52 *Financial Times*, 7 November 1992.

53 John Peter, *The Sunday Times*, 8 November 1992.

54 Kirsty Milne, the *Sunday Telegraph*, 8 November 1992.

55 Peter Holland, 'Shakespeare Performances in England, 1989–90', *Shakespeare Survey* 44, Stanley Wells (ed.), Cambridge, Cambridge University Press, 1992, p. 158.

56 In an address to the International Shakespeare Conference, Stratford-upon-Avon, August 1992.

57 Michael Billington, the *Guardian*, 21 May 1991.

58 Dea Birkett, 'Dark Star', the *Guardian*, 19 May 1991.

59 On the stereotype of the 'loose limbed negro' see Richard Dyer on black 'soul' dancing in *White*, p. 6.

60 Hughes-Hallett, *Cleopatra*, pp. 252, 253.

61 Birkett, the *Guardian*, 19 May 1991.

62 On white beauty see Hughes-Hallett, *Cleopatra*, p. 252; Dyer, *White*, p. 72.

63 Martin Bernal, *Black Athena: The Afroasiatic Roots of Classical Civilization* vol. 1, New Brunswick, Rutgers University Press, 1987, p. xv. Accounting for nineteenth-century appropriation, Bernal writes (his italics): '*after the rise of black slavery and racism, European thinkers were concerned to keep black Africans as far as possible from European civilization.* Where men and women in the Middle Ages and the Renaissance were uncertain about the colour of the Egyptians, the Egyptophile Masons tended to see them as white. Next, the Hellenomaniacs of the early 19th century began to doubt their whiteness and to deny that the Egyptians had been civilized. It was only at the end of the 19th century, when Egypt had been entirely stripped of its philosophic reputation, that its African affinities could be re-established. *Notice that in each case the necessary divide between blacks and civilization was clearly demarcated*', p. 30.

64 Edward Said, *Orientalism*, London, Penguin, 1995, pp. 21, 72.

65 Birkett, the *Guardian*, 19 May 1991.

66 By contrast, Nunn's 1972 programme contained twenty pages, three of advertising, the rest relevant to the production.

67 Benedict's Charmian was not noticed by reviewers although, as the production photographs record, she was the one who literally held together the
   'female triumvir' at the heart of the play. Reviewers described her Zenocrate
   as possessing a 'dignified, regal eroticism' (John Peter, *The Sunday Times*,
   6 September 1992); 'a wonderful mixture of passion, eroticism and
   anguish' that 'lends an ache of tenderness to the horror show' (Charles
   Spencer, the *Daily Telegraph*, 3 September 1992). Billington in the
   Guardian, 3 September 1992, thought her 'seductive', and Mark Thornton
   Burnett in the *The Times Higher Education Supplement*, 4 September 1992,
   said she was 'no subservient princess but an oppositional voice, racked by
   Tamburlaine's scouring triumphs'.
68 David Lister, 'To Play the Queen', the *Independent*, Tuesday Review, 1
   December 1998.
69 'Dominant culture,' says Chedgzoy, 'is already gay men's culture', for
   'whereas black people and women have sought to highlight their exclusion
   from cultural privilege and authority, gay men have always had access to
   those things – have, indeed, played a central role in defining and maintain-
   ing them', *Shakespeare's Queer Children*, Manchester, Manchester
   University Press, 1995, p. 190.
70 *Guardian*, 8 December 1998. The reference to 'quota filling' is a bit of
   journalistic nonsense. As it turned out, the Rylance production achieved an
   unexpected 'authenticity' – by casting a black actor to play Charmian in this
   all-male *Antony and Cleopatra*. *Plus ça change*.
71 W.B. Worthen, *Shakespeare and the Authority of Performance*, Cambridge,
   Cambridge University Press, 1997, p. 189.
72 Hawkes, *Meaning by Shakespeare*, p. 154.
73 Joyce Green MacDonald, 'Sex, Race, and Empire in Shakespeare's *Antony
   and Cleopatra*' (unpublished seminar paper), March 1995, p. 2; Lynda E.
   Boose, '"The Getting of a Lawful Race"', p. 47.
74 *OED* 'Egyptian', B.2. For more on the confusion between 'real' Egyptians
   and counterfeit gipsies who turn out to be English vagabonds in blackface see
   John Cowell's 1607 definition in *The Interpreter: or Booke Containing the
   Signification of Words*: 'Egyptions (*Egyptiani*) are in our statute's and lawes of
   England a counterfeit kind of roagues, that, being English or Welch people,
   accompany themselves together, disguising themselves in straunge roabes,
   blacking their faces and bodies, and framing to themselves an unknowne
   language, wander up and downe, and under pretence of telling Fortunes,
   curing diseases, and such like, abuse the ignorant common people', quoted in
   Geraldo U. de Sousa, *Shakespeare's Cross-Cultural Encounters*, Basingstoke,
   Macmillan, 1999. In forthcoming work Sujata Iyengar tracks England's gipsies, finding contemporary observation that cites gipsies as '"white" people in
   ethnic drag' whose 'filthy complexion', says Thomas Dekker, was faked. Sir
   Thomas Browne in *Pseudodoxia Epidemica* called gipsies 'Artificial Negroes'
   or 'Counterfeit Moors' who acquired 'their complexion by anointing their
   bodies with Bacon and fat substances, and so exposing them to the Sun.' The
   ballad of 'The Brave English Jipsie' cites another cosmetic technology: 'we
   doe dye in graine:/ The Walnut tree supplies our lacke, / What was made
   faire, we can make black' – that is, English gipsy 'roadies' acquired their
   blackface by the same means the players used in the theatre. See Iyengar,
   'Cleopatra', unpublished conference paper, pp. 1–11, April 2000.

75 Eldred Jones, *Othello's Countrymen: The African in English Renaissance Drama*, London, Oxford University Press, 1965, p. 28.

76 Hunter, *Dramatic Identities*, pp. 49–50, quoting Pseudo-Bede, *Exceptiones Patrum*.

77 R.A. Foakes and R.T. Rickert (eds), *Henslowe's Diary*, Cambridge, Cambridge University Press, 1968, p. 16 (f. 7). It seems likely that Shakespeare would have known *Zenobia*; his *Henry VI* opened at the Rose some days earlier. For identifying yet another black queen and her Cleopatra connection I am grateful to John Ray, Reader in Egyptology, Selwyn College, Cambridge.

78 Jones, *Othello's Countrymen*, p. 28.

79 T.J.B. Spencer (ed.), *Shakespeare's Plutarch*, London, Penguin, 1968, p. 205. Plutarch notes his 'vain expenses upon women', his 'rioting and banqueting' that finally forced his father to shut his doors to him in Rome; his sojourn in Greece where he adopted 'a manner of . . . speech called Asiatic'; his desire 'to be taken for Hercules, his ancestor' by dressing like him, and for 'Bacchus, father of mirth'. When Antony appeared in Egypt, 'there went a rumour in the people's mouths that the goddess Venus was come to play with the god Bacchus, for the general good of all Asia,' and although 'most men misliked' Antony's levity, 'the Alexandrians . . . liked it well' for 'Antonius showed them a comical face . . . ; and the Romans a tragical face', pp. 175, 198, 202, 206.

80 Barnaby Riche, *The Famous Hystory of Herodotus*, London, Thomas Marshe, 1584, Bodleian Library Douce HH243. Certainly, Ben Jonson knew Herodotus on Egypt by 1605; see his marginal references in *The Masque of Blackness*, C.H. Herford and Percy and Evelyn Simpson (eds), *Ben Jonson* vol. 7, Oxford, Clarendon Press, 1941, p. 161.

81 Ovid, Book III, verse 270; and see note 51 to Henry T. Riley's *The Heroïdes*, London, Bell & Daldy, 1869, p. 444.

82 When 'the foreigner is both a woman and a queen,' writes MacDonald in 'Sex, Race, and Empire', 'hierarchies of gender cancel hierarchies of race', p. 13.

83 E.K. Chambers, *The Elizabethan Stage* vol. 4, Oxford, Oxford University Press, 1923, p. 172.

84 Paul Yachnin, '"Courtiers of Beauteous Freedom": *Antony and Cleopatra* in Its Time,' *Renaissance and Reformation* 26.1, 1991, pp. 1–20, especially pp. 1, 4. See, too, Hamer, *Signs of Cleopatra*, p. 22; Jonathan Goldberg, *James I and the Politics of Literature: Jonson, Shakespeare, Donne and Their Contemporaries*, Stanford, Stanford University Press, 1989; and Hodgdon, *The Shakespeare Trade*, pp. 105–109.

85 Other contemporary commentators conceived the new empire and the king's relationship to it differently, John Chamberlain calling her 'old widow Britain' and wondering whether Parliament finally would succeed in bringing 'this longe wooing . . . to conclusion . . . that the King might be wedded' to her. See Norman E. McClure, *The Letters of John Chamberlain* vol. 1, Philadelphia, American Philosophical Society, 1939, p. 243.

86 B.A. Young, *Financial Times*, 16 August 1972; Robert Cushman, *The Observer*, 15 October 1978; David Roper, the *Daily Express*, 14 October 1982.

87 Chambers, *Elizabethan Stage*, vol. 4, p. 171.

88 McClure, *Letters* vol. 1, pp. 198–9.
89 Herford and Simpson (eds), *Ben Jonson* vol. 7, pp. 161, 169, 170, 174, 177. Inigo Jones's designs for the *Masque,* including one of a 'Daughter of Niger', are published in facsimile in Stephen Orgel and Roy Strong (eds), *Inigo Jones: The Theatre of the Stuart Court* 2 vols., Sotheby Park Vernet, University of California Press, 1973, vol. 1, p. 88.
90 For the best work on Anna's *Masque of Blackness* see three articles by Leeds Barroll, 'Inventing the Stuart Masque' in David Bevington and David Holbrook (eds), *The Politics of the Stuart Court Masque,* Cambridge, Cambridge University Press, 1998, pp. 121–143; 'Theatre as Text: The Case of Queen Anna and the Jacobean Court Masque' in A.L. Magnusson and C.E. McGee (eds), *The Elizabethan Theatre XIV* (1996), pp. 175–193, and 'The Court of the First Stuart Queen' in Linda Levy Peck (ed.), *The Mental World of the Jacobean Court,* Cambridge, Cambridge University Press, 1991, pp. 191–208. See also Boose, '"The Getting of a Lawful Race"'; Hardin Aasand, '"To Blanch an Ethiop, and Revive a Corse": Queen Anne and *The Masque of Blackness*', *Studies in English Literature* 32:2 (1992), pp. 271–285; Clare McManus, '"Defacing the Carcass": Anne of Denmark and Jonson's *The Masque of Blackness*' in Julie Sanders (ed.), *Refashioning Ben Jonson: Gender Politics and the Jonsonian Canon,* Basingstoke, Macmillan, 1998, pp. 93–113. Kim Hall's work on the masque in *Things of Darkness,* London, Cornell University Press, 1995, is unreliable, flawed by a number of factual errors: mistaking Anna's coronation entrance into Edinburgh for her 'wedding pageant'; mis-identifying a number of Anna's female courtiers, including confusing Francis Walsingham with Francis Howard, and claiming 'she later became notorious for poisoning her husband [*sic*] in the "Overbury affair"'; repeating the apocryphal story, passed down without any corroboration from John Gade to Ethel Carlton Williams, and quoted recently by Dympna Callaghan and Stephen Greenblatt, of the Negro boys dancing naked in the Oslo snow for Anna's wedding. Hall's assertions that *Blackness* figured in a 'discursive network' of Jacobean racial awareness, that 'actual black people were an integral part of Scottish court entertainment', and that, when James and Anna reigned in Scotland, 'Blacks were a common feature in the Scottish court, kept there as dehumanized alien curiosities' (p. 128) is not supported by any documentary evidence. On the contrary, I have been able to identify only one black body – 'Ane Moir' – in the royal household in the 1580s and 1590s.
91 Wanting us to learn to read theatre 'texts' sceptically, Leeds Barroll in 'Theatre as Text' queries Carleton as eyewitness: 'there is no indication that his status allowed him entry to the performance . . . invitations for which ambassadors were vying', p. 180. John Chamberlain, however, writing to Ralph Winwood on 26 January 1605, was certain Carleton did attend: 'I doubt not but Dudley Carleton hath acquainted you with all theyre Christmas games at court, for he was a spectator of all the sportes and shewes', McClure, *Letters,* vol. 1, p. 201.
92 For a reading of Carleton's two letters and their (political) differences, see Barroll, 'Theatre as Text', pp. 181–182.
93 Reading this same letter, Boose in '"The Getting of a Lawful Race"', p. 51, hears an 'obsessive', 'curiously punitive narration' marked by a 'fantasized

sense of a "Danger" that female blackness will leave marks on the white male who touches her', but doesn't pick up on Carleton's humour. His remark, later in the passage, about the fish out of water is clearly intended as a joke. Indeed, the entire letter seems to be written tongue in cheek.

94 Herford and Simpson, *Ben Jonson* vol. 10, p. 449.

95 In a future essay I intend to pursue this question by re-reading the Paul van Somer portrait of Queen Anna (one of the Queen's pictures now hanging in St James's) to correct the rather fanciful misreading imposed upon it by Kim Hall, who sees 'sensuality' in Anna's 'stance' and 'excess', even incontinence, in the painting's composition, for 'instead of being spread through the portrait, here the "company" surrounds Anne, almost enclosing her: the dog pawing at her dress . . . and the groom with the horse behind her, almost overtaking her'. 'Clearly,' she comments, Anna 'had a penchant for the unusual and exotic', *Things of Darkness*, pp. 238–239. Hall, however, fails to read the painting's cartouche, doesn't see the significance of Oatlands in the background, and neither sees nor understands the black/white imagery as troping Catholic Jesuit iconography.

96 Herford and Simpson, *Ben Jonson* vol. 10, p. 449.

97 Yachnin, '"Courtiers of Beauteous Freedom"', p. 7.

98 For examples of her 'performances' from her self-inflicted abortion in protest at the removal of baby Prince Henry from her maternal care, to the introduction of a new youth to dazzle the king's roving eye, thus ensuring the downfall of Somerset, see Leeds Barroll, 'The Court of the First Stuart Queen'. The verdict by the Venetian ambassador on Anna in 1607, quoted in Barroll, might have been Caesar's on Cleopatra: 'full of kindness for those who support her, but on the other hand she is terrible, proud, unendurable to those she dislikes', p. 207.

99 Janet Adelman, *Suffocating Mothers: Fantasies of Maternal Origins in Shakespeare's Plays*, Hamlet *to* The Tempest, London, Routledge, 1992, p. 176.

100 McClure, *Letters* vol. 1, pp. 205, 192.

101 McClure, *Letters* vol. 1, pp. 209, 238, 296, 298, 374, 399, 444, 474, 490.

102 McClure, *Letters* vol. 2, pp. 224, 232, 237.

103 Quoted from the RSC souvenir programme to Trevor Nunn's *Antony and Cleopatra*.

104 MacDonald 'Sex, Race, and Empire', pp. 4, 8.

105 I am thinking about Richard Dyer's *White* here, and proposing *Antony and Cleopatra* as the master text for the white racist mythography he traces.

106 Sinden was the last blacked-up Othello at the RSC.

4 DESIGNS ON SHAKESPEARE

1 All the design work I survey in this chapter was produced at the RST. *Measure for Measure* in 1978 was directed by Barry Kyle; in 1983, by Adrian Noble; in 1987, by Nicholas Hytner; in 1991, by Trevor Nunn.

2 I am, of course, remembering the opening of L.P. Hartley's *The Go-Between*.

3 Following Anne Pasternak Slater, who calls him *Shakespeare: The Director*, Sussex, Harvester, 1982, p. 1, I extend her suggestive anachronism. It is a commonplace of theatre history that there were no directors or designers

on Shakespeare's stage, but what is Peter Quince doing if not directing *Pyramus and Thisbe?* And Prince Hamlet is certainly more John-Barton-like than the 'tragedians of the city' might wish. It must have been standard playhouse practice to hold a company read-though so the players could hear the whole play, before the new book was copied into parts and distributed among them so they could learn their lines. Henslowe's *Diary* records one such occasion:

> lent vnto the company..
> .... for the boocke called
> th*e* famos wares of henry th*e* fryste & the prynce of
> walles the some of .... iiij li v s
>
> lent at that tyme vnto the company for to spend at
> th*e* Readynge of that boocke at the sonne in new
> fyshstreat*e* .... v s

I would guess the playwright gave the reading and 'directed' the play as he told it. While it is clear from Henslowe's accounts that the players had a developed sense of production design, the first design team we can identify was the Ben Jonson/Inigo Jones partnership. See R.A. Foakes and R.T. Rickert, *Henslowe's Diary*, Cambridge, Cambridge University Press, 1986, p. 88.

4 Extracts from the Proclamations of Apparel, 6 July 1597, 39 Elizabeth I, are re-printed in Carol Chillington Rutter, *Documents of the Rose Playhouse*, Manchester University Press, 1984, rpt. 1999, pp. 233–234. The statute in full appears in P.L. Hughes and J.F. Larkin (eds), *Tudor Royal Proclamations 1588–1603*, New Haven, Yale University Press, 1969. Given that Elizabeth's government found it necessary to reiterate the Act nine times during her reign, it may be supposed that it was regularly flouted. Jacques' quillet about the 'city-woman' who 'bears the cost of princes on unworthy shoulders' (*As You Like It*, 2.7.75) clearly hit a target. See also Peter Stallybrass, 'Patriarchal Territories: The Body Enclosed' in Margaret Ferguson, Maureen Quilligan, and Nancy J. Vickers (eds), *Rewriting the Renaissance: The Discourses of Sexual Difference in Early Modern Europe*, Chicago, University of Chicago Press, 1986, pp. 123–142, and 'Worn Worlds: Clothes and Identity on the Renaissance Stage' in Margreta de Grazia, Maureen Quilligan and Peter Stallybrass (eds), *Subject and Object in Renaissance Culture*, Cambridge, Cambridge University Press, 1996, pp. 289–320.

5 These accounts refer to Worcester's Men and the Admiral's Men at the Rose; see Rutter, *Documents of the Rose Playhouse*, pp. 156, 180, 182, 209, and Foakes and Rickert, *Diary*, pp. 178, 179. An inventory, now lost but doubtless authentic, of properties and costumes belonging to the Admiral's Men at the Rose itemized a variety of design effects, large and small: 'a gown to goe invisible', 'the sitte of Rome', 'Harey the fyftes vellet gowne', 'Kentes woden leage', 'j dragon in fostes', and 'j frame for the [be]heading in Black Jone'. See Foakes and Rickert, *Diary*, pp. 317–325.

6 Neither F (1623) nor Q (1609) contains act or scene divisions. Arden, New Penguin, New Shakespeare (Cambridge), Alexander, and Riverside follow Nicholas Rowe (1709) in making the 4.2 the 'morning after' scene; 4.3 the 'knocking up Cressida' scene; and 4.4 the 'rail and farewell' scene. Wells

and Taylor (Oxford) and after them, Greenblatt *et al.* (Norton) follow Q
and F in marking a general Exeunt at 4.2.76, then indicate a new scene (4.3
/ sc. 12) with the subsequent entrance of Pandarus and Cressida. This
throws off the traditional scene-numbering for the remainder of the Act but
also necessitates a new exit for Pandarus (not in Q or F) that complicates his
moves in the scene. All quotation from *Troilus and Cressida* follows the
Arden edition, Kenneth Palmer (ed.), London, Methuen, 1982.

7 Shakespeare's contemporaries, if they were men, slept in their shirts; if
women, in their smocks. Nightgowns – made of woollen or worsted fabrics,
sometimes with a hood – were seen as intimate garments, worn, says Janet
Arnold in her excellent *Queen Elizabeth's Wardrobe Unlock'd*, Leeds,
Maney, 1988, 'as an informal gown during the day', p. 139. When the
French Ambassador from Henri IV gained an audience with Queen
Elizabeth in December 1597 he recorded that 'She excused herself because
I found her attired in her night-gown [sa robe de nuit], and began to
rebuke those of her Council who were present saying, "What will these gentlemen say" – speaking of those who accompanied me – "to see me so
attired? I am much disturbed that they should see me in this state"' (quoted
in Arnold, p. 7).

8 The glove, like the sleeve, is an anachronism; Shakespeare's Greeks and
Trojans are end-of-reign Elizabethan makeovers of Chaucerian originals.
But it's also a piece of theatrical shorthand. Where gloves are represented
in early modern English portraiture they are usually ornamental, held or
worn on one hand only (see Arnold, *Queen Elizabeth's Wardrobe Unlock'd*,
pp. 126, 136, 140, 148), signifying public dress. Gloves, though, were necessary gear for the traveller, being, says Arnold, 'absolutely essential for
protection on horseback, in summer as well as winter', p. 217. If a playwright wanted to signify a character in transit, giving her a pair of gloves
would make this instantly legible.

9 A 'Prefatory Letter' to the 1609 Quarto describes *Troilus* as 'never staled
with the stage, never clapper-clawed with the palms of the vulgar'. William
Poel's 1913 production was the first full-scale *Troilus* ever recorded.
Productions in Stratford followed in 1936, 1948 and 1954. In 1960 Barton
co-directed with Peter Hall a production that toured in 1962, then re-
directed the play in 1968 (designed by Timothy O'Brien) and 1976
(designed by Chris Dyer). RST productions followed in 1981 (Terry
Hands/Farrah); 1985 (Howard Davies/Ralph Koltai with Liz da Costa);
1990 (Sam Mendes/Anthony Ward); 1996 (Ian Judge/John Gunter with
Deirdre Clancy); and 1998 (Michael Boyd/Tom Piper).

10 A phrase Billington has repeated in his reviews; see, for example, the
Guardian 19 August 1976; 8 July 1981; 26 July 1996.

11 *Independent*, 30 April 1990.

12 *New Statesman*, 16 August 1968.

13 Whether the betrayal the woman is accused of in Shakespeare is political or
domestic, the language that constructs her betrayal is always sexualized. For
the move that turns the female 'traitor' into the strumpet, see Iago's manipulation of Emilia in *Othello*, first urging her complicity in his lies, 'Go to,
charm your tongue'; then invalidating her truth as insanity, 'What, are you
mad?', and advising, 'Be wise, and get you home.' Her persistence in speaking out against her husband marks her 'betrayal' – figured in sexualized

imagery: 'Villanous whore!'; 'Filth, thou liest!' (5.2.179, 191, 221, 234, 236).

14 Eve Kosofsky Sedgwick, *Between Men: English Literature and Male Homosocial Desire*, New York, Columbia University Press, 1985, p. 44.

15 Only Cassandra and Andromache appear on stage together – in 5.3, for some forty lines.

16 Marlowe in *Dr. Faustus* (5.2.97–98). It is inconceivable that Shakespeare did not know (and glance at?) Marlowe's seductive, subversive Helen – Helen as succubus – when he created his own 'mortal Venus'.

17 Quoted in Kathleen Tynan, *The Life of Kenneth Tynan*, London, Phoenix, 1995, pp. 278–279.

18 Ronald Bryden, *The Observer*, 11 August 1968.

19 Harold Hobson, *The Sunday Times*, 11 August 1968.

20 The doll and the business around her are recorded in the prompt book (Shakespeare Centre Library, Stratford-upon-Avon). Later, 'Helen' returned. Pandarus delivered the final speech bequeathing the audience his diseases then covered his face with a hideously carbuncled death mask and, in a slow *danse macabre*, descended into a grave-like vault that closed over him. Behind it stood Thersites fondling a doll that could have been Helen – or Cressida.

21 Irving Wardle, *The Times*, 9 August 1968.

22 W.A. Darlington, the *Daily Telegraph*, 10 August 1968.

23 Michael Billington, the *Guardian*, 19 August 1976.

24 Robert Cushman, *The Observer*, 22 August 1976; Wardle, 1976.

25 Michael Billington, the *Guardian*, 8 July 1981.

26 Sedgwick, *Between Men*, p. 26, quoting Gayle Rubin, 'The Traffic in Women: Notes Toward a Political Economy of Sex' in Rayna Reiter (ed.), *Toward an Anthropology of Women*, New York, Monthly Review Press, 1975, pp. 157–210.

27 Sedgwick, *Between Men*, pp. 34, 38. In the Sonnets as in Greek culture, male–male love is not an alternative or oppositional lifestyle; it is rather set within a structure of institutionalized social relations performed through women (marriage, family, lineage) that do not affect his relationship with the man.

28 *Stratford upon Avon Herald*, 2 August 1968; Ronald Bryden, *The Observer*, 11 August 1968; Milton Shulman, the *Evening Standard*, 9 August 1968.

29 'The Purpose of Playing: Reflections on a Shakespearean Anthropology', *Helios*, n.s. 7 (1980), pp. 51–74, esp. p. 64, developed further in *The Purpose of Playing*, Chicago, University of Chicago Press, 1996. Montrose takes the term 'anti-structure' from the anthropologist Victor Turner in *Dramas, Fields and Metaphors*, Ithaca, Cornell University Press, 1974.

30 Larkin's 'Annus Mirabilis' (1974) continues, ruefully:

> (Which was rather late for me) –
> Between the end of the *Chatterley* ban
> And the Beatles' first LP.

31 Quoted by Jonathan Dollimore, 'The Challenge of Sexuality', in Alan Sinfield (ed.), *Society and Literature 1945–1970*, London, Methuen, 1983, pp. 51–85.

32 Dollimore, 'The Challenge of Sexuality', p. 52.

33 W.A. Darlington, the *Daily Telegraph*, 19 August 1968; Milton Shulman, the *Evening Standard*, 19 August 1968.
34 Harold Hobson, *The Sunday Times*, 11 August 1968; Ronald Bryden, *The Observer*, 11 August 1968.
35 'Homoeroticism' has no entry in the *OED*; an entry for 'homosexuality' appears in the *OED* for the first time in the 1971 Supplement.
36 Ronald Bryden, *The Observer*, 11 August 1968.
37 *New Statesman*, 16 August 1968. W.A. Darlington was even more offended, calling the production 'vandalism', an 'outrageous travesty': 'Shakespeare nowhere shows any sign at all of intending to make homosexuals' of Achilles and Patroclus. 'This idea has been read into the play by modern or not-so-modern theatrical directors, and has hardened into a stage tradition', the *Daily Telegraph*, 19 August 1968.
38 Alan Bray, *Homosexuality in Renaissance England*, London, Gay Men's Press, 1982.
39 See particularly 'Breaking the Code' in Marjorie Garber's *Vested Interests: Cross-Dressing and Cultural Anxiety*, London, Routledge, 1992: 'clinical, psychological, and medicalized distinctions notwithstanding, the confusion between – or conflation of – transvestism and gay identity becomes evident virtually whenever transvestism becomes a topic for public debate . . . [N]either can simply be transhistorically "decoded" as a sign for the other', p. 131. Crisp eschewed drag because it made him look less feminine. He wanted, he said, to present 'to the world . . . a brand image of homosexuality that was outrageously effeminate', but not transvestite (quoted in Garber, p. 138). Coincidentally, Crisp's memoirs were published as *The Naked Civil Servant* in 1968, the same year as Barton's *Troilus and Cressida*.
40 See Bray, *Homosexuality*, esp. Introduction. The Wolfenden Report on Homosexual Offences and Prostitution was published in 1967; the Stonewall riots followed in 1970.
41 *Stratford upon Avon Herald*, the *Daily Mail*, both 2 August 1968.
42 In *White*, London, Routledge, 1997, Richard Dyer analyses these peplum films in terms of class address, white colonialism and fascism, and observes that while white male nudity might be represented in such 'socially sanctioned or cordoned-off images' as were regularly on view in 'The art gallery, sports and pornography', in cinema, whites appeared naked only in boxing films and adventure films in colonial settings – films that featured 'a star possessed of a champion or built body', p. 146. The stars of the peplum whose representation made good white culture's claim to racial superiority in post-war Europe were invariably American: Steve Reeves, Mark Forrest, Dan Vadis.
43 Milton Shulman, the *Evening Standard*, 9 August 1968.
44 Irving Wardle, *The Times*, 19 August 1976.
45 Francis King, the *Sunday Telegraph*, 12 July 1981.
46 Robert Cushman, *The Observer*, 12 July 1981.
47 *Sunday Telegraph* headline 28 July 1996; the *Independent on Sunday* headline 28 July 1996; Michael Billington, the *Guardian*, 26 July 1996; Robert Butler, the *Independent on Sunday*, 28 July 1996.
48 Dollimore, 'The Challenge of Sexuality', p. 61.
49 Paul Taylor, the *Independent*, 30 April 1990.

50 Paul Taylor, the *Independent*, 7 November 1998.
51 Paul Taylor, the *Independent*, 7 November 1998; Charles Spencer, the *Daily Telegraph*, 9 November 1998. Michael Billington called it 'orgiastic', the *Guardian*, 10 November 1998. I am grateful to Janet Costa, Amelia Marriette and Michiyo Kato, of the Shakespeare Institute, Stratford-upon-Avon, for sharing their reading of this scene with me.

5 REMEMBERING EMILIA

1 I am thinking here of John Arden's observation on *Henry V*, that there are so many corrections to the view of Agincourt as a 'lovely war' within the structure of the play that 'one is forced to wonder if the author had not written a secret play inside the official one'. Quoted in Carol Chillington Rutter, 'Kate, Bianca, Ruth and Sarah: Playing the Woman's Part in Shakespeare's *The Taming of the Shrew*' in Michael Collins (ed.), *Shakespeare's Sweet Thunder*, Newark, University of Delaware Press, 1997, pp. 176–215; see, too, for more on 'secret' plays inside 'official' ones.
2 Maureen Quilligan, 'Staging Gender: William Shakespeare and Elizabeth Cary' in James Grantham Turner (ed.), *Sexuality and Gender in Early Modern Europe: Institutions, Texts, Images*, Cambridge, Cambridge University Press, 1993, pp. 208–232, esp. 211. See also Ruth Kelso, *Doctrine for the Lady of the Renaissance*, Urbana, University of Illinois Press, 1978; Carolyn Lenz, Ruth Swift, Gayle Green and Carol Thomas Neely (eds), *The Woman's Part: Feminist Criticism of Shakespeare*, Urbana, University of Illinois Press; Lisa Jardine, *Still Harping on Daughters: Women and Drama in the Age of Shakespeare*, Brighton, Harvester, 1983; Patricia Parker, *Literary Fat Ladies: Rhetoric, Gender, Property*, London, Routledge, 1987; Karen Newman, *Fashioning Femininity*, Chicago, University of Chicago Press, 1991; and Carol Chillington Rutter, 'Eel Pie and Ugly Sisters in *King Lear*, Parts 1 and 2', *Essays in Theatre* 13:2 (May 1995), pp. 135–158 and 14:1 (November 1995), pp. 49–63. See, too, Laura Gowing, *Domestic Dangers: Women, Words, and Sex in Early Modern London*, Oxford, Clarendon Press, 1998: her title makes my point for me.
3 M.R. Ridley (ed.) *Othello*, London, Methuen, 1958, rpt. 1984 (all references are to this edition); E.A.J. Honigmann (ed.), Walton-on-Thames, Thomas Nelson and Sons, 1997, p. 47. Even more astonishingly, Honigmann effects the editorial change Ridley merely conjectures – there being no authority for it in either Folio or Quarto – and reassigns Desdemona's line, 'This Lodovico is a proper man' (4.3.33) to Emilia, (who immediately adds, 'A very handsome man'), giving as his reason, 'For Desdemona to praise Lodovico at this point seems out of character', p. 291. Ridley, too, worried about Desdemona's propriety, but confined his speculations to rhetorical questions in a note: 'What did Shakespeare intend by this sudden transition to Lodovico? Is Desdemona for a moment "matching Othello with her country forms"? One is tempted to wonder whether there has not been a misattribution of speeches, so that this line as well as the next should be Emilia's', p. 116. Ridley asks the right opening question, but doesn't go on seriously to contemplate the effect of Shakespeare's deliberate project to destabilize the women's text by writing the line for Desdemona.

NOTES

4 Ridley (ed.), *Othello*, p. 54.
5 Quoted in Peter Stallybrass, 'Patriarchal Territories: The Body Enclosed', in Margaret Ferguson, Maureen Quilligan, and Nancy J. Vickers (eds), *Rewriting the Renaissance: The Discourses of Sexual Difference in Early Modern Europe*, Chicago, University of Chicago Press, 1986, p. 94.
6 See also James Calderwood, 'Speech and Self in *Othello*', *Shakespeare Quarterly* 38:3, (Fall 1987), pp. 293–303.
7 For a brilliant reading of the handkerchief, see Lynda E. Boose, 'Othello's Handkerchief: "The Recognizance and Pledge of Love"', *English Literary Renaissance* 5, 1975, pp. 360–374.
8 For a psychoanalytic structuring of the argument I am making performatively, see Janet Adelman, 'Iago's Alter Ego: Race as Projection in *Othello*', *Shakespeare Quarterly* 48:2 (Summer 1997), pp. 125–144.
9 John Cleaver, 'A godly form of household government' (1614), in Kate Aughterson (ed.), *Renaissance Woman: Constructions of Femininity in England*, London, Routledge, 1995, p. 79.
10 Henry Smith, 'A preparative to marriage' (1591), in Aughterson, *Renaissance Woman*, p. 83.
11 Quoted in Bernard Capp, 'Separate Domains? Women and Authority in Early Modern England' in Paul Griffiths, Adam Fox and Steve Hindle (eds), *The Experience of Authority in Early Modern England*, London, Macmillan, 1996, p. 118.
12 Aughterson, *Renaissance Woman*, p. 81.
13 Norman E. McClure, *The Letters of John Chamberlain* vol. 1, Philadelphia, American Philosophical Society, 1939, p. 178.
14 *The Prayer-Book of Queen Elizabeth 1559*, John Grant, Edinburgh, 1909, p. 113. For a detailed discussion of the sacramental and social rituals surrounding baptism culled from contemporary sources see David Cressy, *Birth, Marriage and Death: Ritual, Religion, and the Life-Cycle in Tudor and Stuart England*, Oxford, Oxford University Press, 1999, 149–172.
15 McClure, *Letters* vol. 1, pp. 415–416.
16 Alan Brissenden (ed.), Thomas Middleton, *A Chaste Maid in Cheapside*, London, Ernest Benn, 1968, pp. 45–56. The gossips' feast begins with their return from church, telling Mrs Allwit, who lies in '*A bed thrust out upon the stage*', 'We have brought you home / A kursen [i.e., Christian] soul' (3.2.1–2). Gossiping belonged to the aristocracy as to the plebs; as Chamberlain writes of Sir Arthur Ingrams' son, 'the earle of Suffolke, the earle of Somerset and the Countesse of Nottingham were gossips', McClure, *Letters* vol. 1, p. 545.
17 Allwit's children, of course, are all bastards, and the 'tattle' the women exchange, congratulating him on a daughter 'so like the father' that she might have 'been spit out of his mouth' (3.2.12, 13), is just that. But then, as Richard Wilson observes in *Will Power: Essays on Shakespearean Authority*, Detroit, Wayne State University Press, 1993, p. 172, such tales, like the paternity they 'affirm', are unverifiable; both 'gestate in a matrix that is beyond the light of masculine observation'. Here, however, the joke is on the gossips, not the (complicit) cuckold.
18 Cressy, *Birth, Marriage, and Death*, p. 164.
19 Capp, 'Separate Domains?' pp. 117, 129–130, 131, 139.

20 Patricia M. Spacks, *Gossip*, Chicago, University of Chicago Press, 1985, pp. 5, 8, 11, 23, 34.
21 Spacks, *Gossip*, p. 12.
22 For a brilliant discussion of pregnancy, midwifery, obstetrics and their connection to the authority of Shakespeare's 'tales', see Wilson, *Will Power*.
23 My thinking here is indebted to Roach's *Cities of the Dead*, particularly pp. 28 and 25 where he expands Barthes and Arac into his own notion of 'genealogies of performance'.

BIBLIOGRAPHY

Aasand, Hardin, '"To Blanch an Ethiop, and Revive a Corse": Queen Anne and *The Masque of Blackness*', *Studies in English Literature* 32:2, 1992, pp. 271–285.

Adelman, Janet, *The Common Liar: An Essay on Antony and Cleopatra*, Oxford, Oxford University Press, 1973.

——, 'Iago's Alter Ego: Race as Projection in *Othello*', *Shakespeare Quarterly* 48:2 (Summer 1997), pp. 125–144.

——, *Suffocating Mothers: Fantasies of Maternal Origins in Shakespeare's Plays*, Hamlet *to* The Tempest, London, Routledge, 1992.

Arnold, Janet, *Queen Elizabeth's Wardrobe Unlock'd*, Leeds, Maney, 1988.

Auerbach, Nina, *Woman and the Demon*, Cambridge, Massachusetts, Harvard University Press, 1982.

Aughterson, Kate (ed.), *Renaissance Woman: Constructions of Femininity in England*, London, Routledge, 1995.

Bakhtin, Mikhail, *Rabelais and His World*, trans. Helene Iswolsky, Bloomington, Indiana University Press, 1984.

Barker, Felix, *The Oliviers: A Biography*, London, Hamish Hamilton, 1953.

Barroll, Leeds, 'The Court of the First Stuart Queen' in Linda Levy Peck (ed.), *The Mental World of the Jacobean Court*, Cambridge, Cambridge University Press, 1991, pp. 191–208.

——, 'Inventing the Stuart Masque' in David Bevington and David Holbrook (eds), *The Politics of the Stuart Court Masque*, Cambridge, Cambridge University Press, 1998, pp. 121–143.

——, 'Theatre as Text: The Case of Queen Anna and the Jacobean Court Masque' in A.L. Magnusson and C.E. McGee (eds), *The Elizabethan Theatre XIV*, 1996, pp. 175–193.

Barthelemy, Antony Gerard, *Black Face, Maligned Race: The Representation of Blacks in English Drama from Shakespeare to Southerne*, Baton Rouge, Louisiana State University Press, 1987.

Beauman, Sally, *The Royal Shakespeare Company: A History of Ten Decades*, Oxford, Oxford University Press, 1982.

Bernal, Martin, *Black Athena: The Afroasiatic Roots of Classical Civilization* 2 vols, New Brunswick, Rutgers University Press, 1987, 1991.

Berry, Philippa, *Shakespeare's Feminine Endings: Disfiguring Death in the Tragedies*, London, Routledge, 1999.

Berry, Ralph, *On Directing Shakespeare*, London, Hamish Hamilton, 1989.

Bevington, David (ed.), *The Complete Works of Shakespeare*, New York, Harper Collins, 1992.

Billington, Michael, *Peggy Ashcroft*, London, John Murray, 1988.

Boose, Lynda E., 'The Father and the Bride in Shakespeare', *PMLA* 97, 1982, pp. 325–347.

——, '"The Getting of a Lawful Race": Racial Discourse in Early Modern England and the Unrepresentable Black Woman' in Margo Hendricks and Patricia Parker (eds), *Women, 'Race', and Writing in the Early Modern Period*, London, Routledge, 1994, pp. 35–54.

——, 'Othello's Handkerchief: "The Recognizance and Pledge of Love"', *English Literary Renaissance* 5, 1975, pp. 360–374.

Bray, Alan, *Homosexuality in Renaissance England*, London, Gay Men's Press, 1982.

Brissenden, Alan (ed.), Thomas Middleton, *A Chaste Maid in Cheapside*, London, Ernest Benn, 1968.

Bristol, Michael D., *Carnival and Theatre: Plebeian Culture and the Structure of Authority in Renaissance England*, London, Routledge, 1985.

Bronfen, Elisabeth, *Over Her Dead Body: Death, Femininity and the Aesthetic*, Manchester, Manchester University Press, 1992.

Calderwood, James, 'Speech and Self in *Othello*', *Shakespeare Quarterly* 38:3, (Fall 1987), pp. 293–303.

Calendar of State Papers Venetian IX, 1592–1603, Horatio Brown (ed.), London, HM Stationery Office, 1897.

Calendar of State Papers Venetian X, 1603–1607, Horatio Brown (ed.), London, HM Stationery Office, 1900.

Capp, Bernard, 'Separate Domains? Women and Authority in Early Modern England' in Paul Griffiths, Adam Fox and Steve Hindle (eds), *The Experience of Authority in Early Modern England*, London, Macmillan, 1996.

Chambers, E.K., *The Elizabethan Stage* 4 vols, Oxford, Clarendon Press, 1923.

Charnes, Linda, *Notorious Identity: Materializing the Subject in Shakespeare*, London, Harvard University Press, 1993.

Chedgzoy, Kate, *Shakespeare's Queer Children*, Manchester, Manchester University Press, 1995.

Cloud, Random, 'The Marriage of Good and Bad Quartos,' *Shakespeare Quarterly* 33: 4 (Winter 1982), pp. 421–431.

Coursen, H.R., *Shakespearean Performance as Interpretation*, Newark, University of Delaware Press, 1992.

Cressy, David, *Birth, Marriage and Death: Ritual, Religion, and the Life-Cycle in Tudor and Stuart England*, Oxford, Oxford University Press, 1999.

——, *Travesties and Transgressions in Tudor and Stuart England: Tales of Discord and Dissension*, Oxford, Oxford University Press, 2000.

D'Amico, Jack, *The Moor in English Renaissance Drama*, Tampa, University of South Florida Press, 1991.

Dawson, Anthony B., 'Performance and Participation: Desdemona, Foucault, and the Actor's Body' in James C. Bulman, (ed.), *Shakespeare, Theory, and Performance*, London, Routledge, 1996, pp. 29–45.

De Sousa, Geraldo U., *Shakespeare's Cross-Cultural Encounters*, Basingstoke, Macmillan, 1999.

Dollimore, Jonathan, 'The challenge of sexuality', in Alan Sinfield (ed.), *Society and Literature 1945–1970*, London, Methuen, 1983, pp. 51–85.

Donaldson, Peter, *Shakespearean Films/Shakespearean Directors*, London, Unwin Hyman, 1990.

Douglas, Mary, *Natural Symbols: Explorations in Cosmology*, New York, Pantheon, 1970.

Dyer, Richard, *White*, London, Routledge, 1997.

Elam, Keir, '"In what chapter of his bosom?": Reading Shakespeare's Bodies' in Terence Hawkes (ed.), *Alternative Shakespeares 2*, London, Routledge, 1996, pp. 140–163.

Foakes, R.A. and R.T. Rickert (eds), *Henslowe's Diary*, Cambridge, Cambridge University Press, 1968.

Foucault, Michel, *Discipline and Punish: The Birth of the Prison*, trans. Alan Sheridan, Harmondsworth, Penguin, 1977.

Freeman, Rosemary, *English Emblem Books*, London, Chatto, 1948.

Frye, Roland Mushat, *The Renaissance Hamlet: Issues and Responses in 1600*, Princeton, Princeton University Press, 1984.

Garber, Marjorie, *Coming of Age in Shakespeare*, London, Routledge, 1981, rpt. 1997.

——, *Vested Interests: Cross-Dressing and Cultural Anxiety*, London, Routledge, 1992.

Geertz, Clifford, 'Thick Description: Toward an Interpretive Theory of Culture', in *The Interpretation of Cultures*, New York, Basic Books, 1973, pp. 3–32.

Gittings, Clare, *Death, Burial and the Individual in Early Modern England*, Beckenham, Croom Helm, 1984.

Goldberg, Jonathan, *James I and the Politics of Literature: Jonson, Shakespeare, Donne and Their Contemporaries*, Stanford, Stanford University Press, 1989.

——, *Sodometries: Renaissance Texts, Modern Sexualities*, Stanford, Stanford University Press, 1992.

Goodwin, John (ed.), *British Theatre Design: The Modern Age*, London: Weidenfeld and Nicolson, 1989.

Gowing, Laura, *Domestic Dangers: Women, Words, and Sex in Early Modern London*, Oxford, Clarendon Press, 1998.

Greenblatt, Stephen (ed.), *The Norton Shakespeare*, London, Norton, 1997.

Halio, Jay, 'Three Filmed *Hamlet*s,' *Literature and Film Quarterly* 1:4 1973, pp. 316–320.

Hall, Kim, *Things of Darkness*, London, Cornell University Press, 1995.

Hamer, Mary, *Signs of Cleopatra: History, Politics, Representation*, London, Routledge, 1993.

Hawkes, Terence, *Meaning by Shakespeare*, London, Routledge, 1992.

Herford, C.H. and Percy and Evelyn Simpson (eds), *Ben Jonson Volume VII, The Sad Shepherd, The Fall of Mortimer, Masques and Entertainments*, Oxford, Clarendon Press, 1941, pp. 161–184.

Herford, C.H. and Percy and Evelyn Simpson (eds), *Ben Jonson, Volume X, Play Commentary, Masque Commentary*, Oxford, Clarendon Press, 1950, pp. 445–455.

Hill, Errol, *Shakespeare in Sable: A History of Black Shakespearean Actors*, Amherst, Massachusetts, University of Massachusetts Press, 1984.

Hodgdon, Barbara, '"Here Apparent": Photography, History, and the Theatrical Unconscious' in Edward Petcher (ed.), *Textual and Theatrical Shakespeare: Questions of Evidence*, Iowa City, University of Iowa Press, 1996, pp. 181–209.

——, 'Replicating Richard: Body Doubles, Body Politics', *Theatre Journal 50* (1998), pp. 207–225.

——, *The Shakespeare Trade: Performances and Appropriations*, Philadelphia, Pennsylvania University Press, 1998.

——, 'Two *King Lears*: Uncovering the Filmtext,' *Literature and Film Quarterly* 11:3, 1983, pp. 143–151.

——, '*William Shakespeare's Romeo and Juliet*: Everything's Nice in America', *Shakespeare Survey 52*, Stanley Wells (ed.), Cambridge, Cambridge University Press, 1999, pp. 88–98.

Holland, Peter, *English Shakespeares: Shakespeare on the English Stage in the 1990s*, Cambridge, Cambridge University Press, 1997.

——, 'Shakespeare Performances in England, 1989–90', *Shakespeare Survey 44: Shakespeare and Politics*, Stanley Wells (ed.), Cambridge, Cambridge University Press, 1992, pp. 157–190.

——, 'Two-Dimensional Shakespeare: *King Lear* on Film', in *Shakespeare and the Moving Image: The Plays on Film and Television*, Anthony Davies and Stanley Wells (eds), Cambridge, Cambridge University Press, 1994, pp. 50–68.

Holleram, J.V., 'Maimed Funeral Rites in *Hamlet*,' *English Literary Renaissance* 19, 1989, pp. 65–93.

Honigmann, E.A.J. (ed.), *Othello*, Walton-on-Thames, Thomas Nelson and Sons, 1997, rpt. 1999.

hooks, bell, *Black Looks: Race and Representation*, Boston, South End Press, 1992.

Howard, Jean, 'Crossdressing, the Theatre, and Gender Struggle in Early Modern England', *Shakespeare Quarterly* 39:4 (Winter 1988), pp. 418–440.

Huggett, Richard, *Binkie Beaumont: Eminence Grise of the West End Theatre 1933–1972*, London, Hodder and Stoughton, 1989.

Hughes, P.L. and J.F. Larkin (eds), *Tudor Royal Proclamations 1588–1603*, New Haven, Yale University Press, 1969.

Hughes, Ted, *The Birthday Letters*, London, Faber and Faber, 1998.

Hughes-Hallett, Lucy, *Cleopatra: Histories, Dreams and Distortions*, London, Vintage, 1990.

Hunter, G.K., *Dramatic Identities and Cultural Tradition*, Liverpool, Liverpool University Press, 1978.

Iyengar, Sujata, 'Cleopatra', unpublished conference paper, April 2000.

Jardine, Lisa, *Still Harping on Daughters: Women and Drama in the Age of Shakespeare*, Brighton, Harvester, 1983.

Jenkins, Harold (ed.), *Hamlet*, London, Routledge, 1993.

Jensen, Michael P., 'Mel Gibson on Hamlet,' *Shakespeare on Film Newsletter* 15:2, 1991, pp.1–6.

Jones, Eldred, *Othello's Countrymen: The African in English Renaissance Drama*, London, Oxford University Press, 1965.

Jordanova, Ludmilla, 'Happy Marriages and Dangerous Liaisons: Artists and Anatomy' in Deanna Petherbridge (ed.), *The Quick and the Dead*, Manchester, Cornerhouse Publications, 1997.

Jorgens, Jack J., 'Image and Meaning in the Kozintsev *Hamlet*,' *Literature and Film Quarterly* 1:4, 1973, pp. 307–315.

——, *Shakespeare on Film*, Bloomington, Indiana University Press, 1977.

Kelso, Ruth, *Doctrine for the Lady of the Renaissance*, Urbana, University of Illinois Press, 1978.

Kozintsev, Grigori, *Shakespeare: Time and Conscience*, trans. Joyce Vining, New York, Hill and Wang, 1966.

Laqueur, Thomas, *Making Sex: Body and Gender from the Greeks to Freud*, Cambridge, Massachusetts, Harvard University Press, 1990.

Lee, Sidney, *Stratford on Avon*, London, Seeley & Co, 1885.

Lenz, Carolyn, Ruth Swift, Gayle Green and Carol Thomas Neely (eds), *The Woman's Part: Feminist Criticism of Shakespeare*, Urbana, University of Illinois Press, 1980.

Levine, Laura, *Men in Women's Clothing: Anti-theatricality and Effeminization 1579–1642*, Cambridge, Cambridge University Press, 1986.

Lindley, Arthur, 'The Unbeing of the Overreacher', *Modern Language Review* 84, 1989, pp. 1–17.

Litten, Julian, *The English Way of Death: The Common Funeral Since 1450*, London, Robert Hale, 1991.

Loomba, Ania, *Gender, Race, Renaissance Drama*, Oxford, Oxford University Press, 1989.

Loomis, Catherine, 'Elizabeth Southwell's Manuscript Account of the Death of Queen Elizabeth [with text]', *English Literary Renaissance* 26:1, 1996, pp. 482–509.

MacDonald, Joyce Green, 'Sex, Race, and Empire in Shakespeare's *Antony and Cleopatra*', unpublished seminar paper, March 1995.

MacDonald, Michael, 'Ophelia's Maimed Rites,' *Shakespeare Quarterly* 38:3, (Autumn 1986), 308–317.

MacDonald, Michael and Terence Murphy, *Sleepless Souls: Suicide in Early Modern England*, Oxford, Clarendon Press, 1990.

McClure, Norman Egbert (ed.), *The Letters of John Chamberlain* 2 vols, Philadelphia, American Philosophical Society, 1939.

McManus, Clare, '"Defacing the Carcass": Anne of Denmark and Jonson's *The Masque of Blackness*' in Julie Sanders (ed.), *Refashioning Ben Jonson: Gender, Politics and the Jonsonian Canon*, Basingstoke, Macmillan, 1998, pp. 93–113.

Montrose, Louis A., 'The Purpose of Playing: Reflections on a Shakespearean Anthropology', *Helios*, n.s.7, 1980, pp. 51–74.

——, *The Purpose of Playing*, Chicago, University of Chicago Press, 1996.

Motion, Andrew, *Wainewright the Poisoner*, London, Faber and Faber, 2000.

Muir, Kenneth (ed.), *King Lear*, London, Routledge, 1991.

Mullin, Michael, *Design by Motley*, Newark, University of Delaware Press, 1996.

Neill, Michael (ed.), *Antony and Cleopatra*, Oxford, Oxford University Press, 1994.

——, *Issues of Death: Mortality and Identity in English Renaissance Tragedy*, Oxford, Clarendon Press, 1998.

Newman, Karen, *Fashioning Femininity*, Chicago, University of Chicago Press, 1991.

Olivier, Laurence, 'An Essay in Hamlet', in Brenda Cross (ed.), *The Film* Hamlet: *A Record of its Production*, London, Saturn Press, 1948, pp. 9–15.

——, *Confessions of an Actor: An Autobiography*, New York, Simon and Schuster, 1982.

——, *On Acting*, London, Weidenfeld and Nicolson, 1986.

Orgel, Stephen, 'Nobody's Perfect, Or, Why Did the English Stage Take Boys for Women?', *South Atlantic Quarterly* 88.1 (Winter 1989), pp. 7–30.

Orgel, Stephen and Roy Strong (eds), *Inigo Jones: The Theatre of the Stuart Court* 2 vols, Sotheby Park Bernet, University of California Press, 1973.

Palmer, Kenneth (ed.), *Troilus and Cressida*, London, Methuen, 1982.

Parker, Patricia, *Literary Fat Ladies: Rhetoric, Gender, Property*, London, Routledge, 1987.

Paster, Gale Kern, *The Body Embarrassed: Drama and the Disciplines of Shame in Early Modern England*, Ithaca, Cornell University Press, 1993.

Pieterse, Jan Nederveen, *White on Black: Images of Africa and Blacks in Western Popular Culture*, New Haven, Yale University Press, 1992.

The Prayer-Book of Queen Elizabeth 1559, John Grant, Edinburgh, 1909; with an Introduction by Edward Benham, DD.

Quilligan, Maureen, 'Staging Gender: William Shakespeare and Elizabeth Cary' in James Grantham Turner (ed.), *Sexuality and Gender in Early Modern Europe: Institutions, Texts, Images*, Cambridge, Cambridge University Press, 1993, pp. 208–232.

Quinn, Edward, 'Zeffirelli's *Hamlet*,' *Shakespeare on Film Newsletter* 15:2, 1991, pp. 1–12.

Ratcliffe, Michael, see John Goodwin (ed.), *British Theatre Design: The Modern Age*, London, Weidenfeld and Nicolson, 1989.

Riche, Barnaby, *The Famous Hystory of Herodotus: Conteyning the Discourse of dyuers Countreys, The succession of theyr Kyngs: The actes and exploytes atchieued by them: The lawes and customes of euery Nation: with the true Description and Antiquities of the same*, London, Thomas Marshe, 1584, Bodleian Library Douce HH243.

Ridley, M.R., (ed.), *Antony and Cleopatra*, London, Methuen, 1954, rpt. 1967.

——, (ed.), *Othello*, London, Methuen, 1958, rpt. 1984.

Riley, Henry T. (ed.), *The Heroïdes*, London, Bell & Daldy, 1869.

Ripa, Caesar, *Iconologia*, 1603.

Roach, Joseph, *Cities of the Dead: Circum-Atlantic Performance*, New York, Columbia University Press, 1996.

Rothwell, Kenneth S., 'Representing *King Lear* on Screen: From Metatheatre to "Meta-Cinema"' in Anthony Davies and Stanley Wells (eds), *Shakespeare and the Moving Image: The Plays on Film and Television*, Cambridge, Cambridge University Press, 1994, pp. 211–233.

Royster, Francesca T., 'Cleopatra as Diva: African-American Women and Shakespearean Tactics' in Marianne Novy (ed.), *Transforming Shakespeare: Contemporary Women's Re-Visions in Literature and Performance*, New York, St Martin's Press, 1999, pp. 103–125.

Rubin, Gayle, 'The Traffic in Women: Notes Toward a Political Economy of Sex' in Rayna Reiter (ed.), *Toward an Anthropology of Women*, New York, Monthly Review Press, 1975, pp. 157–210.

Rutter, Carol Chillington, *Documents of the Rose Playhouse*, Manchester, Manchester University Press, 1984, rpt. 1999.

——, 'Eel Pie and Ugly Sisters in *King Lear*, Part 1', *Essays in Theatre* 13:2 (May, 1995), pp. 135–158.

——, 'Eel Pie and Ugly Sisters in *King Lear* Part 2', *Essays in Theatre* 14:1 (November, 1995), pp. 49–63.

——, 'Kate, Bianca, Ruth and Sarah: Playing the Woman's Part in Shakespeare's *The Taming of the Shrew*' in Michael Collins (ed.), *Shakespeare's Sweet Thunder*, Newark, University of Delaware Press, 1997, pp. 176–215.

Sacks, Peter M., *The English Elegy: Studies in the Genre from Spenser to Yeats*, London, Johns Hopkins University Press, 1985.

Said, Edward, *Orientalism*, London, Penguin, 1995; first published 1978.

Sawday, Jonathan, *The Body Emblazoned: Dissection and the Human Body in Renaissance Culture*, London, Routledge, 1995.

Scott, Mrs Maxwell, *The Tragedy of Fotheringay*, London, Sands & Co, 1925; first published 1895.

Sedgwick, Eve Kosofsky, *Between Men: English Literature and Male Homosocial Desire*, New York, Columbia University Press, 1985.

Showalter, Elaine, 'Representing Ophelia: Women, Madness, and the Responsibilities of Feminist Criticism', in Patricia Parker and Geoffrey Hartman (eds), *Shakespeare and the Question of Theory*, London, Routledge, 1991, pp. 77–94.

Slater, Anne Pasternak, *Shakespeare: The Director*, Sussex, Harvester, 1982.

Soyinka, Wole, 'Shakespeare and the Living Dramatist', *Shakespeare Survey 36*, Stanley Wells (ed.), Cambridge, Cambridge University Press, 1983, pp. 1–10.

Spacks, Patricia M., *Gossip*, Chicago, University of Chicago Press, 1985.

Spencer, T.J.B. (ed.), *Shakespeare's Plutarch*, London, Penguin, 1968.

Stallybrass, Peter, 'Worn Worlds: Clothes and Identity on the Renaissance Stage' in Margreta de Grazia, Maureen Quilligan and Peter Stallybrass (eds), *Subject and Object in Renaissance Culture*, Cambridge, Cambridge University Press, 1996, pp. 289–320.

——, 'Patriarchal Territories: The Body Enclosed' in Margaret Ferguson, Maureen Quilligan and Nancy J. Vickers (eds), *Rewriting the Renaissance: The Discourses of Sexual Difference in Early Modern Europe*, Chicago, University of Chicago Press, 1986, pp. 123–142.

——, 'Transvestism and the "Body Beneath": Speculating on the Boy Actor' in Susan Zimmerman (ed.), *Erotic Politics: Desire on the Renaissance Stage*, London, Routledge, 1992, pp. 64–83.

Stoker, Bram, *Dracula*, Harmondsworth, Penguin, 1984; first published 1897.

Turner, Victor, *Dramas, Fields and Metaphors*, Ithaca, Cornell University Press, 1974.

Tynan, Kathleen, *The Life of Kenneth Tynan*, London, Phoenix, 1995.

Urkowitz, Steven, 'Good News about "Bad" Quartos', in Maurice Charney (ed.), *"Bad" Shakespeare: Revaluations of the Shakespeare Canon*, London, Associated University Presses, 1988, pp. 189–206.

Wainwright, Patricia, *Trinity Tales*, the Parochial Church Council of Holy Trinity, Stratford-upon-Avon, 1983.

Wilders, John (ed.), *Antony and Cleopatra*, London, Routledge, 1995.

Wilson, Richard, *Will Power: Essays on Shakespearean Authority*, Detroit, Wayne State University Press, 1993.

Worthen, W.B., *Shakespeare and the Authority of Performance*, Cambridge, Cambridge University Press, 1997.

Yachnin, Paul, '"Courtiers of Beauteous Freedom": *Antony and Cleopatra* in its Time,' *Renaissance and Reformation* 26.1, 1991, pp. 1–20.

Filmography

Hamlet, 1948, UK, directed by Laurence Olivier, Two Cities Films, designed by Roger Furse. Hamlet: Laurence Olivier; Ophelia: Jean Simmons; Gertrude: Eileen Hurley; Claudius: Basil Sydney; Polonius: Felix Alymer; Laertes: Terence Morgan.

Hamlet, 1964, Soviet Union, directed by Grigori Kozintsev, Lenfilm. Hamlet: Innokenti Smoktunovsky; Ophelia: Anastasia Vertinskaya; Gertrude: Elza Radzin; Claudius: Mikhail Nazvanov; Polonius: Yuri Tolubeev; Laertes: C. Olesenko.

Hamlet, 1990, UK, directed by Franco Zeffirelli, Warner Brothers. Hamlet: Mel Gibson; Ophelia: Helena Bonham-Carter; Gertrude: Glenn Close; Claudius: Alan Bates; Polonius: Ian Holm; Laertes: Nathaniel Parker.

Hamlet, 1996, UK, directed by Kenneth Branagh, Castlerock Entertainment. Hamlet: Kenneth Branagh; Ophelia: Kate Winslet; Gertrude: Julie Christie; Claudius: Derek Jacobi; Polonius: Richard Briers; Laertes: Michael Maloney.

King Lear, 1971, directed by Peter Brook, Columbia Pictures in association with the Royal Shakespeare Company, designed by Wahkevitch and Anggard. Lear: Paul Scofield; Goneril: Irene Worth; Regan: Susan Engel; Cordelia: Anne-Lise Gabold; Fool: Jack McGowran. Released 22 July 1971. Distributed by RCA Columbia on video.

Othello, 1990, directed by Trevor Nunn, BBC Channel Four in association with the Royal Shakespeare Company, designed by Bob Crowley. Othello: Willard White; Desdemona: Imogen Stubbs; Iago: Ian McKellen; Emilia: Zoe Wanamaker. Distributed by Primetime Television/BBC.

Production Credits

Antony and Cleopatra, directed by Glen Byam Shaw, designed by Motley. Antony: Michael Redgrave; Cleopatra: Peggy Ashcroft; Octavius: Marius Goring; Enobarbus: Harry Andrews; Iras: Mary Watson; Charmian: Jean Wilson; Mardian: Mervyn Blake. Opened Shakespeare Memorial Theatre, 28 April 1953.

Antony and Cleopatra, directed by Trevor Nunn, designed by Christopher Morley, costumes designed by Ann Curtis. Antony: Richard Johnson; Cleopatra: Janet Suzman; Octavius: Corin Redgrave; Enobarbus: Patrick Stewart; Iras: Mavis Taylor Blake; Charmian: Rosemary McHale; Eros: Joe Marcell. Opened RST, 15 August 1972.

Antony and Cleopatra, directed by Adrian Noble, designed by Nadine Baylis. Antony: Michael Gambon; Cleopatra: Helen Mirren; Octavius: Jonathan Hyde; Enobarbus: Bob Peck; Iras: Josette Simon; Charmian: Sorcha Cusack; opened The Other Place, 13 October 1982.

Antony and Cleopatra, directed by John Caird, designed by Sue Blane. Antony, Richard Johnson; Cleopatra: Clare Higgins; Octavius: John Nettles; Enobarbus: Paul Jesson; Iras: Susie Lee Hayward; Charmian: Claire Benedict. Opened RST, 5 November 1992.

King Lear, directed by Nick Hytner, designed by David Fielding. Lear: John Wood; Goneril: Estelle Kohler; Regan: Sally Dexter; Cordelia: Alex Kingston; Fool: Linda Kerr Scott. Opened RST, 11 July 1990.

King Lear, directed by Adrian Noble, designed by Anthony Ward. Lear: Robert Stephens; Goneril: Janet Dale; Regan: Jenny Quayle; Cordelia: Abigail McKern; Fool: Ian Hughes. Opened RST, 20 May 1993.

Othello, directed by Trevor Nunn, designed by Bob Crowley. Othello: Willard White; Desdemona: Imogen Stubbs; Iago: Ian McKellen; Emilia: Zoe Wanamaker. Opened The Other Place, 24 August 1989.

Troilus and Cressida, directed by John Barton, designed by Timothy O'Brien. Troilus: Michael Williams; Cressida: Helen Mirren; Helen: Sheila Allen; Paris: Bernard Lloyd; Achilles: Alan Howard; Ulysses: Sebastian Shaw; Pandarus: David Waller; Thersites: Norman Rodway; Patroclus: John Shrapnel; Hector: Patrick Stewart. Opened RST, 8 August 1968.

Troilus and Cressida, directed by John Barton, designed by Chris Dyer. Troilus: Mike Gwilym; Cressida: Francesca Annis; Helen: Barbara Leigh-Hunt; Achilles: Rosin Ellis; Ulysses: Tony Church; Pandarus: David Waller: Thersites: John Nettles; Patroclus: Paul Moriarty; Hector: Michael Pennington. Opened RST, 8 August 1976.

Troilus and Cressida, directed by Howard Davies, designed by Ralph Koltai, costumes designed by Liz da Costa. Troilus: Anton Lesser; Cressida: Juliet Stevenson; Helen: Lindsay Duncan; Paris: Sean Baker; Achilles: Alan Rickman; Ulysses: Peter Jeffrey; Pandarus: Clive Merrison; Thersites: Alan Armstrong; Patroclus: Hilton McRae; Hector: David Burke. Opened RST, 25 June 1985.

Troilus and Cressida, directed by Sam Mendes, designed by Anthony Ward. Troilus: Ralph Fiennes; Cressida: Amanda Root; Helen: Sally Dexter; Paris: John Warnaby; Achilles: Ciaran Hinds; Ulysses: Paul Jesson; Pandarus: Norman Rodway; Thersites: Simon Russell Beale; Patroclus: Paterson Joseph; Hector: David Troughton. Opened Swan, 26 April 1990.

Troilus and Cressida, directed by Ian Judge, designed by John Gunter, costumes designed by Deirdre Clancy. Troilus: Joseph Fiennes; Cressida: Victoria Hamilton; Helen: Katia Caballero; Paris: Ray Fearon; Achilles: Philip Quast; Ulysses: Philip Voss; Pandarus: Clive Francis; Thersites: Richard McCabe; Patroclus: Jeremy Sheffield; Hector: Louis Hilyer. Opened RST, 24 July 1996.

Troilus and Cressida, directed by Michael Boyd, designed by Tom Piper. Troilus: William Houston; Cressida: Jayne Ashbourne; Helen: Sara Stewart; Achilles: Darren D'Silva; Ulysses: Colin Hurley; Pandarus: Roy Hanlon; Thersites: Lloyd Hutchinson; Patroclus: Elaine Pyke; Hector: Alistair Petrie. Opened Swan, 5 November 1998.

INDEX